8th Workshop on NLP for Similar Languages, Varieties and Dialects (VarDial '2021)

Online
20 April 2021

ISBN: 978-1-7138-2971-3

Printed from e-media with permission by:

Curran Associates, Inc.
57 Morehouse Lane
Red Hook, NY 12571

Some format issues inherent in the e-media version may also appear in this print version.

Printed with permission by Curran Associates, Inc. (2021)

For permission requests, please contact the Association for Computational Linguistics at the address below.

Association for Computational Linguistics
209 N. Eighth Street
Stroudsburg, Pennsylvania 18360

Phone: 1-570-476-8006
Fax: 1-570-476-0860

acl@aclweb.org

Additional copies of this publication are available from:

Curran Associates, Inc.
57 Morehouse Lane
Red Hook, NY 12571 USA
Phone: 845-758-0400
Fax: 845-758-2633
Email: curran@proceedings.com
Web: www.proceedings.com

EACL 2021

Proceedings of the 8th VarDial Workshop on NLP for Similar Languages, Varieties and Dialects

Co-located with the 16th European Chapter of the Association for Computational Linguistics (EACL)

April 20, 2021

Preface

These proceedings include the 16 papers presented at the Eighth Workshop on NLP for Similar Languages, Varieties and Dialects (VarDial), which was co-located with the 16th Conference of the European Chapter of the Association for Computational Linguistics (EACL). VarDial and EACL were originally scheduled to take place in Kiev, Ukraine, but the COVID-19 situation eventually forced a switch to a virtual format.

We are happy to see that after many years, VarDial keeps serving the community as an important venue for researchers interested in the computational processing of diatopic language variation. The papers accepted this year deal with a wide variety of topics such as language identification, part-of-speech tagging, machine translation, distributional semantic models, and corpus similarity.

As in previous years, together with the workshop, we organized another iteration of the popular VarDial Evaluation Campaign with four shared tasks: Dravidian Language Identification (DLI), Romanian Dialect Identification (RDI), Social Media Variety Geolocation (SMG), and Uralic Language Identification (ULI). Each of these tasks addressed an important challenge in dialect and language identification. Eight teams prepared system description papers that are included in this volume, along with a report paper written by the campaign organizers summarizing the results and the main findings of the evaluation campaign.

Finally, we would like to take this opportunity to thank the VarDial Evaluation Campaign shared task organizers and the task participants for their hard work. We further thank our amazing VarDial program committee members for their thorough reviews. They have been a very important part of the workshop's success in these eight years.

The VarDial workshop organizers:

Marcos Zampieri, Preslav Nakov, Nikola Ljubešić, Jörg Tiedemann, Yves Scherrer, and
Tommi Jauhiainen

`http://sites.google.com/view/vardial2021/`

Organizers:

Marcos Zampieri - Rochester Institute of Technology (USA)
Preslav Nakov - Qatar Computing Research Institute, HBKU (Qatar)
Nikola Ljubešić - Jožef Stefan Institute (Slovenia) and University of Zagreb (Croatia)
Jörg Tiedemann - University of Helsinki (Finland)
Yves Scherrer - University of Helsinki (Finland)
Tommi Jauhiainen - University of Helsinki (Finland)

Program Committee:

Željko Agić (Corti, Denmark)
Cesar Aguilar (Pontifical Catholic University of Chile, Chile)
Laura Alonso y Alemany (University of Cordoba, Argentina)
Eric Atwell (University of Leeds, United Kingdom)
Jorge Baptista (University of Algarve and INESC-ID, Portugal)
Eckhard Bick (University of Southern Denmark, Denmark)
Johannes Bjerva (University of Copenhagen, Denmark)
Francis Bond (Nanyang Technological University, Singapore)
Aoife Cahill (Educational Testing Service, United States)
David Chiang (University of Notre Dame, United States)
Paul Cook (University of New Brunswick, Canada)
Çağrı Çöltekin (University of Tübingen)
Marta Costa-Jussà (Universitat Politècnica de Catalunya, Spain)
Jon Dehdari (Think Big Analytics, United States)
Liviu Dinu (University of Bucharest, Romania)
Stefanie Dipper (Ruhr University Bochum, Germany)
Sascha Diwersy (University of Montpellier, France)
Mark Dras (Macquarie University, Australia)
Tomaž Erjavec (Jožef Stefan Institute, Slovenia)
Pablo Gamallo (University of Santiago de Compostela, Spain)
Binyam Gebrekidan Gebre (Phillips Research, The Netherlands)
Cyril Goutte (National Research Council, Canada)
Nizar Habash (New York University Abu Dhabi, UAE)
Chu-Ren Huang (Hong Kong Polytechnic University, Hong Kong)
Radu Ionescu (University of Bucharest, Romania)
Jeremy Jancsary (Nuance Communications, Austria)
Tommi Jauhiainen (University of Helsinki, Finland)
Surafel Melaku Lakew (FBK , Italy)
Ekaterina Lapshinova-Koltunski (Saarland University, Germany)
Lung-Hao Lee (National Taiwan Normal University, Taiwan)
John Nerbonne (University of Groningen, Netherlands and University of Freiburg, Germany)
Kemal Oflazer (Carnegie-Mellon University in Qatar, Qatar)
Maciej Ogrodniczuk (IPAN, Polish Academy of Sciences, Poland)
Petya Osenova (Bulgarian Academy of Sciences, Bulgaria)
Santanu Pal (Saarland University, Germany)
Francisco Rangel (Autoritas Consulting, Spain)
Taraka Rama (University of North Texas, United States)

Reinhard Rapp (University of Mainz, Germany and University of Aix-Marsaille, France)
Paolo Rosso (Technical University of Valencia, Spain)
Rachel Edita O. Roxas (National University, Phillipines)
Fatiha Sadat (Université du Québec à Montréal (UQAM), Canada)
Tanja Samardžić (University of Zurich, Switzerland)
Kevin Scannell (Saint Louis University, United States)
Yves Scherrer (University of Helsinki, Finland)
Serge Sharoff (University of Leeds, United Kingdom)
Miikka Silfverberg (University of Helsinki, Finland)
Kiril Simov (Bulgarian Academy of Sciences, Bulgaria)
Milena Slavcheva (Bulgarian Academy of Sciences, Bulgaria)
Marco Tadić (University of Zagreb, Croatia)
Liling Tan (Rakuten Institute of Technology, Singapore)
Joel Tetreault (Dataminr, United States)
Francis Tyers (Indiana University, United States)
Taro Watanabe (Google Inc., Japan)
Pidong Wang (Google Inc., United States)

Table of Contents

Conference Program

Tuesday, April 20, 2021

10:30–10:40 ***Opening Session***

10:40–11:00 *Findings of the VarDial Evaluation Campaign 2021*
Bharathi Raja Chakravarthi, Gaman Mihaela, Radu Tudor Ionescu, Heidi Jauhiainen, Tommi Jauhiainen, Krister Lindén, Nikola Ljubešić, Niko Partanen, Ruba Priyadharshini, Christoph Purschke, Eswari Rajagopal, Yves Scherrer and Marcos Zampieri

11:00–11:30 ***Coffee break***

11:30–12:30 ***Invited Talk by Jack Grieve***

Oral Presentations

12:30–12:45 *Hierarchical Transformer for Multilingual Machine Translation*
Albina Khusainova, Adil Khan, Adín Ramírez Rivera and Vitaly Romanov

12:45–13:00 *Regression Analysis of Lexical and Morpho-Syntactic Properties of Kiezdeutsch*
Diego Frassinelli, Gabriella Lapesa, Reem Alatrash, Dominik Schlechtweg and Sabine Schulte im Walde

13:00–13:15 *Representations of Language Varieties Are Reliable Given Corpus Similarity Measures*
Jonathan Dunn

13:15–13:30 *Whit's the Richt Pairt o Speech: PoS tagging for Scots*
Harm Lameris and Sara Stymne

13:30–15:00 ***Lunch break***

Tuesday, April 20, 2021 (continued)

15:00–16:00 Poster Session

Efficient Unsupervised NMT for Related Languages with Cross-Lingual Language Models and Fidelity Objectives
Rami Aly, Andrew Caines and Paula Buttery

Fine-tuning Distributional Semantic Models for Closely-Related Languages
Kushagra Bhatia, Divyanshu Aggarwal and Ashwini Vaidya

Discriminating Between Similar Nordic Languages
René Haas and Leon Derczynski

Naive Bayes-based Experiments in Romanian Dialect Identification
Tommi Jauhiainen, Heidi Jauhiainen and Krister Lindén

UnibucKernel: Geolocating Swiss German Jodels Using Ensemble Learning
Gaman Mihaela, Sebastian Cojocariu and Radu Tudor Ionescu

Optimizing a Supervised Classifier for a Difficult Language Identification Problem
Yves Bestgen

Comparing the Performance of CNNs and Shallow Models for Language Identification
Andrea Ceolin

Dialect Identification through Adversarial Learning and Knowledge Distillation on Romanian BERT
George-Eduard Zaharia, Andrei-Marius Avram, Dumitru-Clementin Cercel and Traian Rebedea

Comparing Approaches to Dravidian Language Identification
Tommi Jauhiainen, Tharindu Ranasinghe and Marcos Zampieri

N-gram and Neural Models for Uralic Language Identification: NRC at VarDial 2021
Gabriel Bernier-Colborne, Serge Leger and Cyril Goutte

Social Media Variety Geolocation with geoBERT
Yves Scherrer and Nikola Ljubešić

Tuesday, April 20, 2021 (continued)

16:00–17:00 *Invited Talk by Katharina Kann*

17:00–17:15 *Closing Remarks*

Findings of the VarDial Evaluation Campaign 2021

Bharathi Raja Chakravarthi[1], Mihaela Găman[2], Radu Tudor Ionescu[2], Heidi Jauhiainen[3], Tommi Jauhiainen[3,9], Krister Lindén[3], Nikola Ljubešić[4,5], Niko Partanen[3], Ruba Priyadharshini[6], Christoph Purschke[7], Eswari Rajagopal[8] Yves Scherrer[3], Marcos Zampieri[9]

[1]National University of Ireland Galway, [2]University of Bucharest, [3]University of Helsinki, [4]Jožef Stefan Institute, [5]University of Ljubljana, [6]Madurai Kamaraj University, [7]University of Luxembourg, [8]National Institute of Technology Tiruchirappalli, [9]Rochester Institute of Technology

`vardialworkshop@gmail.com`

Abstract

This paper describes the results of the shared tasks organized as part of the VarDial Evaluation Campaign 2021. The campaign was part of the eighth workshop on Natural Language Processing (NLP) for Similar Languages, Varieties and Dialects (VarDial), co-located with EACL 2021. Four separate shared tasks were included this year: Dravidian Language Identification (DLI), Romanian Dialect Identification (RDI), Social Media Variety Geolocation (SMG), and Uralic Language Identification (ULI). DLI was organized for the first time and the other three continued a series of tasks from previous evaluation campaigns.

1 Introduction

The computational processing of similar languages, varieties and dialects is a vibrant area of research discussed in a recent survey (Zampieri et al., 2020). Co-located with international conferences, the workshop series on NLP for Similar Languages, Varieties and Dialects (VarDial) has become the main workshop on this topic reaching its eighth edition in 2021. Since its first edition, VarDial has included well-attended shared tasks on topics such as language and dialect identification, morphosyntactic tagging, and cross-lingual parsing. These shared tasks became part of the VarDial Evaluation Campaigns featuring multiple shared tasks organized yearly with the workshop (Zampieri et al., 2017, 2018, 2019; Găman et al., 2020).

Together with VarDial 2021, we organized the fifth edition of the VarDial Evaluation Campaign.[1] The VarDial Evaluation Campaign 2021 featured four shared tasks addressing different aspects of language and dialect identification. In this paper, we present the results and main findings of these shared tasks. Section 4 presents the Dravidian Language Identification (DLI) shared task included for the first time at VarDial 2021. The Romanian Dialect Identification (RDI) shared task is described in Section 5 and the Social Media Variety Geolocation (SMG) task is presented in Section 6. These two tasks are task re-runs from VarDial 2020 with augmented datasets prepared for VarDial 2021. Finally, the Uralic Language Identification (ULI) shared task, described in Section 7, is an open leaderboard shared task that ran between VarDial 2020 and 2021. We include references to the 8 system description papers written by the participants of the campaign in Table 1.

2 Shared Tasks at VarDial 2021

Dravidian Language Identification (DLI): Dravidian languages are a language family spoken mainly in the south of India (Chakravarthi, 2020). The four major literary Dravidian languages are Tamil (ISO 639-3: tam), Telugu (ISO 639-3: tel), Malayalam (ISO 639-3: mal), and Kannada (ISO 639-3: kan). Tamil, Malayalam, and Kannada are closely related belonging to the Tamil-Kannada subgroup. All three languages have official status in the Government of India. Outside India, Tamil also has official status in Sri Lanka and Singapore. These languages are widely considered to be under-resourced (Thavareesan and Mahesan, 2019, 2020a,b). The DLI shared task provides participants with a collection of 16,672 YouTube comments as training set. The comments contain code-mixed sentences with English and one of the South Dravidian languages (Tamil, Malayalam or Kannada). All comments were written in the Latin script (Non-native script). The task is to identify the language of each comment.

[1]`https://sites.google.com/view/vardial2021/evaluation-campaign`

Proceedings of the 8th VarDial Workshop on NLP for Similar Languages, Varieties and Dialects, pages 1–11
April 20, 2021 ©2021 Association for Computational Linguistics

Romanian Dialect Identification (RDI): The 2021 Romanian Dialect Identification shared task is at the third iteration, following the 2019 Moldavian vs. Romanian Cross-Dialect Topic identification (MRC) (Zampieri et al., 2019) and the 2020 Romanian Dialect Identification (RDI) (Găman et al., 2020) shared tasks. The 2021 RDI shared task is formulated as a cross-domain binary classification by dialect problem, in which a classification model is required to discriminate between the Moldavian (MD) and the Romanian (RO) subdialects. This year, we provided participants with an augmented version of the MOROCO data set (Butnaru and Ionescu, 2019) for training, which contains Moldavian and Romanian samples of text collected from the news domain. Last year's test set of tweets (Găman and Ionescu, 2020b) is used for validation. A new set of tweets has been collected for the 2021 shared task. The task has two formats, open and closed. In the closed format, participants are not allowed to use external data to train their models. In the open format, participants are allowed to use external resources such as unlabeled corpora, lexicons and pre-trained embeddings (e.g. BERT), but the use of additional labeled data is still not allowed.

Social Media Variety Geolocation (SMG): In contrast to most past and present VarDial tasks, the SMG task is framed as a geolocation task: given a text, the participants have to predict its geographic location in terms of latitude and longitude coordinates. This setup addresses the common issue that defining a set of discrete labels is not trivial for many language areas where there is a continuum between varieties rather than clear-cut borders. The SMG task is split into three subtasks covering different language areas: the **BCMS** subtask is focused on geolocated tweets published in the area of Croatia, Bosnia and Herzegovina, Montenegro and Serbia in the Serbo-Croatian (HBS) macrolanguage (Ljubešić et al., 2016); the **DE-AT** subtask focuses on Jodel conversations initiated in Germany and Austria, which are written in standard German but commonly contain regional and dialectal forms; the **CH** subtask is based on Jodel conversations initiated in Switzerland, which were found to be held majoritarily in Swiss German dialects (Hovy and Purschke, 2018). All three subtasks used the same data format and evaluation methodology.

Uralic Language Identification (ULI): This task focuses on discriminating between the languages in the Uralic group as defined by the ISO 639-3 standard. Following VarDial 2020, ULI 2021 was an open public leaderboard competition where participants were able to submit at any point until the final submission date. A leaderboard page was set up to inform the participants of the current high scores and as a way to get more detailed information.[2] The task included 29 individual relevant languages, some of which are very closely related, such as Erzya (myv) and Moskha (mdf), or Livvi (olo) and Ludian (lud). The languages are spoken in Scandinavia, Estonia and Finland, and within the Russian Federation in a region that extends far into Siberia. In addition to the relevant languages, the task featured 149 non-relevant languages.

3 Participating Teams

A total of nine teams submitted runs to one or more shared tasks in this year's VarDial evaluation campaign. In Table 1, we list the teams that participated in the shared tasks, including references to the 8 system description papers which will be published as parts of the VarDial workshop proceedings. Detailed information about the submissions in each respective task is included in the following sections of this report.

4 Dravidian Language Identification (DLI)

4.1 Dataset

The DLI task is based on three datasets from YouTube comments (Chakravarthi et al., 2020b,a; Hande et al., 2020). In the 2021 (DLI) shared task, participants have to train a model on comments written in Roman script. Our corpora contains all the three types of code-mixed sentences: Inter-Sentential switch, Intra-Sentential switch and Tag switching. All comments were written in Roman script (Non-native script) with either one of the south Dravidian (Tamil, Malayalam, and Kannada) grammar with English lexicon or English grammar with south Dravidian lexicons (Jose et al., 2020; Priyadharshini et al., 2020). The comments were written in the Latin Script with different types of code-mixing. The language tag of the comment were given. The challenge of the task was to identify the language of the given comment. It was

[2] `http://urn.fi/urn:nbn:fi:lb-2020102201`

Team	DLI	RDI	SMG	ULI	System Description Papers
HeLju			✓		(Scherrer and Ljubešić, 2021)
HWR	✓				(Jauhiainen et al., 2021b)
LAST	✓		✓		(Bestgen, 2021)
NAYEL	✓				
NRC				✓	(Bernier-Colborne et al., 2021)
Phlyers	✓	✓	✓		(Ceolin, 2021)
SUKI		✓			(Jauhiainen et al., 2021a)
UnibucKernel			✓		(Găman et al., 2021)
UPB		✓			(Zaharia et al., 2021)

Table 1: The teams that participated in the VarDial Evaluation Campaign 2021.

a challenging task, since Tamil, Malayalam and Kannada are closely related languages, some of the words being common in all these languages. The participants had to train a system to identify the language of each comment. Our dataset size is 16,672 comments for training and 4,588 for testing. There were three language tags such as Tamil, Malayalam and Kannada. A new category **Not in intended language** was added to include comments written in a language other than the Dravidian languages.

A sample comment from our dataset provided is displayed below. The original sentence was annotated in Tamil and it contains the English word *movie*. The corresponding English gloss is *You will see what is the movie*.

(1) Paka thana poro **movie** la Enna irukunu baki ellam.

4.2 Participants and Approaches

Due to the short time between the announcement of the shared task and the submission deadline, the participation was lower than we expected. Four teams submitted results to the shared task.

Bestgen (2021) proposed a logistic regression model based on *n*-grams of characters with maximum length as features to classify the comments. The authors achieved a high score with simple techniques. The authors also analyzed the results in detail. For more information, the reader should look at the working notes of the author.

Jauhiainen et al. (2021b) submitted results using two models, a Naïve Bayes (NB) classifier with adaptive language models, which was shown to obtain competitive performance in many language and dialect identification tasks, and a transformer-based model, which is widely regarded as the state-of-the-art in a number of NLP tasks. Their first submission was sent in the closed submission track, using only the training set provided by the shared task organisers. In contrast, the second submission is considered to be open, as it used a pre-trained model trained with external data. Their team attained a shared second position in the shared task with the submission based on Naïve Bayes.

4.3 Results

Results for the DLI task are presented in Table 2.

Rank	Team	Run	Macro-F1
1	LAST	1	0.93
	LAST	2	0.92
	LAST	3	0.92
2	HWR	1	0.92
2	NYAEL	1	0.92
	NAYEL	2	0.91
4	Phlyers	1	0.89
	Phlyers	2	0.89
	HWR	2	0.89
	NAYEL	3	0.84

Table 2: The results of all entries by the four team participating in the DLI shared task in terms of Macro-F1.

Given the difficulty of the DLI 2021 task, the level of performance achieved by the systems is appreciable. Identifying the Other-language category was particularly difficult because it may be thought that it is not homogeneous but composed of different languages in varying proportions. It is not even certain that all the other languages present in the test set were also present in the learning set. Logistic Regression and Naive Bayes methods were used to win the competition. Regarding the systems proposed by Jauhiainen et al. (2021b), even though the difference in performance between the NB model and the transformers was only 3% on the test set, the fact that the transformers did not outperform the simple NB classifier deserves special attention. One of the reasons behind the inferior performance of the pre-trained models is that the comments contain code-mixed sentences, which were not seen before by pre-trained language models such as BERT or XLM-R.

4.4 Summary

We are glad to see non-native speakers of Dravidian language participating in the DLI task. The DLI shared task showed the difficulty of identifying language in a code-mixed setting. We will continue to add more data to the DLI dataset to improve the language identification for the Dravidian languages in the code-mixed settings in the future.

5 Romanian Dialect Identification (RDI)

5.1 Dataset

As training data, we used an extended version of the Moldavian and Romanian Dialectal Corpus (MOROCO)[3] (Butnaru and Ionescu, 2019), which comprises news articles collected from the top five news websites from Romania and the Republic of Moldova. To automatically annotate the news articles with dialect labels, Butnaru and Ionescu (2019) used the web domains (*.md* or *.ro*) of the news websites. As development data, we used the short text samples from MOROCO-Tweets[4] (Găman and Ionescu, 2020b). The tweets were collected from Romania and the Republic of Moldova, the labels being assigned according to the geographical location. As test data, we collected a new set of tweets, which was compiled in the same manner as MOROCO-Tweets. With these choices as training, development and test corpora, we can evaluate participants on a challenging cross-genre binary dialect identification task: Moldavian (MD) vs. Romanian (RO). The number of samples in the training, the development and the test sets are shown in Table 3. All text samples were automatically pre-processed to replace each named entity with the special token NE.

Dialect	Training	Development	Test
Moldavian	18,121	2,612	2,665
Romanian	21,366	2,625	2,617
Total	**39,487**	**5,237**	**5,282**

Table 3: Number of text samples in the training, the development and the test sets of the RDI shared task.

5.2 Participants and Approaches

Phlyers: The Phlyers (Ceolin, 2021) submitted two runs based on a simple convolutional neural network (CNN). The CNN is first trained on news articles from the official training set, and then fine-tuned on tweets from the official development set. For the first run, the team performed data augmentation by creating ten additional versions of the development set, where the words in each sentence are shuffled. For the second run, the model is trained with even more data augmentation. Both submissions are closed.

SUKI: The predictions submitted by the SUKI team (Jauhiainen et al., 2021a) were produced by a custom coded language identifier based on the product of relative frequencies of character *n*-grams. The model is essentially a Naïve Bayes classifier that uses the relative frequencies as probabilities (Jauhiainen et al., 2019c). The length of the character *n*-grams ranges from 2 to 5. SUKI summed up the negative logarithms of the relative frequencies instead of multiplying them. As a smoothing value, they used the negative logarithm of an *n*-gram appearing only once multiplied by a penalty modifier equal to 1.61. SUKI submitted two closed runs in which they used 50% of the development data as training material and the other 50% for hyperparameter tuning. For the first run, in addition to the basic classifier, they used a blacklist of lowercase character *n*-grams generated from the training and the development data. For the second run, they added the language model adaptation technique described by (Jauhiainen et al., 2018). They used one epoch of language model adaptation to the test data.

UPB: The UPB team (Zaharia et al., 2021) submitted three open runs. For the first run, UPB fine-tuned a Romanian BERT model on the training set, which was split into sentences. After the initial training, they filtered the training set considering only the entries that the model correctly predicted with high confidence for the second round of training. At the same time, they used a prediction threshold to classify an entry as Moldavian or

[3] `https://github.com/butnaruandrei/MOROCO`

[4] `https://github.com/raduionescu/MOROCO-Tweets`

Romanian. For the second run, UPB proposed an ensemble formed by training or fine-tuning multiple models, including a Romanian BERT based on adversarial training, a distilled model as well as a method based on generative adversarial networks. For the third run, they submitted the predictions of a student model resulting from knowledge distillation using TextBrewer on Romanian BERT.

5.3 Results

Rank	Team	Run	Macro-F1
1	SUKI	2	0.777182
2	UPB	2	0.732467
	UPB	1	0.731909
	SUKI	1	0.726556
	UPB	3	0.674343
3	Phlyers	1	0.653171
	Phlyers	2	0.513287

Table 4: Macro F_1 scores attained by the teams participating in the 2021 RDI shared task.

As shown in Table 4, the best results in the 2021 RDI shared task were attained by the SUKI team. Compared with their own results Jauhiainen et al. (2020a) obtained in the first edition of the RDI shared task (Găman et al., 2020), the SUKI team improved their performance by a considerable margin. It seems that the main drivers for improvement were (i) the decision to use the development data for training and (ii) the idea of adapting the language model to the test set. The team that was ranked in the second place is UPB. Their best submission is an ensemble that comprises several deep models, including a Romanian BERT. Different from their last year's participation (Zaharia et al., 2020), they carefully split the training set into sentences. This idea was borrowed from top-ranked teams of the 2020 RDI shared task. Phlyers ranked on the third place in the 2021 ranking, without significant differences in terms of performance with respect to their previous participation (Ceolin and Zhang, 2020). Despite having access to significantly more in-domain data compared with the previous RDI shared task, the participants were not able to report significant performance gains. Indeed, the top scoring team (Çöltekin, 2020) in 2020 reached a macro F_1 score of 0.7876, while the top scoring team in 2021 achieved a macro F_1 score of 0.7772. Although the test sets are not identical, we expect them to be equally difficult, since they were collected in the same manner. We thus conclude that Romanian dialect identification remains a difficult task when it comes to short text samples such as tweets, even when in-domain data is available.

5.4 Summary

For the Romanian Dialect Identification shared task, we proposed a cross-domain binary classification task. We had a total of 8 submissions coming from 3 different teams. Each team submitted between 2 and 3 runs. Compared with the 2020 RDI shared task, we observed a decreased interest which can be attributed to the extremely short time given to participants for model development. Looking at the results, we conclude that the set of 5 thousand in-domain text samples (MOROCO-Tweets) can compensate for the much larger set of out-of-domain training samples (MOROCO). However, we did not observe any significant performance boosts compared with last year's RDI shared task, in which the in-domain data available for development was scarce.

6 Social Media Variety Geolocation (SMG)

6.1 Dataset

The SMG task is based on three datasets from two Social Media platforms, Jodel and Twitter. Since its first edition in 2020, the datasets have been expanded.

- The **BCMS subtask** is focused on geolocated tweets published in the area of Croatia, Bosnia and Herzegovina, Montenegro and Serbia in the Serbo-Croatian macrolanguage (ISO acronym HBS, code 639-3). While the training and development data comes from the pool of the 2020 data (Ljubešić et al., 2016), new data collected during 2020 is used for the test set. The training and development data is also divided by the time of publication, the whole train:dev:test setup thereby being significantly more realistic in this iteration of the subtask.

- The **DE-AT subtask** focuses on Jodel conversations initiated in Germany and Austria, which are written in standard German but commonly contain regional and dialectal forms. The training, development and test sets are created by resampling the 2020 dataset (Hovy and Purschke, 2018).[5]

- The **CH subtask** focuses on Jodel conversations from Switzerland, which were found to be held majoritarily in Swiss German dialects. This dataset is considerably smaller, but we expect it to contain more dialect-specific cues than the DE-AT one. The training, development and test sets are created by resampling the 2020 dataset (Hovy and Purschke, 2018).

All three subtasks use the same data format: each instance consists of three fields, the unprocessed text of the message or conversation, the latitude coordinate and the longitude coordinate. Table 5 shows the key figures of the datasets.

Subtask	Number of instances			Tokens /
	Training	Devel.	Test	instance
BCMS	353,953	38,013	4,189	13
DE-AT	318,487	29,122	31,515	69
CH	25,261	2,416	2,438	50

Table 5: SMG datasets.

6.2 Participants and Approaches

Unfortunately, the participation was much lower than in 2020, due to the short time between the announcement of the shared task and the submission deadline: one team (HeLju) submitted to all three subtasks, whereas another team (UnibucKernel) submitted only to the CH subtask.

HeLju: The HeLju systems (Scherrer and Ljubešić, 2021) rely on the BERT architecture, where the classification output is replaced by a double regression output. HeLju proposes constrained submissions, for which the BERT models are trained from scratch using the SMG training data, as well as unconstrained submissions, for which pre-trained models are used.

UnibucKernel: The UnibucKernel team (Găman et al., 2021) submitted an ensemble system based on XGBoost, whose components are a ν-SVR model trained on top of n-gram string kernels, a CNN with character-level and word-level filters, and a pre-trained BERT model. All components provide double regression outputs. The model represents an upgrade of the previously proposed ensemble (Găman and Ionescu, 2020a) for the 2020 SMG-CH geolocation shared task.

[5]Unfortunately, the Jodel API does not currently allow the collection of new data.

6.3 Results

The test set predictions were evaluated on the basis of median and mean distance to the gold coordinates. Submissions are ranked by decreasing median distance, which is the official metric. For comparison, we also mention the distance values obtained from a simple centroid baseline, which predicts the center point (measured on the training data) for each test instance. Results and rankings for the three tasks are presented in Table 6.

Subtask /	Rank	Submission	Median dist. (km)	Mean dist. (km)
BCMS	1	HeLju unconstr.	15.49	76.04
	2	HeLju constr.	52.06	98.74
		Baseline	*118.33*	*160.78*
DE-AT	1	HeLju unconstr.	149.33	172.52
	2	HeLju constr.	161.13	184.97
		Baseline	*206.42*	*226.13*
CH	1	HeLju unconstr.	17.55	25.84
	2	HeLju constr.	20.70	29.62
	3	UnibucKernel	23.60	29.75
		Baseline	*53.13*	*51.50*

Table 6: SMG task results. The official metric is median distance in kilometers, i.e., lower values are better.

The low number of submissions does not allow us to draw reliable conclusions, but the general findings are similar to last year's: the CH subtask turned out to be the easiest one and the DE-AT the most difficult one, with BCMS lying between the two. All submissions managed to beat the baseline by a large margin, and unconstrained systems again tend to beat constrained ones.

The median distance value of the best-ranked BCMS submission seems surprisingly low. The reason for this outlier is probably to be found in the way the 2021 data were obtained. The test set consists entirely of tweets published after March 2020. Thus, it is likely that the limitation in population movements due to COVID restrictions led to a more skewed geographical distribution of the test instances, which in turn makes it easier to reach low median values.

6.4 Summary

The second edition of the SMG task attracted fewer participants than the first, and as a consequence, the variety of explored solutions and algorithms is also narrower. Nevertheless, we believe that a geolocation task has its justification within VarDial, in particular for pluricentric languages without clear-cut variety borders. Thanks to its reliance on easily available geolocated messages from social media services, future editions of the SMG task can be envisaged, possibly focusing on different language areas.

7 Uralic Language Identification (ULI)

The ULI shared task focuses on 29 rare Uralic languages and especially the difficulties of finding such languages amongst a huge amount of textual material in more common languages. In ULI, the 29 rare Uralic languages are considered relevant. In addition to them, there are 149 non-relevant languages.

The shared task was first organized as part of the VarDial Evaluation Campaign 2020 (Găman et al., 2020). Due to low participation, we decided to keep the shared task open even after the campaign was over. Only the NRC team had submitted results and they were all well below the baseline. We constructed a leaderboard page with the best results updated as soon as they were evaluated.

The ULI 2021 shared task contained three separate subtasks: **ULI-RLE**, **ULI-RSS**, and **ULI-178**. In **ULI-RLE** (relevant languages as equals), the defining measure was the macro F_1 score calculated for the relevant languages present in the training set. In **ULI-RSS** (relevant sentences as equals), the measure used was the micro F_1 score calculated for sentences either written in or predicted to be written in the relevant languages. In **ULI-178** (All 178 languages as equals), the macro F_1 score was calculated as an average over all the 178 languages part of the training set repertoire.

We were accepting submissions until the end of the evaluation phase of the VarDial Evaluation Campaign 2021 on February 2, 2021. Participants who submitted results were all invited to submit a system description paper to appear in the proceedings of VarDial 2021.

7.1 Dataset

The dataset for the 2021 competition was the same as earlier. It is described by Găman et al. (2020) and in more detail by Jauhiainen et al. (2020b). In short, the training set consists of two parts, the relevant and the non-relevant languages. The training data for the relevant languages comes from the Wanca 2016 collection (Jauhiainen et al., 2019a).[6] Wanca 2017 containing the test data for relevant languages remains unpublished, but the publication is expected to occur in 2021. The training and the test data for the non-relevant languages comes from the Leipzig Corpora Collection (Richter et al., 2006).[7] The ULI leaderboard contains links to the download locations of the training and the test sets.

7.2 Participants and Approaches

Three teams submitted new results during the ULI 2021 evaluation period.

NRC: The NRC team was the only one submitting results for the initial ULI shared task (Bernier-Colborne and Goutte, 2020). In 2020, they used a system based on the one they had used to win the Cuneiform Language Identification (CLI) shared task in the 2019 VarDial Evaluation Campaign (Jauhiainen et al., 2019b; Bernier-Colborne et al., 2019; Zampieri et al., 2019). However, the ULI task turned out to be much more difficult for the BERT based language classifier system. For the ULI 2021, they set out to further improve the results produced by the deep learning architecture (Bernier-Colborne et al., 2021). In addition, they submitted results using a probabilistic classifier similar to Naïve Bayes. They used this NB style classifier already in the DSL shared task of 2014 (Zampieri et al., 2014) to predict the language group before handing the task over to SVMs (Goutte et al., 2014).

LAST: The LAST team submitted several runs using Logistic Regression (LR) classifiers and their ensembles (Bestgen, 2021). As features, the classifiers used character n-grams, either word internal or word spanning, which were weighted with BM25. BM25 weighted character n-grams were used successfully by the CECL team in Discriminating between Similar Languages (DSL) and GDI shared tasks of VarDial 2017 (Bestgen, 2017). Then they were used as features for their SVM based classifiers.

[6] http://urn.fi/urn:nbn:fi:lb-2020022901

[7] https://corpora.uni-leipzig.de/

Rank	Team	Method	Relevant Macro-F1
1	NRC	Probabilistic classifier (similar to Naive Bayes) using character 5-grams	0.8138
2	Phlyers	Ensemble of SVM and Naive Bayes classifiers using character *n*-grams 3-5.	0.8085
	baseline	HeLI	0.8004
	Phlyers	Naive Bayes classifier trained on character 5grams	0.7977
3	LAST	Ensemble of LR classifiers trained on char *n*-grams 1-3 weighted with BM25	0.7758
	LAST	LR classifier trained on char *n*-grams 1-3 weighted with BM25	0.7755
	Phlyers	SVM (char *n*-grams 3-4) followed by Naive Bayes classifier (char *n*-grams 3-5)	0.7740
	LAST	LR classifier trained on word internal char *n*-grams 1-4 weighted with BM25	0.7727
	Phlyers	Naive Bayes classifier trained on character 3grams and 4grams	0.7584
	NRC	BERT-style deep neural network with early stopping	0.7430
	NRC	BERT-style deep neural network	0.6866
	Phlyers	SVM (char *n*-grams 5-7) followed by Naive Bayes classifier (char *n*-grams 3-5)	0.6783

Table 7: ULI shared task 2021 - RLE results.

Rank	Team	Method	Relevant Micro-F1
1	NRC	Probabilistic classifier (similar to Naive Bayes) using character 5-grams	0.9668
	baseline	HeLI	0.9632
	NRC	BERT-style deep neural network with early stopping	0.9530
2	LAST	Ensemble of LR classifiers trained on char *n*-grams 1-3 weighted with BM25	0.9496
	LAST	LR classifier trained on word internal char *n*-grams 1-4 weighted with BM25	0.9492
	LAST	LR classifier trained on char *n*-grams 1-3 weighted with BM25	0.9484
3	Phlyers	SVM (char *n*-grams 3-4) followed by Naive Bayes classifier (char *n*-grams 3-5)	0.8389
	NRC	BERT-style deep neural network	0.8177
	Phlyers	SVM (char *n*-grams 5-7) followed by Naive Bayes classifier (char *n*-grams 3-5)	0.7595
	Phlyers	Naive Bayes classifier trained on character 5grams	0.5934
	Phlyers	Ensemble of SVM and Naive Bayes classifiers using character *n*-grams 3-5.	0.5932

Table 8: ULI shared task 2021 - RSS results.

Rank	Team	Method	Macro-F1
	baseline	HeLI	0.9252
1	LAST	LR classifier trained on word internal char *n*-grams 1-4 weighted with BM25	0.9164
	LAST	Ensemble of LR classifiers trained on char *n*-grams 1-3 weighted with BM25	0.9131
	LAST	LR classifier trained on char *n*-grams 1-3 weighted with BM25	0.9125
2	NRC	Probabilistic classifier (similar to Naive Bayes) using character 5-grams	0.9079
	NRC	BERT-style deep neural network with early stopping	0.9039
3	Phlyers	Ensemble of SVM and Naive Bayes classifiers using character *n*-grams 3-5.	0.8847
	Phlyers	Naive Bayes classifier trained on character 5grams	0.8831
	Phlyers	Naive Bayes classifier trained on character 3grams and 4grams	0.8753
	NRC	BERT-style deep neural network	0.8366

Table 9: ULI shared task 2021 - 178 results.

Phlyers: The Phlyers team used different combinations and ensembles of Naïve Bayes and SVM classifiers (Ceolin, 2021). As features, they used varying sized character *n*-grams. They experimented with similar systems in their submissions to the RDI shared task in 2020 (Ceolin and Zhang, 2020).

7.3 Results

Tables 7, 8, and 9 show the VarDial 2021 Evaluation Campaign end results for the ULI 2021 competition. As baseline, we used a HeLI based language identifier using parameters presented by Jauhiainen et al. (2017). Relative frequencies were calculated from the training data for character *n*-grams and words, but the baseline was not tuned using the training set.

In the ULI-RLE subtask, both the NRC and the Phlyers teams managed to beat the HeLI baseline. The NRC team's probabilistic classifier using character 5-grams is the new state of the art in ULI-RLE. In ULI-RSS, the Phlyers teams submission was not competetive at all, but the NRC team surpassed the baseline with the same system as they had used to win the ULI-RLE. For the third subtask, ULI-178, the submitted results failed to improve on the strong baseline provided by the HeLI based language identifier. The best submission was by the LAST team using an LR classifier with BM25-weighted word internal character n-grams.

7.4 Summary

We were glad to see more active participation in the ULI task than during the previous Evaluation Campaign. The ULI shared task proved again to be too difficult for the deep learning based classifiers and the more traditional approaches won all the subtasks. We will continue to keep the ULI leaderboard open and the results list can be updated again after the VarDial 2021 workshop is over. During 2021, we are aiming to produce a joint error analysis of several systems which have participated so far and design a new dataset for ULI 2022.

8 Conclusion

This paper presented the results and findings of the four shared tasks organized as part of the VarDial Evaluation Campaign 2021: Dravidian Language Identification (DLI), Romanian Dialect Identification (RDI), Social Media Variety Geolocation (SMG), and Uralic Language Identification (ULI). Each of these tasks addressed an important challenge in language and dialect identification providing participants with either new or augmented versions of existing datasets that are made freely available to the community.

We included short descriptions for each team's systems in this report and references to all 8 system description papers published in the VarDial workshop proceedings in Table 1. Despite the state-of-the-art performance obtained by deep learning models in a wide range of NLP tasks, in VarDial 2021 we observed that traditional machine learning models once again outperformed deep learning models for language and dialect identification. This corroborates the findings of previous editions of the campaign (Zampieri et al., 2019; Găman et al., 2020) and of the survey by Jauhiainen et al. (2019d).

Acknowledgments

We thank all the participants for their interest in the evaluation campaign.

The work related to the ULI shared task has been partly funded by the Kone Foundation, The Finnish Research Impact Foundation, and the University of Helsinki in cooperation with Lingsoft.

References

Gabriel Bernier-Colborne and Cyril Goutte. 2020. Challenges in neural language identification: NRC at VarDial 2020. In *Proceedings of the 7th Workshop on NLP for Similar Languages, Varieties and Dialects*, pages 273–282, Barcelona, Spain (Online). International Committee on Computational Linguistics (ICCL).

Gabriel Bernier-Colborne, Cyril Goutte, and Serge Léger. 2019. Improving cuneiform language identification with BERT. In *Proceedings of the Sixth Workshop on NLP for Similar Languages, Varieties and Dialects*, pages 17–25, Ann Arbor, Michigan. Association for Computational Linguistics.

Gabriel Bernier-Colborne, Serge Léger, and Cyril Goutte. 2021. N-gram and neural models for uralic language identification: NRC at VarDial 2021. In *Proceedings of the Eighth Workshop on NLP for Similar Languages, Varieties and Dialects (VarDial)*. Association for Computational Linguistics.

Yves Bestgen. 2017. Improving the character ngram model for the dsl task with bm25 weighting and less frequently used feature sets. In *Proceedings of the Fourth Workshop on NLP for Similar Languages, Varieties and Dialects (VarDial)*, pages 115–123, Valencia, Spain.

Yves Bestgen. 2021. Optimizing a Supervised Classifier for a Difficult Language Identification Problem. In *Proceedings of the Eighth Workshop on NLP for Similar Languages, Varieties and Dialects (VarDial)*. Association for Computational Linguistics.

Andrei M. Butnaru and Radu Tudor Ionescu. 2019. MOROCO: The Moldavian and Romanian Dialectal Corpus. In *Proceedings of ACL*, pages 688–698.

Andrea Ceolin. 2021. Comparing the performance of CNNs and shallow models for language identification. In *Proceedings of the Eighth Workshop on NLP for Similar Languages, Varieties and Dialects (VarDial)*. Association for Computational Linguistics.

Andrea Ceolin and Hong Zhang. 2020. Discriminating between standard Romanian and Moldavian tweets using filtered character ngrams. In *Proceedings of the 7th Workshop on NLP for Similar Languages, Varieties and Dialects*, pages 265–272, Barcelona, Spain (Online). International Committee on Computational Linguistics (ICCL).

Bharathi Raja Chakravarthi. 2020. *Leveraging orthographic information to improve machine translation of under-resourced languages*. Ph.D. thesis, NUI Galway.

Bharathi Raja Chakravarthi, Navya Jose, Shardul Suryawanshi, Elizabeth Sherly, and John Philip McCrae. 2020a. A sentiment analysis dataset for code-mixed Malayalam-English. In *Proceedings of the 1st Joint Workshop on Spoken Language Technologies for Under-resourced languages (SLTU) and*

Collaboration and Computing for Under-Resourced Languages (CCURL), pages 177–184, Marseille, France. European Language Resources association.

Bharathi Raja Chakravarthi, Vigneshwaran Muralidaran, Ruba Priyadharshini, and John Philip McCrae. 2020b. Corpus creation for sentiment analysis in code-mixed Tamil-English text. In *Proceedings of the 1st Joint Workshop on Spoken Language Technologies for Under-resourced languages (SLTU) and Collaboration and Computing for Under-Resourced Languages (CCURL)*, pages 202–210, Marseille, France. European Language Resources association.

Çağrı Çöltekin. 2020. Dialect Identification under Domain Shift: Experiments with Discriminating Romanian and Moldavian. In *Proceedings of the 7th Workshop on NLP for Similar Languages, Varieties and Dialects*, pages 186–192, Barcelona, Spain (Online). International Committee on Computational Linguistics (ICCL).

Cyril Goutte, Serge Léger, and Marine Carpuat. 2014. The nrc system for discriminating similar languages. In *Proceedings of the First Workshop on Applying NLP Tools to Similar Languages, Varieties and Dialects (VarDial)*, pages 139–145, Dublin, Ireland.

Mihaela Găman, Sebastian Cojocariu, and Radu Tudor Ionescu. 2021. UnibucKernel: Geolocating Swiss German Jodels Using Ensemble Learning. In *Proceedings of the Eighth Workshop on NLP for Similar Languages, Varieties and Dialects (VarDial)*. Association for Computational Linguistics.

Mihaela Găman, Dirk Hovy, Radu Tudor Ionescu, Heidi Jauhiainen, Tommi Jauhiainen, Krister Lindén, Nikola Ljubešić, Niko Partanen, Christoph Purschke, Yves Scherrer, and Marcos Zampieri. 2020. A Report on the VarDial Evaluation Campaign 2020. In *Proceedings of the Seventh Workshop on NLP for Similar Languages, Varieties and Dialects (VarDial)*.

Mihaela Găman and Radu Tudor Ionescu. 2020a. Combining Deep Learning and String Kernels for the Localization of Swiss German Tweets. In *Proceedings of the 7th Workshop on NLP for Similar Languages, Varieties and Dialects*, pages 242–253.

Mihaela Găman and Radu Tudor Ionescu. 2020b. The Unreasonable Effectiveness of Machine Learning in Moldavian versus Romanian Dialect Identification. *arXiv preprint arXiv:2007.15700*.

Adeep Hande, Ruba Priyadharshini, and Bharathi Raja Chakravarthi. 2020. KanCMD: Kannada CodeMixed dataset for sentiment analysis and offensive language detection. In *Proceedings of the Third Workshop on Computational Modeling of People's Opinions, Personality, and Emotion's in Social Media*, pages 54–63, Barcelona, Spain (Online). Association for Computational Linguistics.

Dirk Hovy and Christoph Purschke. 2018. Capturing regional variation with distributed place representations and geographic retrofitting. In *Proceedings of the 2018 Conference on Empirical Methods in Natural Language Processing*, pages 4383–4394, Brussels, Belgium. Association for Computational Linguistics.

Heidi Jauhiainen, Tommi Jauhiainen, and Krister Linden. 2019a. Wanca in Korp: Text corpora for under-resourced Uralic languages. In *Proceedings of the Research data and humanities (RDHUM) 2019 conference*, number 17 in Studia Humaniora Ouluensia, pages 21–40, Finland. University of Oulu.

Tommi Jauhiainen, Heidi Jauhiainen, Tero Alstola, and Krister Lindén. 2019b. Language and dialect identification of cuneiform texts. In *Proceedings of the Sixth Workshop on NLP for Similar Languages, Varieties and Dialects*, pages 89–98. Association for Computational Linguistics.

Tommi Jauhiainen, Heidi Jauhiainen, and Krister Lindén. 2018. HeLI-based experiments in Swiss German dialect identification. In *Proceedings of the Fifth Workshop on NLP for Similar Languages, Varieties and Dialects (VarDial 2018)*, pages 254–262, Santa Fe, New Mexico, USA. Association for Computational Linguistics.

Tommi Jauhiainen, Heidi Jauhiainen, and Krister Lindén. 2020a. Experiments in Language Variety Geolocation and Dialect Identification. In *Proceedings of the 7th Workshop on NLP for Similar Languages, Varieties and Dialects*, pages 220–231, Barcelona, Spain (Online). International Committee on Computational Linguistics (ICCL).

Tommi Jauhiainen, Heidi Jauhiainen, and Krister Lindén. 2021a. Naive Bayes-based Experiments in Romanian Dialect Identification. In *Proceedings of the Eighth Workshop on NLP for Similar Languages, Varieties and Dialects (VarDial)*. Association for Computational Linguistics.

Tommi Jauhiainen, Heidi Jauhiainen, Niko Partanen, and Krister Lindén. 2020b. Uralic Language Identification (ULI) 2020 shared task dataset and the Wanca 2017 corpus. In *Proceedings of the Seventh Workshop on NLP for Similar Languages, Varieties and Dialects (VarDial)*, pages 688–698.

Tommi Jauhiainen, Krister Lindén, and Heidi Jauhiainen. 2017. Evaluation of Language Identification Methods Using 285 Languages. In *Proceedings of the 21st Nordic Conference on Computational Linguistics (NoDaLiDa 2017)*, pages 183–191, Gothenburg, Sweden. Linköping University Electronic Press.

Tommi Jauhiainen, Krister Lindén, and Heidi Jauhiainen. 2019c. Discriminating between Mandarin Chinese and Swiss-German varieties using adaptive language models. In *Proceedings of the Sixth Workshop on NLP for Similar Languages, Varieties and*

Dialects, pages 178–187, Ann Arbor, Michigan. Association for Computational Linguistics.

Tommi Jauhiainen, Marco Lui, Marcos Zampieri, Timothy Baldwin, and Krister Lindén. 2019d. Automatic Language Identification in Texts: A Survey. *Journal of Artificial Intelligence Research*, 65:675–782.

Tommi Jauhiainen, Tharindu Ranasinghe, and Marcos Zampieri. 2021b. Comparing Approaches to Dravidian Language Identification. In *Proceedings of the Eighth Workshop on NLP for Similar Languages, Varieties and Dialects (VarDial)*. Association for Computational Linguistics.

Navya Jose, Bharathi Raja Chakravarthi, Shardul Suryawanshi, Elizabeth Sherly, and John P. McCrae. 2020. A Survey of Current Datasets for Code-Switching Research. In *2020 6th International Conference on Advanced Computing and Communication Systems (ICACCS)*, pages 136–141.

Nikola Ljubešić, Tanja Samardžić, and Curdin Derungs. 2016. TweetGeo - a tool for collecting, processing and analysing geo-encoded linguistic data. In *Proceedings of COLING 2016, the 26th International Conference on Computational Linguistics: Technical Papers*, pages 3412–3421, Osaka, Japan. The COLING 2016 Organizing Committee.

Ruba Priyadharshini, Bharathi Raja Chakravarthi, Mani Vegupatti, and John P. McCrae. 2020. Named Entity Recognition for Code-Mixed Indian Corpus using Meta Embedding. In *2020 6th International Conference on Advanced Computing and Communication Systems (ICACCS)*, pages 68–72.

Matthias Richter, Uwe Quasthoff, Erla Hallsteinsdóttir, and Christian Biemann. 2006. Exploiting the leipzig corpora collection. In *Proceedings of the Information Society Language Technologies Conference*, Ljubljana.

Yves Scherrer and Nikola Ljubešić. 2021. Social media variety geolocation with geobert. In *Proceedings of the Eighth Workshop on NLP for Similar Languages, Varieties and Dialects (VarDial)*. Association for Computational Linguistics.

Sajeetha Thavareesan and Sinnathamby Mahesan. 2019. Sentiment Analysis in Tamil Texts: A Study on Machine Learning Techniques and Feature Representation. In *2019 14th Conference on Industrial and Information Systems (ICIIS)*, pages 320–325.

Sajeetha Thavareesan and Sinnathamby Mahesan. 2020a. Sentiment Lexicon Expansion using Word2vec and fastText for Sentiment Prediction in Tamil texts. In *2020 Moratuwa Engineering Research Conference (MERCon)*, pages 272–276.

Sajeetha Thavareesan and Sinnathamby Mahesan. 2020b. Word embedding-based Part of Speech tagging in Tamil texts. In *2020 IEEE 15th International Conference on Industrial and Information Systems (ICIIS)*, pages 478–482.

George-Eduard Zaharia, Andrei-Marius Avram, Dumitru-Clementin Cercel, and Traian Rebedea. 2020. Exploring the Power of Romanian BERT for Dialect Identification. In *Proceedings of the 7th Workshop on NLP for Similar Languages, Varieties and Dialects*, pages 232–241, Barcelona, Spain (Online). International Committee on Computational Linguistics (ICCL).

George-Eduard Zaharia, Andrei-Marius Avram, Dumitru-Clementin Cercel, and Traian Rebedea. 2021. Dialect Identification through Adversarial Learning and Knowledge Distillation on Romanian BERT. In *Proceedings of the Eighth Workshop on NLP for Similar Languages, Varieties and Dialects (VarDial)*. Association for Computational Linguistics.

Marcos Zampieri, Shervin Malmasi, Nikola Ljubešić, Preslav Nakov, Ahmed Ali, Jörg Tiedemann, Yves Scherrer, and Noëmi Aepli. 2017. Findings of the VarDial Evaluation Campaign 2017. In *Proceedings of the Fourth Workshop on NLP for Similar Languages, Varieties and Dialects (VarDial)*, Valencia, Spain.

Marcos Zampieri, Shervin Malmasi, Preslav Nakov, Ahmed Ali, Suwon Shuon, James Glass, Yves Scherrer, Tanja Samardžić, Nikola Ljubešić, Jörg Tiedemann, Chris van der Lee, Stefan Grondelaers, Nelleke Oostdijk, Antal van den Bosch, Ritesh Kumar, Bornini Lahiri, and Mayank Jain. 2018. Language Identification and Morphosyntactic Tagging: The Second VarDial Evaluation Campaign. In *Proceedings of the Fifth Workshop on NLP for Similar Languages, Varieties and Dialects (VarDial)*, Santa Fe, USA.

Marcos Zampieri, Shervin Malmasi, Yves Scherrer, Tanja Samardžić, Francis Tyers, Miikka Silfverberg, Natalia Klyueva, Tung-Le Pan, Chu-Ren Huang, Radu Tudor Ionescu, Andrei Butnaru, and Tommi Jauhiainen. 2019. A Report on the Third VarDial Evaluation Campaign. In *Proceedings of the Sixth Workshop on NLP for Similar Languages, Varieties and Dialects (VarDial)*. Association for Computational Linguistics.

Marcos Zampieri, Preslav Nakov, and Yves Scherrer. 2020. Natural language processing for similar languages, varieties, and dialects: A survey. *Natural Language Engineering*, 26(6):595–612.

Marcos Zampieri, Liling Tan, Nikola Ljubešić, and Jörg Tiedemann. 2014. A report on the dsl shared task 2014. In *Proceedings of the First Workshop on Applying NLP Tools to Similar Languages, Varieties and Dialects (VarDial)*, pages 58–67, Dublin, Ireland.

Hierarchical Transformer for Multilingual Machine Translation

Albina Khusainova
Innopolis University,
Innopolis, Russia
a.khusainova@innopolis.ru

Adil Khan
Innopolis University,
Innopolis, Russia
a.khan@innopolis.ru

Adín Ramírez Rivera
University of Campinas
Campinas, Brazil
adin@ic.unicamp.br

Vitaly Romanov
Innopolis University,
Innopolis, Russia
v.romanov@innopolis.ru

Abstract

The choice of parameter sharing strategy in multilingual machine translation models determines how optimally parameter space is used and hence, directly influences ultimate translation quality. Inspired by linguistic trees that show the degree of relatedness between different languages, the new general approach to parameter sharing in multilingual machine translation was suggested recently. The main idea is to use these expert language hierarchies as a basis for multilingual architecture: the closer two languages are, the more parameters they share.

In this work, we test this idea using the Transformer architecture and show that despite the success in previous work there are problems inherent to training such hierarchical models. We demonstrate that in case of carefully chosen training strategy the hierarchical architecture can outperform bilingual models and multilingual models with full parameter sharing.

1 Introduction

Machine translation (MT) today is gradually approaching near-human quality; however, this holds true only when massive parallel corpus is available. As for the low-resource machine translation, the main way to improve it is to use additional data such as monolingual texts or parallel data in other languages. One of the ways to use the latter is to build a multilingual model: instead of training separate models for each translation direction, multiple parallel corpora can be combined to train a single model where languages can share some parameters to help each other learn. Given that languages have a lot in common, a properly organized parameter sharing strategy could compensate for the lack of training examples in low-resource pairs.

Exploiting language relatedness can substantially improve translation quality (Tan et al., 2019). The question is which architectural setup allows getting the most benefit from between-language commonalities. While there are different approaches to this problem, such as full parameter sharing (Johnson et al., 2017) or shared encoder side with language-specific decoders (Dong et al., 2015), we find the recent approach by Azpiazu and Pera (2020) promising because it accounts for the degree of relatedness between languages in a multilingual model in a systematic way.

Linguistic trees organize languages in hierarchies by the degree of kinship, and the same approach can be applied to multilingual machine translation models. The idea is to organize both encoder and decoder in a hierarchical fashion, reflecting the degree of relatedness between languages, such that the most related languages share the largest number of parameters. Figure 1 shows the outline of such model (will be explained in more detail in section 3.1).

Unlike Azpiazu and Pera (2020), who used Long Short Term Memory (LSTM) recurrent neural network as a basic architecture, we implemented this idea using the state-of-the-art Transformer (Vaswani et al., 2017) architecture. Our experiments demonstrated some persistent training problems associated with the hierarchical architecture—namely, the model is prone to early overfitting in low-resource directions leading to low translation scores. Given that one of the main goals of introducing multilingual models in general and the hierarchical model in particular is improving

Proceedings of the 8th VarDial Workshop on NLP for Similar Languages, Varieties and Dialects, pages 12–20
April 20, 2021

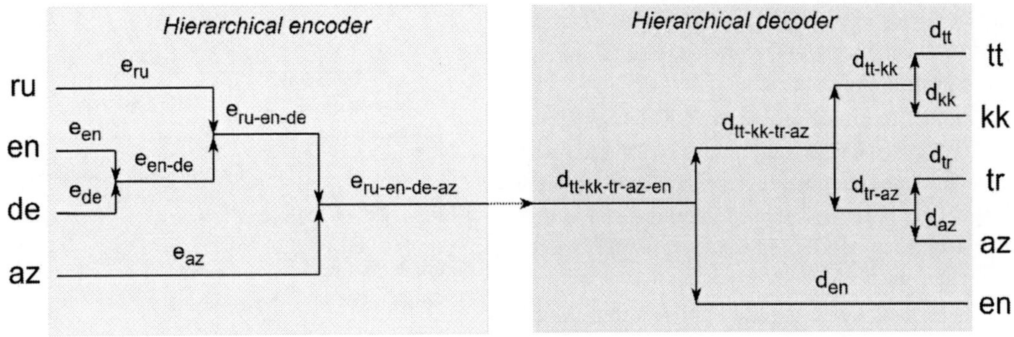

Figure 1: A high-level view of a sample multilingual hierarchical model. Horizontal lines denote encoder/decoder blocks, vertical lines and arrows show points of merging/splitting, and subscripts clarify which languages share a particular encoder/decoder. BCP-47 language codes are given here and below (Phillips and Davis, 2009).

translation accuracy for low-resource directions, this problem is critical and needs a solution.

These are the main contributions of this work:

1. Testing the hierarchical multilingual translation model using the Transformer architecture;

2. Identifying and analyzing problems related to the hierarchical nature of the model—namely, overfitting in low-resource directions;

3. Suggesting and testing a number of solutions, which could be summarized as various forms of regularization.

2 Related Work

In this section, we review the existing approaches to parameter sharing in multilingual MT models to contrast them with the hierarchical approach.

Probably, the simplest form of parameter sharing was introduced by Johnson et al. (2017), where all parameters are shared and identifier tokens are used to distinguish between languages. While being easy to implement, such model may require more resources to capture relationships between languages, as no architectural hints are given.

Dong et al. (2015) views the translation problem as a multi-task one, with a shared encoder and separate decoders for each target language. Here the potential knowledge sharing between target languages is not considered.

Firat et al. (2016) and Wang et al. (2019) introduce shared parameters between the encoder and decoder. This is an interesting idea that can be considered in the future.

Sachan and Neubig (2018) propose a one-to-many model, where parameters are partially shared between the multiple decoders. This is similar in spirit to the hierarchical approach; however, instead of having shared parts between individual decoders, the idea is to build a hierarchy of decoders.

Many other recent works, such as Bapna et al. (2019) and Fan et al. (2020) add language-specific components/layers to the decoder side of a model.

We observe that in these works languages on the encoder/decoder side of multilingual models are treated the same, regardless of the degree of their relatedness. In fact, Fan et al. (2020) do group languages by vocabulary overlap, nevertheless, in their model close languages may end up being in different groups. In the hierarchical model, however, the number of shared parameters directly depends on the degree of kinship between languages.

3 Approach

Using trees to model genealogical relationships between different languages has historically been a common approach in linguistics (Schleicher and Schleicher, 1853). Although this is not the only model, and there exist alternatives such as wave model (Schmidt, 1872), tree structure naturally suits for depicting origination of languages one from another over time.

This expert knowledge of relationships between languages can be utilized when building a multilingual MT model. The current trend in natural language processing is to make models learn linguistic rules and patterns on their own, without explicitly guiding them. However, in this case, when supervision does not really cost anything and language relatedness information is readily available, this expert knowledge can let models train faster and manage parameter space better.

Belinkov et al. (2017) found out that different encoder levels specialize in different language aspects: lower-level representations better capture part-of-speech tags, and higher-level ones are better at grasping semantics.

Another recent observation by Kudugunta et al. (2019) showed that in multilingual MT models with a single shared encoder, representations of different languages cluster by language families, and as they move up the encoder, similarity between source languages increases.

These facts taken together suggest that the encoder tries to find a common representation of different languages that initially cluster together by language families. As they move up the encoder, a model finds intermediate representations that smooth out the dissimilarities on different levels - morphological, syntactic, semantic.

This closely resembles the structure of phylogenetic trees, where connections on the bottom level mean the greatest linguistic similarity between languages, and connections on the highest level of a hierarchy indicate that languages are far from each other. See the example of such tree in Figure 2. If we organize the architecture of a multilingual MT model according to language relationships in a phylogenetic tree, this will allow sharing parameters between languages on appropriate levels.

For example, we can take two very close languages, whose vocabularies overlap significantly. Since these languages are highly related, we assume that it will not take long to reduce them to the same representation. So, we "combine" them early on, i.e., introduce shared parameters for these languages in the first layers of the encoder. The third language, let us suppose, comes from the same family, but many base words are different. Still, sentence structure remains the same as in the first two languages. Therefore, we combine this language with the first two in the later stages (parameter sharing starts deeper in encoder layers), and so on. This parameter sharing strategy allows the economic utilization of parameter space and has the potential to lead to better, i.e., source-language-independent representations of different languages on the output level of the encoder.

3.1 Model Description

The principal idea is to organize languages on the encoder and decoder sides according to their linguistic similarity. Namely, each side of the model is built as a hierarchy that corresponds to how languages connect in phylogenetic trees: the closer two languages are, the more parameters they share.

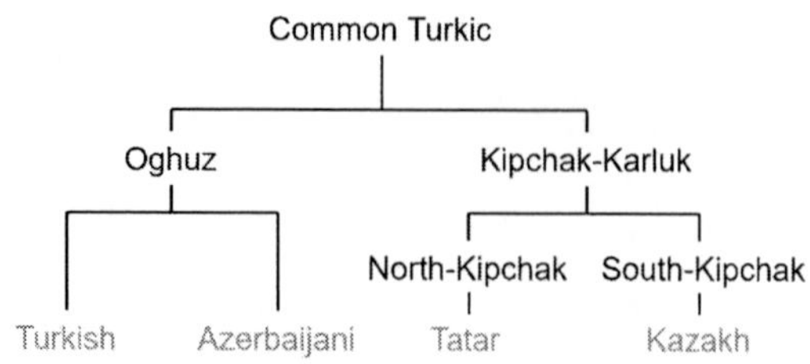

Figure 2: A fragment of the phylogenetic tree for Turkic languages (Savelyev and Robbeets, 2020).

The example of the hierarchical model is given in Figure 1. There are four source and five target languages connected through the chain of hierarchically organized encoders and decoders. Let us consider the encoder side. All source languages have their own respective encoders e_{ru}, e_{en}, e_{de}, e_{az}, and parameters of these encoders are not shared with any other language since they are intended to learn language-specific features. Deeper in the model, the outputs of some encoders are stacked together and passed to shared encoders (connections are denoted with arrows). These encoders (e_{en-de}, $e_{ru-en-de}$) are shared among two or more languages so that they can capture knowledge common to these languages. Finally, there is the last encoder $e_{ru-en-de-az}$ that is shared by all source languages and that combines the outputs of all remaining encoders together.

This architecture is designed to enable knowledge sharing between different languages on different levels. We see that English and German are connected first, as they both come from the Germanic branch of the Indo-European language family. Further in the model, the Russian language mixes in, since it belongs to a different branch of the same language family. Later on, we join these Indo-European languages with Azerbaijani, which comes from an entirely different Turkic language family. Logic on the decoder side is analogous—most dissimilar languages split first.

We suggest having the same number of parameters along any path from source to target. For example, if we compare ru-tt and az-en translation paths in Figure 1, although the latter has considerably less shared parameters, their total number should be the same for both paths. That is why some encoder blocks are longer than others, pointing that, for instance, the number of parameters in e_{az} should be the same as there are cumulatively in

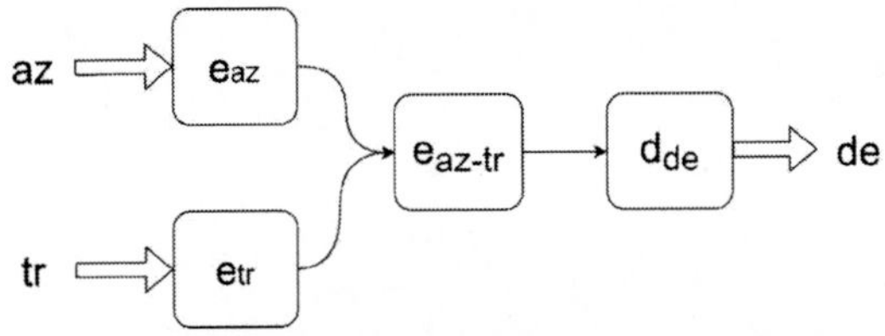

Figure 3: The example of a simple hierarchical model with two source and one target language. Rounded rectangles denote encoder/decoder blocks.

e_{ru} and $e_{ru-en-de}$.

Overall, we can say that the model adheres to the framework by Azpiazu and Pera (2020), but there are important differences. We use a different underlying model—Transformer instead of LSTM, we do not limit the number of layers and do not prune language families. There are also differences in training procedure which will be explained in section 4.2. And, most importantly, we identify the problem specific to training hierarchical models and suggest the improved training techniques for such models, as will be described in section 4.3.

4 Experiments

To test the hierarchical approach to parameter sharing we experimented with several hierarchical setups in multilingual models. Unlike Azpiazu and Pera (2020) who only test complex multi-source multi-target models, we decided to start with simple setups when the hierarchy is just on the one side of the model (encoder or decoder) and then increase the complexity to the general case.

We tested the hierarchical model's performance in three different cases:

1. Simple case with two related source languages and one target language, Figure 3;
2. Simple case with one source language and two related target languages;
3. General case with several languages of different degree of relatedness both on the source and target side, Figure 4.

For each of these cases we trained two hierarchical models using different language sets. Further, when we identified specific training problems of hierarchical models (described in section 4.3.2), we suggested and applied two variations to each hierarchical model.

Each hierarchical model is compared to two baselines: bilingual models and multilingual model with full parameter sharing (will be also called *full sharing model* later). Comparing to bilingual models trained on the same parallel corpora helps to understand whether languages can learn from each other in the hierarchical model. Whereas contrasting hierarchical models to full sharing models, with single shared encoder and decoder for all languages, as in Johnson et al. (2017), answers the question about the use of explicitly introducing the hierarchy into the model.

In every multilingual model we trained there are low-resource and high-resource directions, and we explored whether low-resource ones can learn from high-resource ones, and which model structure better fits for this purpose.

4.1 Data

We used four parallel corpora, all coming from the same JW300 dataset (Agić and Vulić, 2019) to enable fair comparison within the same domain:

- Turkish-German (tr-de), 500k sentences;
- Azerbaijani-German (az-de), 110k;
- English-Polish (en-pl), 500k;
- German-Polish (de-pl), 110k.

Turkish and Azerbaijani languages are related and come from the Oghuz sub-branch of the Turkic language family. English, German, and Polish all belong to the Indo-European language family, however, English and German are more related as they both come from the Germanic branch, while Polish is under the Balto-Slavic branch.

For training simple models with a hierarchy on one side (case 1 and case 2) we used tr-de and az-de corpora together (resulting models can be denoted as az-tr→de (Figure 3) and de→az-tr). Similarly, en-pl and de-pl corpora resulted in en-de→pl and pl→en-de models.

For general hierarchical models (case 3) all four corpora were used together and resulted in 2 models: az-tr-pl→en-de (Figure 4) and en-de→az-tr-pl.

The sizes of corpora are different: tr-de and en-pl are considered as high-resource language pairs, and az-de and de-pl are low-resource pairs.

All corpora were filtered by maximum sentence length of 40 BPE tokens (Sennrich et al., 2016).

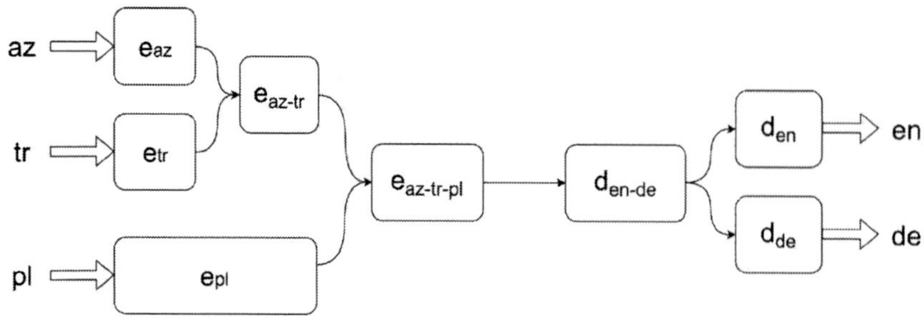

Figure 4: The example of a general multi-source multi-target hierarchical model.

4.2 Model and Training

Our multilingual machine translation system implementation is based on the Transformer architecture (Vaswani et al., 2017) with the reduced number of parameters:

- d_model = 128
- dff = 512
- num_heads = 8
- dropout_rate = 0.1

For all hierarchical and bilingual models there are 6 layers on the path from any source to any target language. Thus, any bilingual model consists of 3 encoder and 3 decoder layers. Case 1 model (with hierarchical encoder) consists of 1 layer in each of the individual encoders, 2 layers in the shared encoder, and 3 layers in the decoder. Adding more languages in the general hierarchical model results in more overall layers, but there are still 6 layers between any pair of source and target languages.

To make the models with full parameter sharing comparable to hierarchical ones, we keep the overall number of layers in the encoder and decoder the same between the models. For example, the full parameter sharing model trained for comparison with case 1 hierarchical model has 4 encoder and 3 decoder layers (corresponds to 1+1+2 and 3). However, when we came to the general case with more layers, the full sharing model could not learn anything. So, for en-de→az-tr-pl doubling batch size solved the problem, and for az-tr-pl→en-de we had to decrease the number of layers in the encoder from 6 to 4.

Azpiazu and Pera (2020) did not mention whether they kept the sizes of the hierarchical model and their baselines comparable, which makes it difficult to analyze the results.

Since training corpora are of different sizes, we oversampled low-resource corpora when training hierarchical models. For full parameter sharing models, however, it turned out that oversampling hurts their performance, so we did not apply it.

As for the training procedure, one way to train the hierarchical model is to alternate between all translation directions in a system (as Azpiazu and Pera (2020)). In this case, the possible concern is that the model parameters may start to oscillate between these directions. Therefore, we decided to simultaneously feed data from all source languages to the respective encoders, stack representations at points where specific encoders merge into shared ones, and pass them through the chain of decoders down to individual decoders. We trained all models with batch size 128 until convergence (for 50 epochs maximum) and report best BLEU scores reached over epochs. When training hierarchical models, we stack full-size (128) batches of different language pairs in the encoder and split them in the decoder.

To facilitate knowledge sharing in multilingual models we use shared vocabularies.

4.3 Results and Analysis

In this section, we present and discuss the results of the experiments.

4.3.1 Evaluating Hierarchical Model

To evaluate the hierarchical approach, we used two baselines: bilingual and full sharing models. We looked at several metrics. First, we calculated the average difference in BLEU scores between multilingual and bilingual models. To do so, we averaged across total 16 translation paths in all trained full sharing models, and, separately, in all hierarchical models. Second, we divided these translation paths to low-resource (8) and high-resource ones (8), and computed average BLEU scores difference across high-resource directions only and, third, across low-resource directions only.

This information is visualized in Figure 5. The height of the bars reflects the magnitude of the difference, and their direction indicates whether scores improve or degrade, compared to a bilingual baseline. For now, we are only interested in full sharing (Full) and basic hierarchical (Hie) models.

On the left of the Figure 5 there are average differences in scores, and we see that full sharing models perform on average almost the same as bilingual ones, and hierarchical are even slightly worse (-0.29). However, the comparison becomes more insightful if we look at high-resource and low-resource directions separately. Although on average full sharing models may seem to behave the same as bilingual, now it is clear that this actually happens because low-resource directions improve, learning from related parallel data (+1.28), and high-resource directions degrade (-1.26).

Exactly the same pattern is observed for hierarchical models: low-resource directions do benefit from multilinguality (+1.31), and high-resource directions are hurt by it (-1.88), even more than in full sharing models.

So, we see two problems here: degradation of high-resource directions in multilingual models in general; and overall low performance of hierarchical models, compared to full sharing models. The first problem is a broad one, it was observed in earlier works on multilingual MT models (Firat et al., 2016) and thus is outside of the scope of this paper. However, the second problem is surprising, since this violates our assumption about the usefulness of the hierarchical organization of a multilingual model, and hence, needs an investigation.

It would be interesting to compare these results with Azpiazu and Pera (2020), however, the way they present their findings does not let us do it. They average BLEU scores across unique source languages, and there is no strict division to high-resource and low-resource pairs. According to their results, the hierarchical model performs better than all other baselines, including bilingual and full sharing ones. However, in the GlobalVoices dataset (Tiedemann, 2012) they used the absolute majority of pairs are very low-resource. Thus, even if high-resource pairs' scores degrade in multilingual models, it would not be seen if for the majority of low-resource pairs scores do improve. The "bad" high-resource score will simply be lost among low-resource improvements. We cannot assert this is the case, but it certainly can be the case that high-resource pairs' scores in their hierarchical models also degrade. This question could have been clarified in Figure 6 of their paper, where they group language pairs by corpus size, but, unfortunately, they decided to omit results for language pairs with relatively big corpus size (more than 100k).

Similarly, it also can be the case that high-resource pairs in their full sharing models (called "one-to-one" there) have higher scores than in hierarchical models.

Overall, it is hard to compare the results in this high/low-resource aspect because settings are very different. Namely, what is low-resource here (100k) could be considered high-resource there. Also, the distribution of high-resource and low-resource directions is different: in our case, half of the directions in multilingual models are high-resource, in their case, they constitute a minority.

So, to sum it up, the identified problems can be the case in Azpiazu and Pera (2020) too, so, our following findings may benefit the overall hierarchical framework they suggested.

4.3.2 Improving Hierarchical Model

The problem we identified and decided to explore here is that the hierarchical model does not outperform the full sharing one as it should have been according to our assumption. The hierarchical idea does not work as expected—it shows almost the same improvements for low-resource pairs and greater degradation for high-resource ones.

In an attempt to solve this problem we investigated training dynamics (train and validation losses) for both model types. It turns out there is a persistent problem with training hierarchical models: for all trained models there is a clear overfitting for low-resource pairs, see Figure 6, whereas high-resource pairs train normally. This is interesting given that low-resource scores improved compared to bilingual baselines. Probably, the hierarchical model allows languages to learn from each other, but this is hindered by overfitting, and if we fix it, scores should grow even higher.

At the same time, this problem never arises in full sharing models (even when low-resource pairs are oversampled). There might be several reasons why this is happening. In hierarchical models, different translation paths have the same number of parameters regardless of the corpus size. This means that low-resource pairs may have too many parameters for the amount of data they have, hence, overfitting. And high-resource pairs may need more

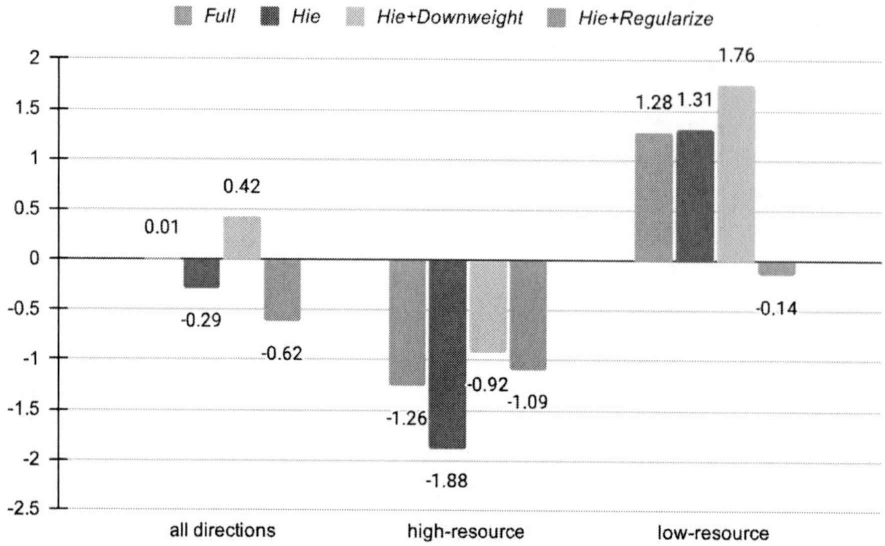

Figure 5: Difference in BLEU scores between multilingual models and bilingual models. Zero level represents average bilingual models' score. Positive values mean improvement over bilingual baseline, negative values, respectively, signify decrease. *Full* denotes models with full parameter sharing, *Hie* stands for hierarchical models, *Hie+Downweight* is for hierarchical models trained by down-weighting low-resource samples, and *Hie+Regularize* is for hierarchical models regularized using high-resource samples.

parameters than low-resource pairs. In this sense, full sharing models may be more effective, since the parameter space is distributed automatically. Another possible explanation is that in full sharing models high-resource data acts as an implicit regularizer, preventing model parameters from being overspecialized in a low-resource pair. This is not exactly so in hierarchical models—there are individual layers, and there can be layers shared by several close low-resource languages.

Yet another concern is oversampling low-resource data when training hierarchical models, which we applied and which itself can be the reason for overfitting. Indeed, we did not observe overfitting in our initial experiments without oversampling; However, in this case, low-resource scores are considerably lower than the ones we reported. Hence, we decided to fight overfitting using a different approach rather than removing oversampling.

Based on this reasoning we suggest two ways to solve the problem of overfitting:

1) Downweight low-resource samples, i.e. decrease their weight in the loss function proportionally to data disbalance. Disbalance here is taken to be the ratio between the low-resource corpus size and the closest high-resource corpus size. For example, if the ratio is 1:5, then low-resource samples have five times less weight in the loss function. The idea is that this will act as a regularization for low-resource directions and at the same time high-resource samples will have more influence in shared parts which will allow improving high-resource scores too.

2) Regularize low-resource paths with high-resource data. This idea is based on the above hypothesis about an implicit regularization happening in full sharing models. Here we explicitly apply this regularization by feeding the closest high-resource data instead of the low-resource data intended for the path. I.e., during the epoch the low-resource path is fed all available low-resource samples (once, we do not oversample here) plus related high-resource samples. We downweight high-resource samples used for regularization proportionally to data disbalance to limit the possible negative effect.

We applied both these ideas. First of all, both of them solved the problem of overfitting. Now let us refer again to Figure 5. As demonstrated there, downweighting low-resource samples turned out to bring a lot of improvement. First, the model now performs on average better than both previous mod-

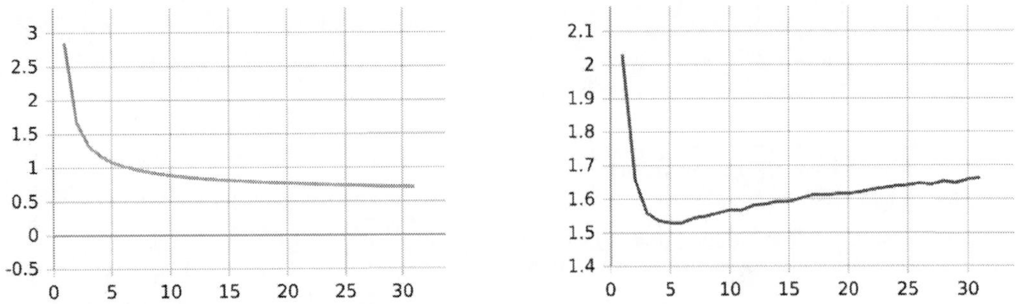

Figure 6: The example of overfitting in hierarchical models. Train *(left)* and validation *(right)* losses for low-resource pl-de pair when training pl→en-de hierarchical model.

els (+0.42). Second, the issue with high-resource pairs is greatly alleviated, from -1.88 to -0.92. And third, low-resource scores have also noticeably increased, from +1.31 to +1.76. As for the second approach, it also improved high-resource scores (-1.09) but severely hit low-resource pairs. Probably, the reason is that the regularization was too strong, which prevented possible learning.

So, to summarize, both approaches solved the problem of overfitting, and while regularization with high-resource data turned out to be too strict, downweighting low-resource samples was able to greatly improve the scores for both high-resource and low-resource directions.

Now, taking the improved version of the hierarchical model as a primary one, we will try to answer the questions we put at the beginning of section 4. We were interested to know whether there is a difference when the hierarchy is on the encoder or decoder side. From our data we can say that there is no substantial difference: the hierarchical model performs at the same level regardless of where the hierarchy is. What is interesting though, simple hierarchical models perform considerably better than bigger ones: high-resource directions degrade less (-0.52 on average versus -1.33), and low-resource improve more (+2.02 versus +1.49). This may happen because adding more languages to a multilingual model inevitably leads to more distant pairs being mixed together, and they may interfere with each other instead of helping.

Comparing hierarchical models to bilingual ones confirmed our supposition that hierarchical architecture allows languages to learn from each other, however, this is true mostly for low-resource pairs. If we look at the exact scores, high-resource directions do not always degrade: in 2 out of 8 cases they improve, although, not by a large margin. Low-resource directions improve in all 8 cases.

As for the comparison of hierarchical models with full sharing ones, the improved hierarchical model surpasses the full sharing model in both high-resource (+0.34) and low-resource (+0.48) pairs. At the same time, the full sharing model is beneficial in the sense that it comes with an intrinsic regularization mechanism, and perhaps this aspect could be further improved in hierarchical models.

5 Conclusion

This work tested a new hierarchical approach in multilingual MT. We implemented the hierarchical model based on the Transformer architecture and contrasted it to bilingual and full parameter sharing baselines. The straightforward approach to training turned out to be hampering the hierarchical model's performance. We found out that there is a problem of overfitting which is specific to training hierarchical models. Regularizing low-resource directions solved the problem, substantially improving the model's performance.

We showed that the hierarchical model greatly improves low-resource pairs' scores, however, at the expense of high-resource pairs. The comparison with the full sharing model provided positive evidence supporting the assumption about the usefulness of explicitly defining parameter sharing strategy in a multilingual model.

Overall, the hierarchical approach looks promising and hence should be further explored and developed. In the future, we would like to analyze how exactly learning happens in hierarchical models and whether hierarchical architecture is indeed capable of capturing different language aspects (morphological, syntactic, semantic) on different levels in a hierarchical manner.

References

Željko Agić and Ivan Vulić. 2019. JW300: A wide-coverage parallel corpus for low-resource languages. In *Proceedings of the 57th Annual Meeting of the Association for Computational Linguistics*, pages 3204–3210, Florence, Italy. Association for Computational Linguistics.

Ion Madrazo Azpiazu and Maria Soledad Pera. 2020. A framework for hierarchical multilingual machine translation.

Ankur Bapna, N. Arivazhagan, and Orhan Firat. 2019. Simple, scalable adaptation for neural machine translation. In *EMNLP/IJCNLP*.

Yonatan Belinkov, Lluís Màrquez, Hassan Sajjad, Nadir Durrani, Fahim Dalvi, and James Glass. 2017. Evaluating layers of representation in neural machine translation on part-of-speech and semantic tagging tasks. In *Proceedings of the Eighth International Joint Conference on Natural Language Processing (Volume 1: Long Papers)*, pages 1–10, Taipei, Taiwan. Asian Federation of Natural Language Processing.

Daxiang Dong, Hua Wu, Wei He, Dianhai Yu, and Haifeng Wang. 2015. Multi-task learning for multiple language translation. In *Proceedings of the 53rd Annual Meeting of the Association for Computational Linguistics and the 7th International Joint Conference on Natural Language Processing (Volume 1: Long Papers)*, pages 1723–1732, Beijing, China. Association for Computational Linguistics.

A. Fan, Shruti Bhosale, Holger Schwenk, Z. Ma, Ahmed El-Kishky, Siddharth Goyal, Mandeep Baines, Onur Çelebi, Guillaume Wenzek, Vishrav Chaudhary, Naman Goyal, Tom Birch, Vitaliy Liptchinsky, Sergey Edunov, E. Grave, M. Auli, and Armand Joulin. 2020. Beyond english-centric multilingual machine translation. *ArXiv*, abs/2010.11125.

Orhan Firat, Kyunghyun Cho, and Yoshua Bengio. 2016. Multi-way, multilingual neural machine translation with a shared attention mechanism. In *Proceedings of the 2016 Conference of the North American Chapter of the Association for Computational Linguistics: Human Language Technologies*, pages 866–875, San Diego, California. Association for Computational Linguistics.

Melvin Johnson, Mike Schuster, Quoc V. Le, Maxim Krikun, Yonghui Wu, Zhifeng Chen, Nikhil Thorat, Fernanda Viégas, Martin Wattenberg, Greg Corrado, Macduff Hughes, and Jeffrey Dean. 2017. Google's multilingual neural machine translation system: Enabling zero-shot translation. *Transactions of the Association for Computational Linguistics*, 5:339–351.

Sneha Kudugunta, Ankur Bapna, Isaac Caswell, and Orhan Firat. 2019. Investigating multilingual NMT representations at scale. In *Proceedings of the 2019 Conference on Empirical Methods in Natural Language Processing and the 9th International Joint Conference on Natural Language Processing (EMNLP-IJCNLP)*, pages 1565–1575, Hong Kong, China. Association for Computational Linguistics.

Addison Phillips and Mark Davis. 2009. Tags for Identifying Languages. RFC 5646.

Devendra Sachan and Graham Neubig. 2018. Parameter sharing methods for multilingual self-attentional translation models. In *Proceedings of the Third Conference on Machine Translation: Research Papers*, pages 261–271, Brussels, Belgium. Association for Computational Linguistics.

Alexander Savelyev and Martine Robbeets. 2020. Bayesian phylolinguistics infers the internal structure and the time-depth of the Turkic language family. *Journal of Language Evolution*. Lzz010.

August Schleicher and S Schleicher. 1853. Die ersten spaltungen des indogermanischen urvolkes [the first splits of the proto-indo-european people].

Johannes Schmidt. 1872. *Die verwantschaftsverhältnisse der indogermanischen sprachen [The Relationship of the Indo-European Languages]*. H. Böhlau.

Rico Sennrich, Barry Haddow, and Alexandra Birch. 2016. Neural machine translation of rare words with subword units. In *Proceedings of the 54th Annual Meeting of the Association for Computational Linguistics, ACL 2016, August 7-12, 2016, Berlin, Germany, Volume 1: Long Papers*. The Association for Computer Linguistics.

Xu Tan, Jianxian Chen, Di He, Yingce Xia, Tao Qin, and Tie-Yan Liu. 2019. Multilingual neural machine translation with language clustering. In *EMNLP/IJCNLP*.

Jörg Tiedemann. 2012. Parallel data, tools and interfaces in opus. In *Proceedings of the Eight International Conference on Language Resources and Evaluation (LREC'12)*, Istanbul, Turkey. European Language Resources Association (ELRA).

Ashish Vaswani, Noam Shazeer, Niki Parmar, Jakob Uszkoreit, Llion Jones, Aidan N Gomez, Ł ukasz Kaiser, and Illia Polosukhin. 2017. Attention is all you need. In I. Guyon, U. V. Luxburg, S. Bengio, H. Wallach, R. Fergus, S. Vishwanathan, and R. Garnett, editors, *Advances in Neural Information Processing Systems 30*, pages 5998–6008. Curran Associates, Inc.

Yining Wang, Long Zhou, Jiajun Zhang, Feifei Zhai, Jingfang Xu, and Chengqing Zong. 2019. A compact and language-sensitive multilingual translation method. In *Proceedings of the 57th Annual Meeting of the Association for Computational Linguistics*, pages 1213–1223, Florence, Italy. Association for Computational Linguistics.

Regression Analysis of Lexical and Morpho-Syntactic Properties of Kiezdeutsch

Diego Frassinelli[1], **Gabriella Lapesa**[2],
Reem Alatrash[2], **Dominik Schlechtweg**[2], **Sabine Schulte im Walde**[2]
[1]Department of Linguistics, University of Konstanz
[2]Institute for Natural Language Processing, University of Stuttgart
[1]`diego.frassinelli@uni-konstanz.de`
[2]`name.surname@ims.uni-stuttgart.de`

Abstract

Kiezdeutsch is a variety of German predominantly spoken by teenagers from multi-ethnic urban neighborhoods in casual conversations with their peers. In recent years, the popularity of Kiezdeutsch has increased among young people, independently of their socio-economic origin, and has spread in social media, too. While previous studies have extensively investigated this language variety from a linguistic and qualitative perspective, not much has been done from a quantitative point of view.

We perform the first large-scale data-driven analysis of the lexical and morpho-syntactic properties of Kiezdeutsch in comparison with standard German. At the level of results, we confirm predictions of previous qualitative analyses and integrate them with further observations on specific linguistic phenomena such as slang and self-centered speaker attitude. At the methodological level, we provide logistic regression as a framework to perform bottom-up feature selection in order to quantify differences across language varieties.

1 Introduction

Over the past 50 years, Europe has seen a substantial increase in the number of immigrants and in the diversity of their origin. A direct consequence of this situation is the rise of the so-called "Urban Youth Languages" (Wiese, 2017): specific linguistic practices used by young people in multi-ethnic urban areas. One example of urban youth languages is Kiezdeutsch ('hood German'), which is a linguistic variety of German spoken primarily by teenagers from multi-ethnic urban neighborhoods in casual conversations with their peers. Kiezdeutsch first appeared over 30 years ago and has since then developed systematic linguistic structures that identify it as an independent variety of German (Wiese et al., 2009).

Recent studies have shown that the stylistic elements of Kiezdeutsch have spread in the repertoires of many young German speakers without immigrant background (Freywald et al., 2011; Stevenson et al., 2017). At the syntactic level, the main differences with standard German are (see examples below): bare noun phrases (1) lacking determiners or (2) lacking prepositions; (3) lack of copula verbs; (4) verb-first declaratives; and (5) subject-verb-object (SVO) word order in sentences beginning with an adverb.

1. Hast du Problem? (vs. Hast du **ein** Problem?)

   Have you problem? (Do you have a problem?)

2. Ich geh Kino. (vs. Ich gehe **ins** Kino.)

   I go cinema. (I go to the cinema.)

   (Wiese and Pohle, 2016)

3. Er aus Kreuzberg. (vs. Er **ist** aus Kreuzberg.)

   He from Kreuzberg. (He is from Kreuzberg.)

4. Wollte ich keine Hektik machen da drinne. (vs. **Ich wollte** keine Hektik machen da drinne.)

   Wanted I no hectic make there inside.
   (I didn't want to make any hectic in there.)

5. Jetzt ich bin 18. (vs. Jetzt **bin ich** 18.)

   Now I am 18. (Now, I am 18.)

In previous work, researchers have studied various linguistic aspects of Kiezdeutsch focusing on either qualitative analyses (Tertilt, 1996; Auer, 2003; Keim and Knöbl, 2011; Wiese et al., 2009; Wiese, 2012, 2013; te Velde, 2017; Preseau, 2018) or small-scale quantitative analyses (Fuchs et al., 2010; Jannedy, 2010; Wiese and Pohle, 2016).

Proceedings of the 8th VarDial Workshop on NLP for Similar Languages, Varieties and Dialects, pages 21–27
April 20, 2021

In this work we suggest logistic regression as a general framework to perform bottom-up data-driven feature selection in order to quantify differences across language varieties. We use Kiezdeutsch as a test case by comparing against standard German, and we deliberately select simple lexical and morpho-syntactic features that can easily be obtained from standard part-of-speech (POS) taggers and lemmatisers. In this vein, we present three studies: morpho-syntactic variation in terms of part-of-speech unigram distributions (Study 1) and in terms of part-of-speech trigram distributions (Study 2); and lexical variation in the usage of nouns and verbs (Study 3).

2 Previous Work on Kiezdeutsch

In the mid-1990s the release of two books sparked interest in migrant varieties of German in Germany, a collection of semi-fictitious interviews with young men from Turkish backgrounds living in Berlin (Zaimoglu, 1995), and a documentation of a Turkish youth gang regarding their daily activities (Tertilt, 1996). Although these ethnographic-centered analyses were not mainly concerned with language change or variation, they brought to light the notion of groups of young people living in the urban centres of Germany who had developed their own language practices as part of their identity.

With the turn of the century, more language-centered studies of this urban vernacular began to appear. In an effort to gain a holistic understanding of Kiezdeutsch, Androutsopoulos (1998a,b, 2001) used media text analyses, ethnographic observations and interviews to analyze the speech style of teenagers speaking Kiezdeutsch. He then compiled a list of language features on the phonological/phonetic, lexical, and grammatical levels. Moreover, Androutsopoulos studied the various socio-cultural aspects of Kiezdeutsch and their effects on the German language. Similarly, Auer (2003) and Keim and Knöbl (2011) identified features of Kiezdeutsch through analyses of speech sequences which were then linked to their social interactions and functions as well as their discourses, in order to asses the social and linguistic effects of these features on the German language. Their research suggested that Kiezdeutsch speakers exhibited a high level of linguistic proficiency and communicative competence, thus contradicting previous views that grammatical simplifications were due to deficiency in language acquisition. These conclusions were in agreement with studies by Freywald et al. (2011) who considered Kiezdeutsch a multi-ethnolect, and by Wiese (2013) who categorized Kiezdeutsch as an urban dialect.

The introduction of a corpus of spoken Kiezdeutsch (Rehbein et al., 2014) led to research across linguistic levels. For example, te Velde (2017) investigated phonological form using syntax of verb-second constructions found in the German dialects Kiezdeutsch, Yiddish, Bavarian, Cimbrian, and colloquial German. More recently, the effects of English on Kiezdeutsch constructions were examined by Preseau (2018) who argued that it was necessary to reconsider Kiezdeutsch as a native dialect of German, given the role of English as a Lingua Franca (ELF) in urban Germany and the effect it has on Kiezdeutsch-speaking communities.

The above-mentioned studies illustrate the broad spectrum of qualitative evidence and analyses on Kiezdeutsch. On the other hand, up to date only a few studies have provided quantitative evidence on Kiezdeutsch. One such study was conducted by Fuchs et al. (2010) who used a Gaussian mixture model to explore the durational properties of the particle *so* in various prosodic positions within utterances of Kiezdeutsch speech. The authors supported their findings by predicting distinctions (e.g., utterance-final and phrase-final) from text using punctuation as marker. The work by Fuchs and her colleagues examined a single test case of a very specific phonological phenomenon using audio signals as the main source of information. Another study by Jannedy (2010) complemented the work by Fuchs and her colleagues by investigating the usage patterns of the particle *so* using a contingency table and χ^2 tests. The usage-patterns of the same particle were also analyzed quantitatively by Wiese (2012) using χ^2 tests. While being close to our studies, the contributions by Jannedy and Wiese focused on a single test case while we focus on large-scale analyses. Moreover, the studies by Fuchs et al. and Jannedy used a closed-access corpus of speech obtained from interviews with teenagers who speak Kiezdeutsch.

The work by Wiese and Rehbein (2016) combined qualitative and quantitative analyses of several well-established phenomena in Kiezdeutsch with the aim of demonstrating the linguistic coherence of this urban vernacular. In their top-down approach, Wiese and Rehbein started with predefined linguistic patterns and then performed a χ^2 test on the raw corpus frequencies of these patterns. The results pointed to systematic differences between data from the sub-corpus of multi-ethnic speakers and the sub-corpus of mono-ethnic speakers of German. In contrast, our study takes a bottom-up approach and does not define features a priori, but instead allows them to emerge in a data-driven fashion. Furthermore, we operate on a large scale and consider all patterns that emerge.

To our knowledge, there have been no studies on Kiezdeutsch which employ logistic regression models to gather large-scale evidence regarding the various claims and theories in the literature.

3 Materials

In our study, we use two transcribed German spoken corpora: the KiDKo corpus containing dialogues in Kiezdeutsch, and the GRAIN corpus containing radio interviews in standard German.

KiDKo The KiezDeutsch Korpus (KiDKo, Rehbein et al. (2014)) is a collection of casual everyday conversations between teenagers (14-17yo) from multi-ethnic and mono-ethnic communities in Berlin. The collection took place from 2008 until 2015 using self-recordings in the absence of adults and non-members of their social group. In order to capture the most salient emerging properties in such a dynamic language variety, in our studies we focus on the multi-ethnic sub-corpus (Rehbein and Schalowski, 2013). In total this part of the corpus contains the transcription of 43 hours of conversations with a total of 63,604 sentences (359,000 normalised tokens). Part-of-speech tagging has been performed with a tagger developed specifically for KiezDeutsch by Rehbein et al. (2014), based on a version of the Stuttgart-Tübingen tagset (STTS) augmented by 11 additional tags tailored to spoken German.

GRAIN The German RAdio INterviews corpus (GRAIN, Schweitzer et al. (2018)) is a collection of interviews broadcast on the German public radio. The hosts from the radio interviews are professionals talking about social and political topics (e.g., a chairman of a council talking about city pollution). In total, 14,097 sentences (221,000 tokens) have been extracted from 23 hours of recordings. The materials have been automatically pos-tagged with the Tree Tagger (Schmid, 1994) and according to the STTS tagset.

KidKo vs. GRAIN GRAIN was selected as the corpus representative of standard (spoken) German because among the available spoken German corpora it is the most comparable to the KiDKo for its size and its collection time frame (see above). Both corpora contain transcriptions of recorded speech, however the dialogues in KiDKo are spontaneous conversations about everyday topics, whereas the dialogues in GRAIN are more controlled in their content and setting. Moreover, speakers of Kiezdeutsch are teenage students, while the speakers in the GRAIN corpus are adults holding professional roles.

With respect to size, both corpora are relatively small, with KiDKo being one third bigger than GRAIN. The sentence length of the two corpora is extremely different: the average sentence length in KidKo (8.8 tokens/sentence) is much shorter than the one in GRAIN (26.7 tokens/sentence). As basis for comparison, we extracted the same number of n-grams (unigrams and trigrams) from GRAIN and KiDKo using a stratified sampling algorithm (Levy and Lemeshow, 2013). In this way, we created a basis for lexical and morpho-syntactic analyses on the individual token level and on a token-sequence level, while maintaining unchanged the underlying distribution of the respective n-grams from the original corpora.

4 Logistic Regression Analyses

To identify the most distinctive features in the two corpora we use logistic regression models. In all the models reported below, we predict the categorical variable `corpus_type` (KidKo vs. GRAIN) using as predictor the presence/absence of one feature at a time. Running a unique model including all the lexicalised features would lead to convergence issues; for this reason, we do not use a bag-of-feature classifier approach consistently in all three studies.

After fitting the model, we take the z-score corresponding to the predicted variable. In logistic regression, a z-score is the ratio of the coefficient estimate divided by its standard error. The larger the z-score, the less uncertain the prediction is and, consequently, the stronger the difference between the feature in the two corpora. Compared to frequency analysis or more traditional estimates like χ^2, the analysis of the z-scores conveys richer information: the sign of the z-score indicates the direction of the effect if the feature is more predictive of the KidKo (positive sign) or of the GRAIN corpus (negative sign); moreover, its absolute value is directly related to the level of uncertainty involved in the prediction: larger numbers indicate more reliable predictions.

For this reason, we systematically look at the largest positive and negative z-scores in the analyses as the most informative ones. In such way, we filter out features that show a comparable distribution in both corpora and consequently have no discriminative power. Finally, by looking at the z-score values it is possible to detect if the probability of selecting one of the two corpora is significantly different from zero (i.e., p-value < 0.001). In order to reduce type I errors (false positives due to chance), we correct the alpha values by dividing our significance threshold (0.001) by the total number of models we run.

5 Studies and Results

Study 1: Unigram POS Analysis The aim of this first study is to compare the unigram POS distributions in the two corpora. We run 10 logistic regression models predicting corpus type given the presence/absence of each POS (such as NOUN).

Given the extreme granularity of the POS types in the original collections, we decided to use a coarse-grained classification of 10 POS types only, encoding the word class but not the inflectional categories: nouns (NOUN), pronouns (PRON), verbs (VERB), adverbs (ADV), adpositions (ADP), determiners (DET), conjunctions (CONJ), adjectives (ADJ), particles (PRT), and numerals (NUM).[1] Besides the fact that it alleviates sparsity, such coarse-grained approach allows us to uncover differences between two corpora that are systematic across classes and go beyond the idiosyncratic use of extremely corpus-specific tags.

Table 1 reports the z-scores associated to each POS. Across the ten POS tags under analysis, five are significantly more predictive of GRAIN (negative values) and five of KidKo (positive values). These results are in line with previous qualitative studies (Wiese and Pohle, 2016): determiners are used significantly less in Kiezdeutsch compared to standard German (see Example (2)); similarly, adpositions (mainly prepositions) are much less used by teenagers than adults (see Example (1)).

[1] For the full set of STTS part-of-speech tags, see `https://www.ims.uni-stuttgart.de/en/research/resources/lexica/germantagsets/`.

GRAIN		**KidKo**	
POS	**z-sc.**	**POS**	**z-sc.**
DET	-54.27	PRT	59.32
NOUN	-44.10	PRON	37.50
ADP	-38.45	ADV	22.10
CONJ	-18.17	VERB	21.92
ADJ	-11.67	NUM	7.30

Table 1: Distribution of z-scores for each coarse-grained POS for standard German (negative) vs. Kiezdeutsch (positive).

Study 2: Trigram POS Analysis In this study we analyse the distribution of trigrams of consequent POS (e.g., DET+ADJ+NOUN) that we extracted from each sentence in the two corpora. In this way we approach syntactic structural differences in the language varieties, while still relying on simple POS information. In total we have 1,245 trigram types and, consequently, we run 1,245 logistic regression models where we predict corpus type using each of those trigrams as binary predictors (0/absence vs. 1/presence of each trigram). Significant level is reached when the z-score is larger than $\pm$ 3.2 (p-value < 0.0008).

Table 2 lists the most predictive trigrams for GRAIN (left) and for KidKo (right). Overall, 178 trigrams are highly significant for GRAIN and 181 for KidKo. Three trigrams of POS have an extremely strong predictive power for Kiezdeutsch: PRON+VERB+PRON, PRON+VERB+ADV, and VERB+PRON+ADV. In line with the evidence from Study 1, we see how trigrams of POS involving verbs and pronouns predominate in KidKo, while nouns and determiners are more predictive of GRAIN. The clear preference for pronouns in Kiezdeutsch, as opposed to nouns, can be explained by the topics of spontaneous speech being much more related to conversations involving self-reference and reference to further actors present in the scene. Corpus examples for the three most predictive KidKo trigrams in this respect are *ich habe deine* 'I have yours' (PRON+VERB+PRON); *wir reden hier* 'we talk here' (PRON+VERB+ADV); and *machen wir jetzt* 'do we now' (VERB+PRON+ADV). Nouns, on the other side, are essential when referring to events far from the proximity of the speech act, as in political interviews, e.g., *Gestaltung des Lebens* 'shaping of life' (NOUN+DET+NOUN); *ein Einsatz in* 'a mission in' (DET+ADP+NOUN); and *Menschen in Sorge* 'humans in fear' (NOUN+ADP+NOUN).

GRAIN		KidKo	
POS	**z-score**	**POS**	**z-score**
NOUN+DET+NOUN	-25.08	PRON+VERB+PRON	37.79
DET+NOUN+ADP	-23.62	PRON+VERB+ADV	33.92
NOUN+ADP+NOUN	-22.99	VERB+PRON+ADV	29.47
NOUN+ADP+DET	-22.96	VERB+PRON+PRON	21.79
DET+ADJ+NOUN	-22.71	PRON+PRON+VERB	19.78
ADP+DET+NOUN	-21.67	VERB+ADV+ADV	19.54
DET+NOUN+DET	-19.07	VERB+PRON+PRT	19.39
ADJ+NOUN+VERB	-18.33	PRON+VERB+PRT	19.25
ADP+DET+ADJ	-17.88	VERB+ADV+PRT	18.03
ADJ+NOUN+ADP	-17.64	PRON+VERB+ADJ	17.21

Table 2: Distribution of z-scores of the most predictive POS trigrams for GRAIN (left) vs. KidKo (right).

Figure 1 shows the distributions of POS trigrams sorted by their relative frequencies. As we can see, even though both lines follow a Zipfian distribution, in KidKo there are three trigrams that are much more frequent than all the rest; we also see a longer tail indicating a higher number of trigrams occurring only once. Moreover, if we look at mid-frequent trigrams (Figure 1), we see how the slope in the distribution from KidKo is much steeper than the one from GRAIN. KidKo thus shows a higher number of extremely frequent and extremely rare trigrams indicating the more idiosyncratic nature of Kiezdeutsch. On the other hand, in GRAIN we can find more mid-frequency trigrams indicating the more standardised nature of the variety of German used in this corpus.

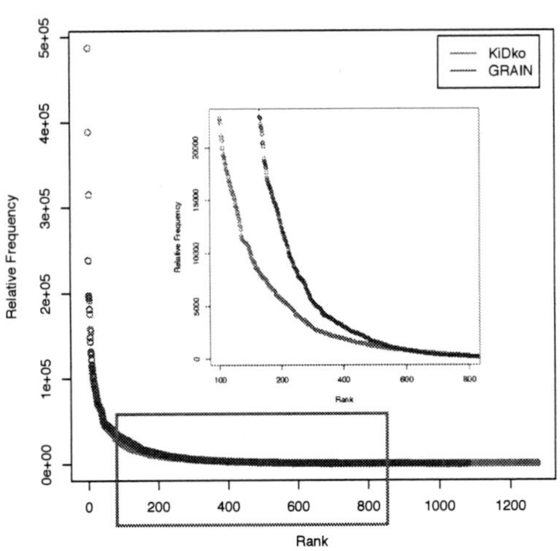

Figure 1: Overall distributions of POS trigrams sorted by relative frequency, accompanied by zoom into mid-values frequency scores.

Study 3: Noun and Verb Distributions In this final study we analyse the distributions of nouns and verbs in the two corpora (Tables 3 and 4). When looking at the most predictive verbs for each corpus, we find that GRAIN contains verbs which are part of more complex structures (such as modal structures requiring the presence of an infinitive form), and more formal nouns.

On the other hand, in KidKo verbs of needing, having, existence and obligation are the most predictive ones, together with nouns referring to typical topics for young people (school, home, fun, games). Important to highlight is the extreme predictive nature of *Alter* as the most frequent form of addressing among members of the younger generation: what the regression model has picked up here is a clear case of slang.

Once more, such distributions highlight the more self-centered type of conversation among teenagers with topics related to everyday life events that affect them, thus directly showing the simplified nature of KidKo. On the other hand, GRAIN shows the usage of more formal and detached forms (human, question, topic).

6 Conclusion

The aim of this study was to introduce logistic regression as a general framework to perform bottom-up data-driven feature selection in order to quantify differences across language varieties. We applied the framework to Kiezdeutsch in comparison to standard German as a test case, which allowed us to identify significant differences at the level of part-of-speech, part-of-speech sequences, as well as lexical choices.

GRAIN		z-score	KidKo		z-score
Menschen	'humans'	-8.23	*Alter*	'age'	11.19
Frage	'question'	-6.23	*Schule*	'school'	8.11
Thema	'topic'	-6.20	*Euro*	'euro'	7.85
Land	'country'	-6.02	*Stunden*	'hours'	7.33
Herr	'Mr.'	-5.99	*Spiel*	'game'	7.23
Prozent	'percent'	-5.65	*Hause*	'home'	7.17
Europa	'Europe'	-5.31	*Ahnung*	'idea'	6.88
Jahren	'years'	-4.70	*Spaß*	'fun'	6.72
Gesellschaft	'society'	-4.29	*Minuten*	'minutes'	6.34
Ende	'end'	-4.07	*Mal*	'times'	6.20

Table 3: The 10 most predictive nouns in GRAIN (left) vs. KidKo (right) with the corresponding z-scores.

GRAIN		z-score	KidKo		z-score
habe	'have'	20.13	*werden*	'will be'	-16.81
war	'was'	11.72	*haben*	'have'	-13.68
weiß	'know'	10.84	*wird*	'will'	-12.61
gesehen	'seen'	6.58	*sind*	'are'	-12.35
warte	'wait'	6.27	*müssen*	'must'	-12.27
mache	'make'	6.18	*gibt*	'give'	-11.34
gesagt	'said'	6.18	*können*	'can'	-9.30
bin	'am'	6.09	*wollen*	'want'	-8.69
mach	'make'	6.05	*brauchen*	'need'	-7.08
gemacht	'made'	5.90	*sagen*	'say'	-7.03

Table 4: The 10 most predictive verbs in GRAIN (left) vs. KidKo (right) with the corresponding z-scores.

Our results show consistent trends: on the one hand, we confirm the predictions drawn from the theoretical literature; on the other hand, our automatic bottom-up process results in a multi-faceted set of observations including slang, specific topics and reporting attitudes. Our studies thus confirm our framework as a useful tool to detect and quantify language variation properties, while relying on simple and easy-to-obtain lexical and morpho-syntactic features.

Current work targets both the scope of the experiments and the methodological investigation. We are further experimenting with the introduction of semi-lexicalised patterns (e.g., PRON+VERB+*Kino*, 'cinema' vs. PRON+VERB+*Schule*, 'school') in the regression to investigate whether specific syntactic patterns are more salient in certain domains, e.g., leisure vs. non-leisure activities. Methodologically, we plan to support our insights with a thorough comparison with other feature selection methodologies, such as random forests Tagliamonte and Baayen (2012).

The relevance of the framework is not limited to the sociolinguistic issues we address: it also proposes a robust strategy to select distinctive features and to demonstrate their use in concrete feature selection settings. Kiezdeutsch is a spoken variety, but we expect its most salient features to emerge also in less controlled varieties of written language, posing a significant challenge to NLP tools developed for standard German. From this perspective, our work has a straightforward application in social-media use-cases, for example in the detection and handling of German/Kiezdeutsch code-switching on Twitter and forums.

Acknowledgments

We thank the three anonymous reviewers for the very detailed and to-the-point comments, and acknowledge funding from the following institutions: G. Lapesa (German Ministry of Education and Research, project E-DELIB); R. Alatrash (CRETA center funded by the German Ministry for Education and Research); D. Schlechtweg (CRETA center and Konrad Adenauer Foundation).

References

Jannis Androutsopoulos. 1998a. *Deutsche Jugendsprache: Untersuchungen zu ihren Strukturen und Funktionen*. Peter Lang, Frankfurt am Main.

Jannis Androutsopoulos. 1998b. Forschungsperspektiven auf Jugendsprache: Ein integrativer Überblick. In Jannis Androutsopoulos and Arno Scholz, editors, *Jugendsprache – Langue des Jeunes – Young People's Language*. Peter Lang, Frankfurt am Main.

Jannis Androutsopoulos. 2001. Ultra korregd Alder! Zur medialen Stilisierung und Aneignung von 'Türkendeutsch'. *Deutsche Sprache*, 29:321–339.

Peter Auer. 2003. "Türkenslang": Ein jugendsprachlicher Ethnolekt des Deutschen und seine Transformationen. In Annelies Häcki-Buhofer, editor, *Spracherwerb und Lebensalter*, pages 255–264. Tübingen: Francke.

Ulrike Freywald, Katharina Mayr, Tiner Özçelik, and Heike Wiese. 2011. Kiezdeutsch as a multiethnolect. *Ethnic Styles of Speaking in European Metropolitan Areas*, pages 45–73.

Susanne Fuchs, Jelena Krivokapic, and Stefanie Jannedy. 2010. Prosodic boundaries in German: Final lengthening in spontaneous speech. *Journal of the Acoustical Society of America*, 127(3):1851–1851.

Stefanie Jannedy. 2010. The usage and distribution of "so" in spontaneous Berlin Kiezdeutsch. *ZASPiL Papers from the Linguistics Laboratory*, 43(52).

Inken Keim and Ralf Knöbl. 2011. Linguistic variation and linguistic virtuosity of young "ghetto"-migrants in Mannheim. In Friederike Kern and Margret Selting, editors, *Ethnic Styles of Speaking in European Metropolitan Areas*, pages 239–264. Amsterdam: Benjamins.

Paul S. Levy and Stanley Lemeshow. 2013. *Sampling of populations: Methods and applications*. John Wiley & Sons.

Lindsay Preseau. 2018. *Kiezdeutsch, Kiezenglish: English in German Multilingual/-ethnic Speech Communities*. Ph.D. thesis, UC Berkeley.

Ines Rehbein and Sören Schalowski. 2013. STTS goes Kiez–Experiments on annotating and tagging urban youth language. *Journal for Language Technology and Computational Linguistics*, 28(1).

Ines Rehbein, Sören Schalowski, and Heike Wiese. 2014. The KiezDeutsch Korpus (KiDKo) Release 1.0.

Helmut Schmid. 1994. Probabilistic part-of-speech tagging using decision trees. In *International Conference on New Methods in Language Processing*, pages 44–49, Manchester, UK.

Katrin Schweitzer, Kerstin Eckart, Markus Gärtner, Agnieszka Falenska, Arndt Riester, Ina Rösiger, Antje Schweitzer, Sabrina Stehwien, and Jonas Kuhn. 2018. German radio interviews: The GRAIN release of the SFB732 Silver Standard Collection. In *Proceedings of the 11th International Conference on Language Resources and Evaluation*.

Patrick Stevenson, Kristine Horner, Nils Langer, and Gertrud Reershemius. 2017. *The German-speaking world: A practical introduction to sociolinguistic issues*. Routledge.

Sali A. Tagliamonte and R. Harald Baayen. 2012. Models, forests, and trees of York English: Was/were variation as a case study for statistical practice. *Language Variation and Change*, 24(2):135–178.

Hermann Tertilt. 1996. *Turkish Power Boys. Ethnographie einer Jugendbande*. Suhrkamp, Frankfurt am Main.

John R. te Velde. 2017. German V2 and the PF-interface: Evidence from dialects. *Journal of Germanic Linguistics*, 29(2):147–194.

Heike Wiese. 2012. *Kiezdeutsch: Ein neuer Dialekt entsteht*. C.H. Beck.

Heike Wiese. 2013. What can new urban dialects tell us about internal language dynamics? The power of language diversity. *Linguistische Berichte*, 19:208–245.

Heike Wiese. 2017. Urban contact dialects. In Salikoko S. Mufwene and Anna Maria Escobar, editors, *Cambridge Handbook of Language Contact*. Cambridge: Cambridge University Press.

Heike Wiese, Ulrike Freywald, and Katharina Mayr. 2009. Kiezdeutsch as a test case for the interaction between grammar and information structure. *Interdisciplinary Studies on Information Structure. Working Papers of the SFB 632*, 12.

Heike Wiese and Maria Pohle. 2016. "Ich geh Kino" oder "... ins Kino"? *Zeitschrift für Sprachwissenschaft*, 35(2):171–216.

Heike Wiese and Ines Rehbein. 2016. Coherence in new urban dialects: A case study. *Lingua*, 172:45–61.

Feridun Zaimoglu. 1995. *Kanak Sprak*. Rotbuch Verlag, Berlin.

Representations of Language Varieties Are Reliable Given Corpus Similarity Measures

Jonathan Dunn
Department of Linguistics
University of Canterbury
jonathan.dunn@canterbury.ac.nz

Abstract

This paper measures similarity both within and between 84 language varieties across nine languages. These corpora are drawn from digital sources (the web and tweets), allowing us to evaluate whether such geo-referenced corpora are reliable for modelling linguistic variation. The basic idea is that, if each source adequately represents a single underlying language variety, then the similarity between these sources should be stable across all languages and countries. The paper shows that there is a consistent agreement between these sources using frequency-based corpus similarity measures. This provides further evidence that digital geo-referenced corpora consistently represent local language varieties.

1 Introduction

This paper evaluates whether digital geo-referenced corpora are consistent across registers (web data vs. tweets). This question is a part of validating the use of digital data to represent local language usage in specific places around the world. In other words, recent work has taken samples of varieties like New Zealand English from social media (Twitter) and the web (Common Crawl). But how closely do these two sources actually match up, both with one another and with New Zealand English in offline settings? The first question is about the *reliability* of geo-referenced corpora and the second is about their *validity*. The question of reliability and validity becomes important when we use geo-located digital corpora to model both lexical variation (Eisenstein et al., 2010; Grieve et al., 2011; Kondor et al., 2013; Eisenstein et al., 2014; Donoso and Sánchez, 2017) and the difference between language varieties (Lui et al., 2014; Gamallo et al., 2016; Dunn, 2018, 2019b; Rangel et al., 2020; Zampieri et al., 2020). These computational approaches are quickly refining our understanding of language variation and change. At the same time, though, both of these lines of work depend on large, reliable sources of geographic language data. This paper evaluates these data sources across nine languages and 84 language varieties in order to determine how reliable they are. The data can be explored further alongside demographic information at earthLings.io.

2 Reliability and Validity

If digital geo-referenced corpora are *reliable*, then both web corpora and Twitter corpora from one location should exhibit similar patterns (as quantified by corpus similarity measures). In other words, no matter how many samples we observe of tweets or web pages from New Zealand, we expect a reliable similarity among samples. If digital corpora are not reliable, then it follows that they are not suitable for modelling linguistic variation. This is because a model of a variety like New Zealand English would depend on arbitrary differences in the specific samples being obeserved.

The further question is whether digital geo-referenced corpora are *valid* representations of an underlying population. In other words, if we observed lexical choices by interviewing speakers in New Zealand, we would expect those same lexical choices to be observed in tweets. If these digital corpora are not reliable, then they are also not valid. But reliability itself does not guarantee a valid representation of the underlying population (Nunnally, 1994). For example, it is possible that register differences lead to different linguistic behaviour, so that lexical choices in written language may never correspond to lexical choices in spoken language. If this were the case, then it would of course never be possible to generalize from patterns in written language to patterns in spoken language.

Proceedings of the 8th VarDial Workshop on NLP for Similar Languages, Varieties and Dialects, pages 28–38
April 20, 2021 ©2021 Association for Computational Linguistics

3 Related Work on Validity

There have been three distinct approaches to the broader problem of validating digital representations of dialects and varieties. First, a *linguistic* approach starts with survey-based dialect studies as a ground-truth. These dialect surveys provide a point of comparison for an underlying variety like American English, one which does not rely on digital language data at all. This line of work has shown that there is a strong correspondence between traditional studies of dialectal variation and both tweets (Grieve et al., 2019) and web-crawled corpora (Cook and Brinton, 2017). This family of results shows that, if we accept dialect surveys as a gold-standard, there is significant justification for substituting digital corpora (like tweets) for much more expensive survey-based data. The correspondence between dialect surveys and tweets, however, is far from perfect. This raises a question: when is the relationship strong enough to justify a purely digital approach to language varieties?

A second *demographic* approach compares digital corpora with ground-truth census data in order to triangulate the similarity between represented populations. For example, given a corpus of tweets from around the world, the geographic density should correspond to some degree with population density (Graham et al., 2014; Dunn, 2020). Otherwise, some locations would be over-represented in the data, thus given more influence. In the same way, a corpus drawn equally from around the world should represent local language use that corresponds to some degree with a census-based study of what languages are used in each country (Dunn and Adams, 2019). The basic idea here is that geo-referenced corpora which correspond with census data are more likely to represent actual local populations, rather than representing non-local populations like tourists or short-term workers (Dunn et al., 2020). This line of work has also shown a strong relationship between demographics and digital corpora. But, again, when is that relationship strong enough to justify using geo-referenced corpora alone to model language varieties?

A third *computational* approach leverages some model of language variation to measure relationships between different partitions of linguistic data. For example, recent work has measured the *linguistic similarity* between varieties of English, like New Zealand English vs. Australian English (Dunn, 2019a; Szmrecsanyi et al., 2019). When expanded across aligned corpora, these models can be used to determine if there is a consistent pattern of variation: does New Zealand English have the same distinctive lexical choices on the web that it has in tweets? The basic idea is that if two sources of data (the web and tweets) accurately represent New Zealand English, both should produce similar models of that variety. On the one hand, even if the models agree (*reliability*) it remains possible that both sources of data are distorting the underlying population (*validity*). But it is more likely that such reliability confirms the validity of a purely digital approach to language varieties. This kind of work has also been systematically evaluated across different similarity measures, with a ground-truth derived from studies in perceptual dialectology (Heeringa et al., 2002, 2006).

This paper expands on these three approaches by systematically experimenting with the reliability of geo-referenced data (i) across register boundaries, (ii) across geographic boundaries, and (iii) across language boundaries. The more reliable the relationship between web data and tweets, the more confidence we can have in computational models of language varieties and linguistic variation.

4 Measuring Corpus Similarity

The approach in this paper is to measure where digital geo-located corpora diverge from one another, across languages and across countries. Unlike previous work, this does not rely on a comparison with an external ground-truth (i.e., dialect surveys, census data, or pre-trained models of variation). First, we collect geo-referenced web data and tweets across 84 varieties of nine languages. Each variety is represented using aligned corpora drawn from web pages and from tweets. These representations are distributed across many individual samples of 1 million words each.

This design allows us to make a direct comparison between samples that have been drawn from the same varieties. Thus, for example, we can measure the similarity of a single variety across register boundaries: New Zealand English on the web and in tweets. And we can also measure the similarity between varieties within a single register: New Zealand English and Australian English in tweets. This is related, for example, to the problem of measuring similarity within a single language variety over time (Pichel Campos et al., 2018). The ultimate goal of the experiments described in this

Lang.	Varieties	Samples TW	Samples CC
ara	13	185	150
deu	7	76	124
eng	14	259	262
fra	15	186	283
ind	3	45	56
nld	2	43	46
por	4	53	71
rus	9	99	216
spa	17	336	322
Total	**84**	**1,282**	**1,530**

Table 1: Varieties and Samples by Language

paper is to examine the reliability of digital representations of language varieties.

We start by drawing on measures of corpus similarity, which calculate the distance between two corpora (Kilgarriff, 2001; Kilgarriff and Rose, 1998). Previous work has shown that frequency-based measures out-perform more sophisticated approaches that make use of language models or topic models (Fothergill et al., 2016). The highest-performing frequency models work by ranking word or character frequencies and using either the Spearman rho or the χ_2 measure between frequency ranks. The χ_2 performs slightly better for samples with the same number of features, but the Spearman rho has more flexibility for dealing with unattested features while experiencing only a minimal impact on performance (Kilgarriff, 2001).

Based on these previous evaluations, we rely on two variants of the Spearman frequency-based similarity measure: one variant uses unigram frequencies and one variant uses character trigram frequencies (motivated by related work on language identification). The experiments in this paper are performed using equal-sized samples, where each sample contains 1 million words. These two measures are labelled as *Word* and *Char* in the tables that follow. The inventory of features (i.e., words or character trigrams) consists of the most common 100k features across all samples from a given language. A higher Spearman value indicates a higher similarity between samples.

In the ideal case, there would be a consistent level of similarity across samples representing all languages and all countries. In other words, we would see a similar impact of register variation (web vs. tweets) regardless of which specific language variety is involved. A result like this would suggest that both sources of geo-located language are representing a single underlying linguistic object (i.e., offline New Zealand English).

The alternate outcome is that there is an arbitrary fluctuation between web usage and tweet usage. For example, it could be the case that New Zealand English is very similar on the web and in tweets, but Australian English shows a wide divergence between the two, with different lexical choices being represented. If this were the case, the digital representation of New Zealand English would be more reliable than the representation of Australian English. This work is related to previous explorations of *noise* in social media (Baldwin et al., 2013), but with a focus on the interaction between geographic variation and register variation. The question is: how consistent are language varieties when sampled from different digital sources?

5 Data and Experimental Design

The experiments draw on existing geographic corpora from the web (ultimately derived from the Common Crawl data) and from tweets (Dunn and Adams, 2020; Dunn, 2020). Both of these data sources are aligned by language and country: for example, each variety like Cuban Spanish or New Zealand English is present from both sources of data. The experiments include nine languages: Arabic (ara), German (deu), English (eng), French (fra), Indonesian (ind), Dutch (nld), Portuguese (por), Russian (rus), and Spanish (spa). These languages each have a different number of varieties, as shown in Table 1, ranging from just 2 (nld) to 17 (spa). In this table, *Varieties* refers to the number of national dialects or varieties (like New Zealand English) that are represented. *Samples* refers to the total number of observations for that language, across all varieties. Finally, *TW* refers to tweets and *CC* to web data.

Each sample contains 1 million words. Some varieties are very well represented, with hundreds of samples (and thus hundreds of millions of words); but other varieties are less well represented, with only a few samples. We restrict the maximum number of samples per variety per register to 20. As shown in Table 2 for Spanish, there is variation in the number of samples per data source. For example, some countries like Mexico have many samples for both tweets and web data (20 and 20, respectively, because of the cap). But other countries are imbalanced: for example, the Dominican

Country	Samples TW	Samples CC
Argentina	20	16
Bolivia	20	16
Chile	20	20
Colombia	20	20
Costa Rica	20	20
Cuba	20	20
Dom. Rep.	4	20
Ecuador	20	20
El Salvador	20	20
Guatemala	20	20
Honduras	20	20
Mexico	20	20
Paraguay	20	2
Peru	20	20
Spain	20	20
United States	12	20
Uruguay	20	19
Venezuela	20	9

Table 2: Number of Samples by Variety for Spanish

Republic has 20 samples from the web but only 4 drawn from tweets. Overall, these experiments are based on approximately 1.2 billion words from tweets and 1.5 billion words from web corpora.

The question behind the experiments in this paper is whether there is a consistent relationship between corpora drawn from the web and from tweets, across many different language varieties. If there is a significantly stable relationship, this increases our confidence that digital corpora accurately represent the underlying geographic language varieties. In other words, the stable relationship would be a result of two different sources that are measuring the same real-world entity (e.g., a single language variety). But, in contexts where this relationship breaks down, we can have less confidence in the validity of digital corpora for modelling language varieties. We present five sets of experiments, each focused on a specific part of this problem.

The first experiment (Section 6), focuses on the internal consistency of each variety-register combination: given similarity relationships between many samples of Mexican Spanish tweets, how stable is the internal similarity between samples? The basic idea is that any variety-register combination with a low internal similarity is less reliable.

The second experiment (Section 7) evaluates the accuracy of both word-frequency and character-frequency measures. The idea in these experiments is to validate the underlying similarity measure to ensure that the later experiments are also valid.

The third experiment (Section 8) is the main part of the paper: measuring the difference between registers (web vs. tweets) for each language variety. Our hypothesis is that only a significantly stable relationship supports the use of digital corpora for representing language varieties.

The fourth experiment (Section 9) looks for differing results by language. It may be the case, for instance, that varieties of English and Spanish are adequately represented by digital corpora, but not varieties of Dutch.

The fifth experiment (Section 10) creates an *average* frequency vector for each language across all varieties and registers. This average is used to situate each national variety according to its relative distance from that center, creating a rank of which varieties are the most divergent or the most unique. There is one rank for each register and the experiment tests where there is a significant relationship between ranks for each language. Taken together, this set of experiments is designed to evaluate the suitability of digital geo-referenced corpora for representing language varieties, building on the validation work discussed in Section 3.

6 Experiment 1: Consistency Across Samples

The first question is the degree to which each language variety-register combination (e.g., Mexican Spanish tweets) is internally consistent. We take 50 observations of unique pairs of samples, each representing the same variety-register combination. Then we measure the similarity between the two samples and look at the distribution of similarity values for each variety-register combination. Varieties with a high average similarity are more internally consistent than varieties with a low average similarity.

The results are shown in Table 3 by language, divided into *Word* and *Character* features as discussed in Section 4. Data from tweets (*TW*) is shown on the left and from the web (*CC* for Common Crawl) is shown on the right. These measures show the stability by language, where each value is drawn from approximately 50 random comparisons between different samples representing the same context. As throughout this paper, higher values indicate higher similarity (here, meaning more internal similarity).

Language	TW Word	TW Char	CC Word	CC Char
ara	0.71	0.84	0.70	0.76
deu	0.66	0.85	0.57	0.72
eng	0.68	0.83	0.63	0.71
fra	0.68	0.82	0.64	0.72
ind	0.71	0.83	0.64	0.73
nld	0.63	0.82	0.53	0.71
por	0.67	0.82	0.64	0.72
rus	0.70	0.83	0.60	0.71
spa	0.65	0.82	0.61	0.71

Table 3: Consistency Within Language Varieties

Language	Word	Character
ara	99.0%	**99.1%**
deu	95.7%	**98.9%**
eng	93.9%	**98.9%**
fra	98.1%	**99.8%**
ind	100.0%	100.0%
nld	94.3%	**100.0%**
por	**98.4%**	96.3%
rus	94.7%	**98.7%**
spa	96.7%	**97.5%**

Table 4: Feature Evaluation by Accuracy

First, this table shows that *character* representations are more consistent across languages, although the accuracy of each type of feature is not evaluated until Section 7. In other words, the average internal similarity for tweets ranges from 0.82 to 0.85 for character features but from 0.63 to 0.71 for word features. At the same time, a smaller range of variation also could mean that character features are less able to discriminate between varieties.

Second, this table shows that tweets from a particular variety have a higher internal similarity than web data from that variety. This is true for all languages and for both word and character features. While this experiment does not indicate *why* this is the case, we can offer some potential reasons: (i) it could be that tweets are more similar in terms of discourse functions, while web data represents a range of different communication purposes; (ii) it could be that tweets represent a more restricted subset of local populations (e.g., Twitter users), which have been shown to be more influenced by demographic attributes like per capita GDP.

Third, all of these Spearman correlations are highly significant, which means that there is at least a strong relationship between representations of each variety drawn from the web and from tweets. At the same time, as discussed in Section 3 in regards to alternate methods of evaluation, it is not clear what threshold for similarity is sufficient. This question is what the remainder of the experiments attempt to address.

7 Experiment 2: Word vs Character Features

The next question is two-fold: First, which frequency-based measure of similarity is more reliable in this setting: words or characters? Previous work on corpus comparison has largely conducted evaluations using only English data and has not included multiple language varieties. Second, regardless of which feature is best, how reliable are the measures? Because the samples are each 1 million words, this is a significantly easier problem than identifying varieties in small samples.

In this experiment we look at the average accuracy for each language for each type of feature. For each variety, we take 100 pairs that come from the same register (tweets against tweets) and 100 pairs that come from different registers (tweets against web pages). If the similarity for a pair is closest to the average similarity for same-register pairs, we predict that each sample comes from the same register (and so on for cross-register pairs). This is a simple framework for evaluating each measure: the percent of correct predictions. This is similar to previous evaluation methods for corpus similarity measures (Kilgarriff, 2001).

The results, shown in Table 4, have a high accuracy in general, as we expect given that each sample is 1 million words. The important question is which similarity measure has the highest accuracy: in every case except for Portuguese the character features are more accurate. For simplicity, we report only the character-based measure in the remainder of the experiments. This experiment also provides a ground-truth confirmation that the measures are meaningful on this data.

8 Experiment 3: Differences in Register

Now that we have established that there is a significant relationship between registers across all varieties and that the character-based measure is generally more accurate, we proceed to the main question: how robust is the relationship between registers? There are two competing hypotheses

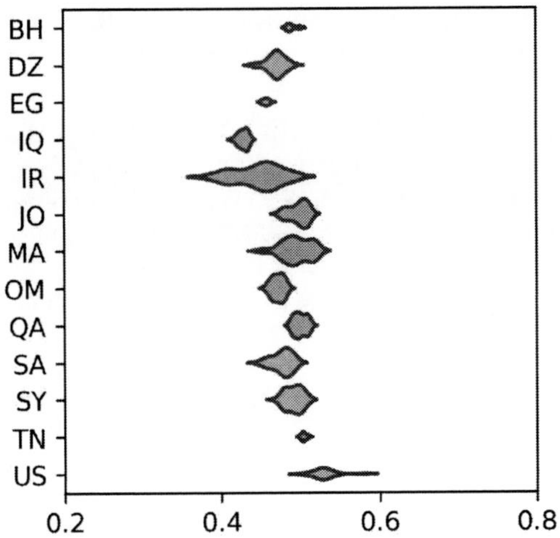

Figure 1: Cross-Register Similarity (Arabic)

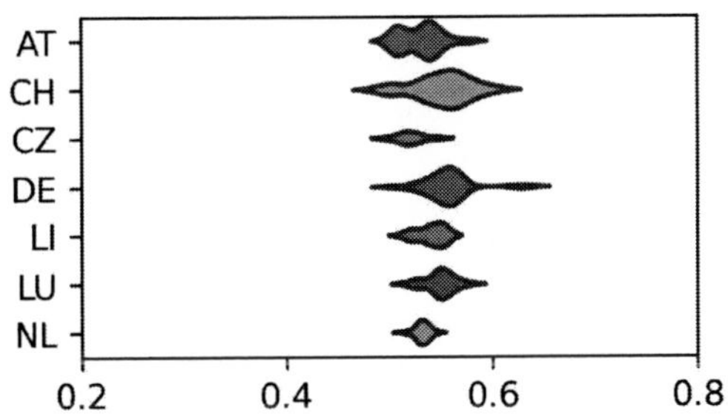

Figure 2: Cross-Register Similarity (German)

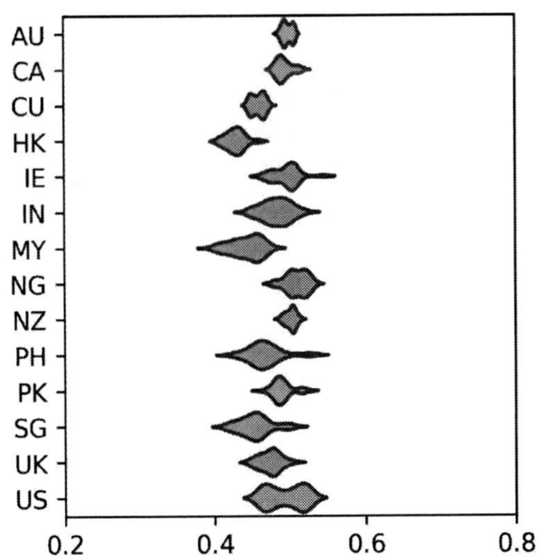

Figure 3: Cross-Register Similarity (English)

here: First, it could be the case that one or both sources of digital data only poorly represent a given language variety. In this case, there would be wide fluctuations in similarity values across varieties and across languages (because the similarity would not be driven by shared populations and shared linguistic patterns). Second, it could be the case that both sources of digital data consistently represent a given language variety. Because of register-based variation, the similarity between sources may not be perfect; but it should be consistent.

We use the samples described above to create a population of cross-register pairs, where each pair consists of two samples from the same variety. For instance, we take 100 random comparisons of Mexican Spanish with other Mexican Spanish samples from a different source (i.e., web vs tweets). This provides a population of between-register scores for each language variety. If the distance between registers is consistent across all contexts, this is evidence for the second hypothesis: that both sources of data are related representations of a single underlying language variety.

The first set of results, for Arabic, is shown in Figure 1 as a violin plot of the distribution of cross-register similarity scores for each country. In the case of Arabic, the average similarity by country ranges from 0.43 (Iraq, IQ) to 0.53 (United States, US). Note the combination here of native varieties and non-native or immigrant varieties. This violin plot shows the distribution of scores, most of which are contained within a tight central band (i.e., are relatively consistent across varieties). Arabic in Iran (IR) and Morocco (MA) have broader distributions, showing that there is more variety within samples from these countries. The US, a non-native variety, has outliers, resulting in thin lines on either side of the plot. There are also differing numbers of samples by country, so that Egypt (EG) and Tunisia (TN) are located in the center but, with few samples, have a small footprint.

Moving on to German, in Figure 2, we see a similar pattern: the distribution (with somewhat higher scores) is centered within the same values across countries. What matters for the hypothesis in this paper is the range of values for cross-register similarity, here with averages ranging from 0.52 (Czechia, CZ) to 0.56 (Germany, DE). This constrained range indicates that there is a stable relationship between digital sources for these varieties.

We next evaluate varieties of English (Figure 3)

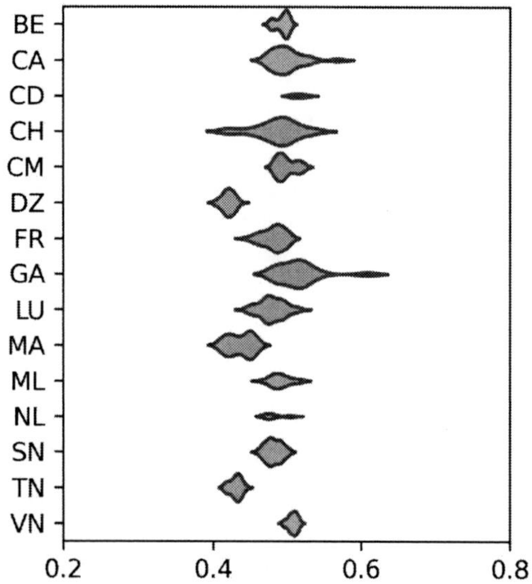

Figure 4: Cross-Register Similarity (French)

and French (Figure 4). Both of these languages are more widely used in digital contexts, thus having a larger number of varieties. English ranges from an average of 0.43 (Hong Kong, HK) to 0.51 (Nigeria, NG). French ranges from an average of 0.42 (Algeria, or DZ) to 0.52 (Gabon, GA, and the Democratic Republic of Congo, CD). In both languages we see a somewhat wider range, with outliers like Hong Kong English or Algerian and Tunisian French; but still the gap between registers remains largely consistent for most varieties.

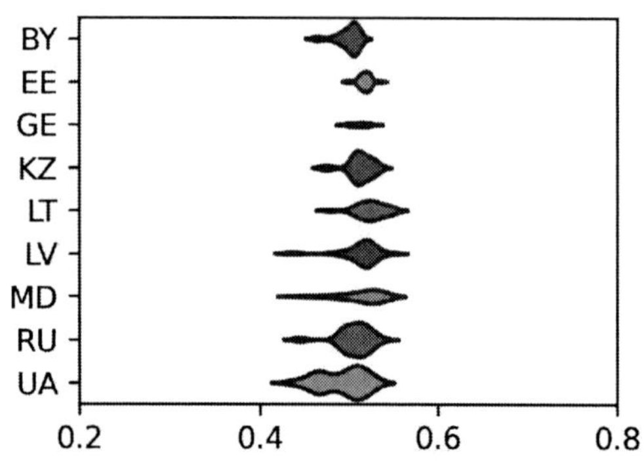

Figure 5: Cross-Register Similarity (Russian)

The results for Russian (Figure 5) and Spanish (Figure 6) continue the same pattern of relative consistency. The figures for Dutch, Indonesian, and Portuguese are excluded because they each have a small number of varieties that largely overlap. The figures for Russian and Spanish show greater consistency across countries, although Russian does have a few outliers for each country (i.e., the narrow tails). Russian averages range from 0.49 (Ukraine, UA) to 0.52 (Estonia, EE). Spanish shows a slightly larger range of averages, from 0.48 (Argentina, AR) to 0.55 (El Salvador, ES). Once again, however, the relationship between registers remains stable.

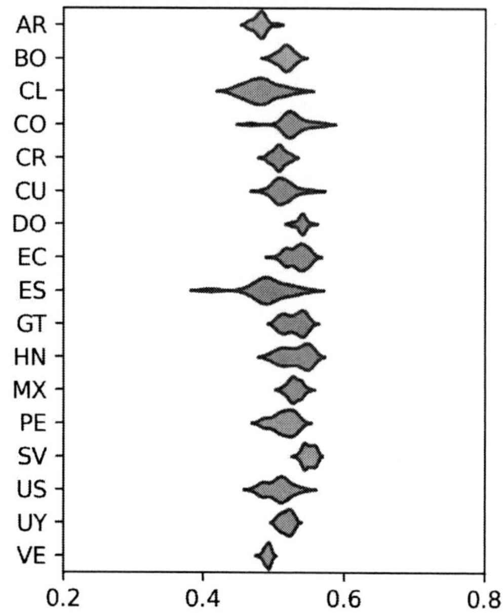

Figure 6: Cross-Register Similarity (Spanish)

The results in this section suggest that both web data and tweets provide reliable representations for a large number of language varieties, regardless of the specific language or country involved. The distance between samples from each source is stable across both categories (language and country). This pattern is what we expect if both sources adequately represent the underlying language variety. This reliability converges with the previous work discussed in Section 3 to suggest that digital georeferenced corpora do in fact represent local language use. As with previous evaluations, however, it is difficult to define a threshold for reliability.

9 Experiment 4: Differences by Language

Our next set of experiments further explores the interaction between dialect variation (e.g., New Zealand vs. Australian English) and register variation (e.g., web data vs. tweets). As we compare

Language	TW Same Varieties	TW Different Varieties	CC Same Varieties	CC Different Varieties
ara	0.84	0.81	0.76	0.67
deu	0.85	0.83	0.72	0.68
eng	0.83	0.80	0.71	0.66
fra	0.82	0.77	0.72	0.66
ind	0.83	0.80	0.73	0.68
nld	0.82	0.80	0.71	0.69
por	0.82	0.80	0.72	0.64
rus	0.83	0.80	0.71	0.68
spa	0.82	0.80	0.71	0.67

Table 5: Variation Within and Across Countries

a large number of samples for each language, how much of the variation comes from register-effects and how much from geographic-effects? The experiments shown in Table 5 compare the similarity of samples drawn from the same variety (thus controlling for geographic effects) with the similarity of samples drawn from different varieties (thus adding geographic effects). The additional similarity of within-variety comparisons can be attributed to geographic variation.

For example, Arabic tweets have 0.03 increased similarity when compared within varieties instead of between varieties. The difference for web data is larger in most cases. We test for significance using a t-test with 50 observed pairs in each condition for each language. In each case there is a highly significant difference. This confirms that we are observing geographic variation across varieties in addition to the register variation that is quantified in the previous section.

This geographic variation is a secondary finding, however, in the sense that much more precise methods of modelling geographic variation exist. The purpose here is simply to confirm that each language shows a significant geographic effect given this measure applied to these sources of data.

10 Experiment 5: Relations Between Varieties

Our final experiment looks at relationships between national varieties or dialects. A final piece of evidence comes from ranks of varieties: if both the web and tweets make Singapore English most similar to Malaysian English, this confirms the reliability digital sources of geo-referenced data.

First, we create an average representation across all samples for a given language using the mean feature frequency. Second, we estimate the average feature frequency for each variety-register combination (like Mexican Spanish tweets). Third, we compare the similarity between (i) the language-based mean feature value and (ii) the average for a specific variety (like Mexican Spanish tweets).

This provides a rank of distance from the average frequency for each variety. For example, what is the most unusual variety of English? We do this for both registers, *TW* and *CC* in Table 6. The question is, do these two sources of data agree about relationships *between* dialects as well as between registers? The Spearman rank correlations are used to measure how well each register ranks varieties in the same manner.

The results for all languages taken together is highly significant, with a correlation of 0.453. Taken individually, some languages are also significant: German, French, Portuguese, and Russian. Given the small number of observations when constrained to individual languages, the lack of significance at that level is not particularly important. What this shows, however, is that even a simple similarity measure can produce, overall, significantly related ranks of varieties. The importance is not the specific ranks, because we know that better methods for modelling language varieties exist. The importance is that we have additional evidence for stability in the relationship between registers and varieties. This is precisely what we would see if both sources of digital data were valid representations of a single underlying linguistic object.

11 Geographic Trends

The focus so far has been on varieties of languages. A different way of framing the question of register similarity is by country: is there a geographic

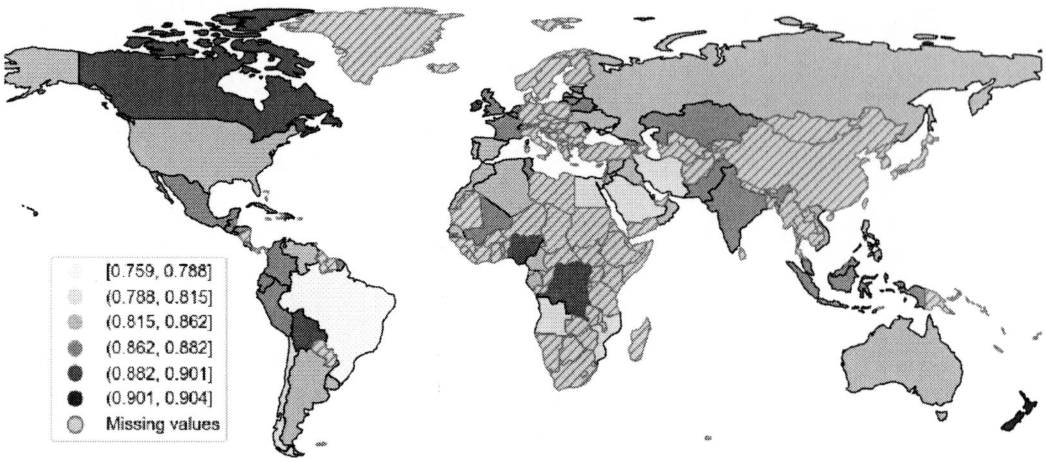

Figure 7: Average cross-domain similarity by country.

Language	Spearman rho	Significance
All	**0.453**	*
ara	0.291	NS
deu	0.785	*
eng	0.428	NS
fra	0.561	*
ind	0.399	NS
nld	0.799	NS
por	0.899	*
rus	0.797	*
spa	0.051	NS

Table 6: Correlation between rankings by register

pattern to where the web and tweets are more or less similar? Here we take cross-register similarity values as described above in Section 8. When we bring all languages together, these experiments represent 66 countries. Of these, 10 are represented by two or more languages; the map in Figure 7 averages the values by country to show geographic trends in cross-register similarity.

When we focus on countries, the average cross-register similarity value is 0.855. Most countries fall with the range of 0.80 to 0.89 (62 out of 66). Only two countries fall below 0.80, meaning that they show a low agreement between registers: Bahrain and Brazil. And only two countries are above 0.90, meaning that they show a higher agreement between registers: Nigeria and New Zealand. Note that the lower value for Brazil likely results from the lower accuracy of character-based measures for Portuguese (c.f., Table 4).

This kind of geographic analysis does not show larger trends. For example, one common trend in digital corpora is that wealthy western countries like the US, Canada, Western Europe, and Australia and New Zealand pattern together. But this is not the case here, with Canada and New Zealand contrasting with the US and Australia. Thus, a geographic analysis further confirms the reliability of geo-referenced corpora in the sense that what little variation we do see does not correspond with expected geographic patterns.

12 Conclusions

The experiments in this paper have shown that there is a consistent relationship between the representation of language varieties across two sources of geo-referenced digital corpora: the web and tweets. In other words, these digital corpora are *reliable*. This finding is important because it disproves the alternate hypothesis that one or both sources is a poor or arbitrary representation of the underlying language varieties. This kind of unreliability would lead to an inconsistent relationship between registers. Reliability is not the same as validity. However, the reliability shown here converges with evidence from dialect surveys and census data and computational models of language varieties, all of which do evaluate the validity of digital corpora.

This robust reliability gives us confidence in the use of digital corpora to study linguistic variation. And this evaluation of both reliability and validity is important because it justifies the use of computational modelling which, in turn, enables global-scale experiments that help us better understand language variation and change.

References

Timothy Baldwin, Paul Cook, Marco Lui, Andrew MacKinlay, and Li Wang. 2013. How Noisy Social Media Text, How Diffrnt Social Media Sources? In *Proceedings of the Sixth International Joint Conference on Natural Language Processing*, pages 356–364.

Paul Cook and Laurel Brinton. 2017. Building and Evaluating Web Corpora Representing National Varieties of English. *Language Resources and Evaluation*, 51(3):643–662.

Gonzalo Donoso and David Sánchez. 2017. Dialectometric analysis of language variation in twitter. In *Proceedings of the Fourth Workshop on NLP for Similar Languages, Varieties and Dialects*, pages 16–25. Association for Computational Linguistics.

Jonathan Dunn. 2018. Finding Variants for Construction-Based Dialectometry: A Corpus-Based Approach to Regional CxGs. *Cognitive Linguistics*, 29(2):275–311.

Jonathan Dunn. 2019a. Global Syntactic Variation in Seven Languages: Toward a Computational Dialectology. *Frontiers in Artificial Intelligence*, 2:15.

Jonathan Dunn. 2019b. Modeling global syntactic variation in english using dialect classification. In *Proceedings of the Sixth Workshop on NLP for Similar Languages, Varieties and Dialects*, pages 42–53. Association for Computational Linguistics.

Jonathan Dunn. 2020. Mapping languages: The Corpus of Global Language Use. *Language Resources and Evaluation*, 54:999–1018.

Jonathan Dunn and Benjamin Adams. 2019. Mapping Languages and Demographics with Georeferenced Corpora. In *Proceedings of Geocomputation 2019*, pages 1–16.

Jonathan Dunn and Benjamin Adams. 2020. Geographically-balanced gigaword corpora for 50 language varieties. In *Proceedings of the 12th Language Resources and Evaluation Conference*, pages 2528–2536. European Language Resources Association.

Jonathan Dunn, Tom Coupe, and Benjamin Adams. 2020. Measuring linguistic diversity during covid-19. In *Proceedings of the Fourth Workshop on Natural Language Processing and Computational Social Science*, pages 1–10. Association for Computational Linguistics.

Jacob Eisenstein, Brendan O'Connor, Noah Smith, and Eric Xing. 2010. A latent variable model for geographic lexical variation. In *Proceedings of the Conference on Empirical Methods in Natural Language Processing*, pages 221–227. Association for Computational Linguistics.

Jacob Eisenstein, Brendan O'Connor, Noah Smith, and Eric Xing. 2014. Diffusion of lexical change in social media. *PloSOne*, 10:1371.

Richard Fothergill, Paul Cook, and Timothy Baldwin. 2016. Evaluating a Topic Modelling Approach to Measuring Corpus Similarity. In *Proceedings of the Tenth International Conference on Language Resources and Evaluation*, pages 273–279. European Language Resources Association.

Pablo Gamallo, Iñaki Alegria, José Ramom Pichel, and Manex Agirrezabal. 2016. Comparing Two Basic Methods for Discriminating Between Similar Languages and Varieties. *Proceedings of the Third Workshop on NLP for Similar Languages, Varieties and Dialects*, pages 170–177.

Mark Graham, Scott Hale, and Devin Gaffney. 2014. Where in the World are You? Geolocation and Language Identification on Twitter. *The Professional Geographer*, 66(4):568–578.

Jack Grieve, Chris Montgomery, Andrea Nini, Akira Murakami, and Diansheng Guo. 2019. Mapping Lexical Dialect Variation in British English Using Twitter. *Frontiers in Artificial Intelligence*, 2:11.

Jack Grieve, Dirk Speelman, and Dirk Geeraerts. 2011. A statistical method for the identification and aggregation of regional linguistic variation. *Language Variation & Change*, 23(1):1–29.

Wilbert Heeringa, Peter Kleiweg, Charlotte Gooskens, and John Nerbonne. 2006. Evaluation of String Distance Algorithms for Dialectology. In *Workshop of the Workshop on Linguistic Distances*, pages 51–62. Association for Computational Linguistics.

Wilbert Heeringa, John Nerbonne, and Peter Kleiweg. 2002. Validating Dialect Comparison Methods. In *Classification, Automation, and New Media*, pages 445–452. Springer, Berlin.

Adam Kilgarriff. 2001. Comparing Corpora. *International Journal of Corpus Linguistics*, 6(1):97–133.

Adam Kilgarriff and Tony Rose. 1998. Measures for Corpus Similarity and Homogeneity. In *Proceedings of the Third Conference on Empirical Methods for Natural Language Processing*, pages 46–52. Association for Computational Linguistics.

Dániel Kondor, István Csabai, László Dobos, János Szüle, Norbert Barankai, Tamás Hanyecz, Tamás Sebők, Zsófia Kallus, and Gábor Vattay. 2013. Using Robust PCA to Estimate Regional Characteristics of Language-use from Geotagged Twitter Messages. In *Proceedings of IEEE 4th International Conference on Cognitive Infocommunications*, pages 393–398. IEEE.

Marco Lui, Ned Letcher, Oliver Adams, Long Duong, Paul Cook, and Timothy Baldwin. 2014. Exploring Methods and Resources for Discriminating Similar Languages. In *Proceedings of the First Workshop on Applying NLP Tools to Similar Languages, Varieties and Dialects*, pages 129–138. Association for Computational Linguistics.

Jum Nunnally. 1994. *Psychometric Theory*, 3rd edition. McGraw-Hill Education.

Jose Ramom Pichel Campos, Pablo Gamallo, and Iñaki Alegria. 2018. Measuring language distance among historical varieties using perplexity. application to european portuguese. In *Proceedings of the Fifth Workshop on NLP for Similar Languages, Varieties and Dialects*, pages 145–155. Association for Computational Linguistics.

Francisco Rangel, Paolo Rosso, Wajdi Zaghouani, and Anis Charfi. 2020. Fine-grained analysis of language varieties and demographics. *Natural Language Engineering*, 26(6):641–661.

Benedikt Szmrecsanyi, Jason Grafmiller, and Laura Rosseel. 2019. Variation-Based Distance and Similarity Modeling: A Case Study in World Englishes. *Frontiers in Artificial Intelligence*, 2:23.

Marcos Zampieri, Preslav Nakov, and Yves Scherrer. 2020. Natural language processing for similar languages, varieties, and dialects: A survey. *Natural Language Engineering*, 26(6):595–612.

Whit's the Richt Pairt o Speech: PoS tagging for Scots

Harm F.K.M. Lameris and Sara Stymne
Uppsala University
Uppsala, Sweden
harm.lameris.2403@student.uu.se, sara.stymne@lingfil.uu.se

Abstract

In this paper we explore PoS tagging for the Scots language. Scots is spoken in Scotland and Northern Ireland, and is closely related to English. As no linguistically annotated Scots data were available, we manually PoS tagged a small set that is used for evaluation and training. We use English as a transfer language to examine zero-shot transfer and transfer learning methods. We find that training on a very small amount of Scots data was superior to zero-shot transfer from English. Combining the Scots and English data led to further improvements, with a concatenation method giving the best results. We also compared the use of two different English treebanks and found that a treebank containing web data was superior in the zero-shot setting, while it was outperformed by a treebank containing a mix of genres when combined with Scots data.

1 Introduction

Part-of-Speech (PoS) tagging is an essential Natural Language Processing (NLP) tool that is often seen as a first step in language analysis (Fang and Cohn, 2017) and can be useful for the analysis of large corpora, for instance in digital humanities (Hinrichs et al., 2019). For high resource languages, PoS tagging is occasionally considered to be a solved task, with recent state-of-the-art PoS taggers reaching high accuracies, such as Andor et al. (2016), who report an average accuracy of 97.5% across seven high-resource languages. However, these strong results are limited to languages and domains with large training data sets. State-of-the-art models commonly use Bi-directional Long Short Term Memory Recurrent Neural Network (Bi-LSTM RNN) architectures that rely on supervised learning methods. In order to obtain a high accuracy, large amounts of labelled data are required (Fang and Cohn, 2017). These resources are not available for low resource languages, and due to the high cost of annotation these are unfeasible to obtain (Garrette et al., 2013).

> Sae a thocht a'd gie ma pynt o view on aw 'is, an 'e story ahint whit caused iz tae stairt the editathon muivement an whit a hink anent the hale hing. On 'e 25t August 2020, a 4chan an Reddit post wis pit oot bi Ryan Dempsey, unner the uisername 'Ultach', fae Ulster, anent an American Wikipedia admin, whase name a willnae mention tae jouk thaim gittin ony mair potential harassment (lat's juist caw thaim Admin fae nou), an hou thay contríbutit near hauf o aw the airticles on 'e Wikipedia, an hou the ither tap fower contríbutors wis American an aw.

Figure 1: Scots excerpt, originally from Clark et al. (2020)

In this paper we focus on the Scots language, a language closely related to English, which is spoken in Scotland and Northern Ireland. Scots lacks linguistic resources and tools. In this paper we take a first step towards overcoming this, by examining PoS tagging for Scots. We investigate how well an English PoS tagger works on Scots, and try to improve on this by using a very small amount of Scots annotated data during training. As part of the study, a small sample of Scots texts were manually PoS tagged. An example of Scots is shown in Figure 1.

While statistics-based PoS taggers are occasionally used for truly low-resource languages (Agić et al., 2015), data scarcity can also successfully be alleviated using transfer learning (Lin et al., 2019). PoS tagging using cross-lingual transfer has proved effective on low-resource simulations of high-resource European languages, and even disparate non-Indo-European languages (Fang and Cohn, 2017). Yet, few attempts have been made to use cross-lingual models to tag European minority

Proceedings of the 8th VarDial Workshop on NLP for Similar Languages, Varieties and Dialects, pages 39–48
April 20, 2021

languages such as Scots, despite the existence of closely related high-resource languages. One exception is Magistry et al. (2019) who focused on PoS tagging for three regional French languages.

We focus on investigating PoS tagging for Scots. First we want to investigate a zero-shot setting, to see how well a PoS tagger trained for English works on Scots, additionally comparing the performance of two different English data sets, the GUM treebank (Zeldes, 2017) and the EWT treebank (Silveira et al., 2014). Secondly, we annotate a small amount of data, 1040 tokens, in order to investigate how much could be gained from adding even a very small amount of data. We compared different methods for combining the Scots and English data, with zero-shot tagging and training only on a tiny amount of Scots data. The main contributions of this work are:

- The first attempt at creating a PoS-tagged Scots corpus. While the size of the corpus is small, it features multiple Scots dialects, and texts from multiple domains, and could therefore easily be expanded upon. This corpus is publicly available at `https://github.com/Hfkml/pos-tagged-scots-corpus`.
- An investigation of combining large English and small Scots data for PoS tagging, leading to the the first NLP tool of its kind developed for the Scots language, including an investigation of two different English training sets.

We believe that our study presents a method that can be used to create NLP tools for many other minority languages with scant resources that are closely related to a high-resource language, such as Low Saxon and Occitan. These NLP tools present a valuable lifeline that enables increased usage of minority languages in digital settings.

2 Scots

Scots is a West-Germanic language spoken by 1.5 million people.[1] While recognized as a language by the Scottish government, Scots' status as a language (Sebba, 2019) is disputed, with 64% of respondents in a 2010 Scottish Government survey seeing Scots as a way of speaking rather than a language.[2]

Scots diverged from English in the 13th century and use of Scots was widespread for both government and literary purposes until the 16th century (Kay, 1988). Since the Union of the Crowns, Scots has undergone a process of Anglicization, and has largely been superseded by Scottish English with which it is spoken on a bipolar spectrum. Currently, Scots is a low-resource language. Scots texts are readily available, but parallel corpora or gold-standard annotations are lacking. This severely complicates the analysis of Scots. In recent years, Scottish identity has experienced a revival, and with it interest in the Scots language. Scots is reemerging as an active language, especially amongst the young rural population of Scotland and amongst Scottish nationalists (Lemeshchenko-Lagoda, 2019). Although this has generated academic interest in the fields of phonology (Lawson et al., 2019) and socio-linguistics (Shoemark et al., 2017a,b), no NLP-tools are available specifically for Scots. The only Scots NLP efforts are two sets of word embeddings, namely Fasttext embeddings (Joulin et al., 2016) and Polyglot Word Embeddings (Al-Rfou et al., 2013).

There are several complications relating to NLP for Scots. Despite attempts at standardization by the *Report & Recommends o the Scots Spellin Comatee* (Allan et al., 1998), Scots does not have a *de jure* standard. As there is no official orthography, major variations in spelling exist, mostly depending on the written dialect of Scots. Additionally, almost no parallel English-Scots texts are publicly available, which excludes approaches relying on such data. Scots grammar and morphology, while similar to and not necessarily more or less complex, differs from English grammar and morphology. Some specific features of Scots is its irregular plural forms for nouns, e.g. *cauf/caur* for "calf/calves", and frequent use of progressive forms, e.g. *who's wantin tae go oot wi you* — "who wants to go out with you"[3],

3 Related Work

3.1 Non-standard Language PoS Tagging

State-of-the-art PoS taggers use a Bi-LSTM RNN configuration, often with a Conditional Random Field, e.g. in Akbik et al. (2018), who achieved an accuracy of 97.85% on the English-language

[1] `https://www.gov.scot/policies/languages/scots/`

[2] *Public Attitudes Towards the Scots Language:* `https://www.webarchive.org.uk/wayback/archive/3000/https://www.gov.scot/Resource/Doc/298037/0092859.pdf`

[3] Example from Anderson et al. (2007)

Wall Street Journal corpus. Most state-of-the-art taggers are trained on newswire articles, and perform poorly on non-standard language or informal language. Gui et al. (2017), for example noticed a performance drop from 97.0% to 73.4% for tweets and other out-of-domain data for a model trained on the Wall Street Journal. This drop was mitigated by training a novel neural network that used an adversarial discriminator on out-of-domain labeled data, unlabeled in-domain data, and labeled in-domain data to achieve 90.92% accuracy.

This performance drop is even greater when examining non-standard English such as African American Vernacular English. In Jørgensen et al. (2016), the performance of the newswire-trained tagger decreased to 63% for AAVE data. The researchers used word representations learned from unlabelled data, as well as partially labelled data generated from lexicons in combination with ambiguous supervision that weighs the probabilities from the partially labelled data to overcome the domain gap.

Similarly, historical texts contain spelling and grammatical constructions that deviate from modern standard language. Moon and Baldridge (2007) achieved an accuracy of 80.5% on Biblical texts and an accuracy 63.9% on other Middle English texts bootstrapping a maximum entropy tagger using alignment projections from the Wycliffe's Middle English Bible and the Modern English NET Bible.

Another method that has shown promise in PoS tagging out-of-domain data, especially historical data, is word normalization. Normalization of non-standard text improves tagging accuracy by lowering the number of out-of-vocabulary words which are substantially more difficult to tag compared to in-vocabulary words. This approached has successfully been applied for several languages including Slovenian (Zupan et al., 2019) and German (Bollmann, 2013). Zupan et al. (2019) further found that for small annotation efforts manual normalization was preferable to manual PoS tagging, while manual PoS tagging was useful in larger annotation projects.

While Scots has been analyzed as non-standard English in the field of sentiment analysis (Shoemark et al., 2017b), this approach is not straightforward for PoS tagging, as the approaches used to fine-tune the models for domain adaptation for PoS tagging in e.g. Gui et al. (2017); Jørgensen et al. (2016) rely on annotated corpora that are unavailable for Scots.

3.2 Low-Resource PoS tagging

Due to the complete absence of annotated data for Scots, its situation in terms of NLP is similar to the situation of many low-resource languages. Multiple methods have been used to alleviate data-scarcity, generally by using multi-task learning or cross-lingual transfer. While this project focuses on cross-lingual transfer learning, multi-task learning bears great relevance to low-resource PoS tagging and so will be briefly discussed.

3.2.1 Multi-task learning

Kann et al. (2018) built on the work of Plank et al. (2016) to hierarchically combine a recurrent network and a character-based sequence-to-sequence model with a corpus of only 478 annotated tokens in the low-resource language. The researchers jointly trained for PoS tagging and alternately unsupervised lemmatization, character-based autoencoding, and character-based random string autoencoding to close the gap on the state-of-the-art PoS tagger by 43%.

3.2.2 Cross-lingual tagging

Yarowsky et al. (2001) first showed the benefit of language transfer, a method in which multiple source languages are used to create a the target language model. Cross-lingual transfer especially improves results for closely related languages, highlighting the applicability for this study. Das (2011) expanded on this study by introducing an graph-based method using unsupervised label propagation that projects syntactic information across languages by constructing a bilingual graph over word-types resulting in a 16.7% error reduction compared to regular HMMs.

Cross-lingual PoS tagging utilizes annotated data available from high resource languages (Kim et al., 2017). This data is supplemented with e.g. parallel corpora to provide linguistic knowledge to aid the transfer. Before the neural era, cross-lingual PoS tagging was applied in low-resource PoS tagging by Agić et al. (2015), who used word alignment from Bible verses in 100 languages in combination with a small amount of manually tagged data to create PoS taggers. For the 25 languages for which test data was available, the models showed an improvement of 20-30% compared to unsupervised models.

Since neural networks perform especially poorly in low-data scenarios, cross-lingual transfer learning is indispensable in the creation of NLP tools such as PoS taggers for low-resource languages. As the aforementioned parallel corpora necessary for cross-lingual tagging are absent, cross-lingual transfer learning can be used. In cross-lingual transfer learning the lower layers of a hierarchical model share knowledge, such as parameters, between the differing input domains.

Yang et al. (2016) explored cross-lingual transfer solely focussed on model transfer between similar languages. Character embeddings were used in order to take advantage of morphological and lexical similarities. The researchers note, however, that fewer parameters were shared for cross-lingual transfer than for cross-domain transfer. Kim et al. (2017) built on Yang et al. (2016)'s research by using knowledge transfer in the Bi-LSTM layers that have as input the character and word embeddings from both a common (shared) Bi-LSTM and a private BiLSTM, as well as language adversarial training. Their best-performing model achieves an average of 88.37% for Germanic languages.

Magistry et al. (2019) attempted to create PoS taggers for three regional French languages. They had no training data available for these languages and relied on data for related high-resource languages, focusing on strategies based on delexicalization and transposition. They use a BiLSTM-CRF tagger, which overall gave better results than two alternative taggers.

4 Data

In this section we describe the data used. We use two existing English data sets, and create a small new set for Scots. The tags used for all the data are the Universal UD PoS tags (Zeman et al., 2019). This tagset consists of 17 tags and only uses basic lexical categories that are seen as applicable to all languages. Examples of categories are: Noun (NOUN), adjective (ADJ), and adposition (ADP).

4.1 English Data

For the English data, we used two data sets: the GUM Treebank (Zeldes, 2017) and the EWT Treebank (Silveira et al., 2014) from the Universal Dependencies project, version 2.5. Both data sets came pre-tagged using the Universal PoS tags from Universal Dependencies (Zeman et al., 2019) and pre-split into a training, development, and test set. The training set of the GUM Treebank contains 73513 tokens and the training set of the EWT Treebank contains 217152 tokens. The GUM Treebank contains multiple text types, including Wiki data, fiction and news, and the EWT Treebank contains web data including blogs and reviews.

4.2 Scots data

No pre-tagged PoS data were available for Scots, so instead the untagged Scots language data were harvested from the Scottish Corpus of Text and Speech (SCOTS) (Anderson et al., 2007), and Scots-language blog Mak Forrit (Clark et al., 2020). SCOTS is a corpus containing 949 texts which were written between 1945 and 2011. It includes texts in Scottish English, Scots, and Scottish Gaelic. The Scots data had to be classified as Broad Scots for it to be included in this project, which was achieved by searching for Scots function words such as *fae* — "from" and *tae* — "to". Mak Forrit is written in a standardized version of Scots. A final selection was arbitrarily made by picking a variety of sentences from the combination of sources. Multiple dialects of Scots, including Doric and West-Central Scots are represented. This results in multiple orthographies being present in the Scots language data. In total, 37 sentences with 1040 tokens were extracted which were divided into a training set of 536 tokens and a test set of 504 tokens. This ratio was chosen to maximize the amount of training and test data available given the time-scope of the project. Due to the small amount of data, we do not have a separate development set, and for the combined models we use the training data also as a development set.

While the option of normalization was considered, we decided on manually PoS tagging Scots as a result of the large number of spelling differences between Scots and English compared to Zupan et al. (2019). The Scots language data were manually tagged by the first author, a non-native Scots speaker with training in linguistics and computational linguistics. The data was tagged on two separate occasions, approximately one month apart so that intra-annotator agreement could be measured. The intra-annotator agreement was 96.5%. The two separate taggings were then consolidated into the final version, by the same annotator. Five retagged tokens were considered outright mistakes due to misinterpretations, for example in: *Kinnin the English airmy wad hae need o great stores*

The problem wis , thair Scots wisnae the best , an thay war relyin on a dictionar tae help thaim oot .
DET NOUN VERB PUNCT DET PROPN VERB DET ADJ PUNCT CCONJ PRON AUX VERB ADP DET NOUN PART VERB PRON ADV PUNCT

Figure 2: Example of a tagged Scots sentence

o supplies —"Knowing the English army would need great stores of supplies", need was tagged as a VERB due to the proceeding verbs that appeared to be auxiliary verbs. The word *o* "of", however makes the construction more akin to "Knowing the English army would have need of great stores of supplies", making *need* a NOUN and was therefore tagged as such. Other differences were attributed to slight ambiguity. In: *The ploy wasnae faur awa fae wirkin* — "The ploy nearly worked", the tokens *faur* "far" and *awa* "away" were initially tagged as ADJ, as *wasnae* — "was not" is a frequently used copula verb that is often followed by an adjective phrase. *Awa* only has ADV entries in *the Dictionary of the Scots Language*,[4] however, and *faur* modifies *awa* making *faur* another ADV. *Faur awa* was therefore reinterpreted as an adverbial phrase and both words were tagged ADV. An example of a tagged Scots sentence can be found in Figure 2.

4.3 Word Embeddings

Both the Scots and English language data were supplemented with Polyglot Word Embeddings (Al-Rfou et al., 2013) which are cross-lingual word embeddings available for over 100 languages trained on Wikipedia. While the Scots Wikipedia has attracted some controversy recently due to the questionable quality of the Scots featured on its pages[5], both sets of word embeddings available for Scots were trained on the Scots Wikipedia. Polyglot Word Embeddings were chosen over Fasttext word embeddings as its usage was recommended for the PoS tagger by Plank et al. (2016). No quality assessment had ever been done on these embeddings, however, and thus the performance of the embeddings could not be verified in advance. We leave a further investigation of word embedding quality to future work.

5 Models & Experiments

All models were run on the Bi-LSTM PoS tagger from Plank et al. (2016) running on the standard settings, bar the addition of the polyglot embeddings (Al-Rfou et al., 2013). Plank et al. (2016)'s tagger uses a Bi-LSTM for character embeddings, the output of which is concatenated with the word embeddings. These embeddings are the input for the BiLSTM which has the softmax for the PoS tags as an output layer.

The network used 100-dimensional character embeddings, 100 dimensional polyglot embeddings, 100-dimensional LSTM hidden states and had one hidden-layer for the encoder and the decoder. During training, stochastic gradient descent was applied with a dropout rate of 0.25 as well as a sigma of 0.2 Gaussian noise. The network used a softmax activation function in the decoder to generate the tags.

All models were trained for 20 iterations with an early stop of four iterations. These hyperparameters were chosen to prevent training from finishing pre-maturely, although no model trained for more than 19 iterations.

For our experiments, we first trained monolingual baseline models for English and Scots. Then we explored three ways of combining data across languages. In all cases we also compare the results with the two English corpora.

5.1 Model 1: Zero-shot

To compare the effect of the different types of model- and data transfer to the monolingual models, we first obtained a zero-shot baseline by training models on the two English training and development sets, and testing the model on the Scots test set. To examine the accuracy of the zero-shot models for English, it was first tested on the English test set from the GUM (Zeldes, 2017) and EWT (Silveira et al., 2014) obtaining an accuracy of of 95.7% and 95.1% respectively.

5.2 Model 2: Scots Only

The second monolingual baseline model was only trained on the Scots training data from the SCOTS corpus (Anderson et al., 2007) and Mak Forrit (Clark et al., 2020). The training set, 536 tokens, was, therefore, much smaller than for the other models, and it did not feature a development set. The purpose of this model was to elucidate fur-

[4]Scottish Language Dictionaries Ltd., `https://dsl.ac.uk/`

[5]https://www.theguardian.com/uk-news/2020/aug/26/shock-an-aw-us-teenager-wrote-huge-slice-of-scots-wikipedia

ther where transfer learning could bring benefits for small data sets.

5.3 Model 3: Concatenated Data

The concatenated data model used a joint-training method. The English and Scots training data were simply concatenated. The Scots training set was additionally also used as the development set during training, as empirical evidence showed that using the English evaluation set resulted in overfitting on the English part of the data set and had poorer results.

5.4 Model 4: Mixed training

In the mixed-training model, the model was first allowed to train to convergence on the English data set. After convergence, an even distribution of the Scots and the English data was used to further fine-tune the parameters. This method was used since it had proved beneficial in improving Neural Machine Translation in low-resource settings (Dabre et al., 2019; Chu and Wang, 2018).

5.5 Model 5: Pure fine-tuned model

In pure fine-tuning (Dabre et al., 2019), the model was first allowed to fully converge on the English training set. These parameters were then transferred to the Scots model by training the converged model on the small Scots training set, to allow convergence on the Scots set. This model used the Scots development set for pre-training and no development set for fine-tuning.

6 Results

Table 1 shows the main results. Training on only the small Scots data gave an accuracy of 60.5%, which is higher than the zero-shot results trained on much larger English data. All cross-lingual models performed remarkably better than the zero-shot models, seeing an improvement in accuracy of 16.9-23.1% for the GUM data set, and an improvement of 5.2-9.9% for the EWT data set. While for both data sets the zero-shot models obtain a low accuracy, the difference is starker for the GUM data set, which sees the best performance for the cross-lingual models, while it is out-performed by EWT for the zero-shot model. A possible explanation for this is the genres of the data. The GUM data set consists of largely curated data, for instance Wikipedia and news, with some non-curated Reddit data, while the EWT data set largely contains non-curated user-generated blogs. This has, most likely, caused the EWT zero-shot model to be more robust. The low accuracy obtained by the zero-shot models is indicative of a large discrepancy between the training and the test data. This strongly suggests that Scots, for NLP purposes, cannot merely be treated as out-of-domain English data. The zero-shot accuracy is much lower and the difference in accuracy between the zero-shot model and the cross-lingual models is a lot larger than in, e.g. Gui et al. (2017)'s models for the PoS tagging of out-of-domain data that obtained an accuracy of 73.4%, and than the 63% accuracy for AAVE-like language in Jørgensen et al. (2016).

	GUM	EWT
Scots only	60.5	
Zero-shot	42.4	**55.7**
Concatenated	**67.4**	65.6
Mixed training	62.2	**63.8**
Pure fine-tune	**63.5**	60.9

Table 1: The accuracy results of each model. Boldface indicates the best model of each type.

As can be seen in Table 1, the cross-lingual models display a slight to moderate improvement on the Scots-only model. The similarity in accuracy scores between the Scots-only and the cross-lingual models could be a sign that the domain overlap between the Scots training and test set was too great. Even though the annotated Scots corpus was created from sources that spanned multiple domains, the division between the training- and test data was made randomly, meaning that segments of the training- and test set could have been taken from the same text. The best-performing model for both data sets were the concatenated models. The concatenated models appear to benefit from first converging to the English training data, with the parameters then being adjusted to the Scots training data. The other models show more frequent under- and overfitting. The GUM Mixed-training mode for example on five occasions predicted an X tag, for example for *faa* "fall" and *e* "he" or "the". The X tag occurs in the Scots training data, as it contains some Catalan words. In the GUM data set the X symbol is nonetheless more sparse. Conversely, *wisnae* "was not" was tagged as a NOUN, despite occurring in the training data as a VERB and AUX.[6]

[6]In this work we have not segmented words not sep-

	Scots Only		Zero-shot				Concatenation			
			GUM		EWT		GUM		EWT	
	Prec.	Recall	Prec.	Recall	Prec.	Recall	Prec.	Recall	Prec.	Recall
INTJ	N/A	0	**100**	*100*	33.0	*100*	0	0	**50.0**	**100**
PUNCT	100	94.0	**100**	100	89.3	100	**100**	100	89.3	100
NOUN	61.5	64.9	33.7	81.1	**47.2**	**90.5**	**64.3**	**87.8**	55.9	83.8
PROPN	50.0	8.3	17.9	**100**	**26.2**	91.7	**50.0**	**91.7**	38.9	58.3
ADP	79.6	78.0	**100**	32.0	85.3	**58.0**	72.3	68.0	**77.8**	**70.0**
DET	86.6	75.0	**100**	48.1	90.6	**55.7**	78.0	**75.0**	**92.3**	69.2
ADJ	36.4	16.0	13.0	12.0	**25.8**	**32.0**	**50.0**	**32.0**	35.0	28.0
VERB	52.2	61.2	**52.2**	31.0	52.1	**35.2**	55.3	43.7	**61.2**	**57.8**
PRON	50.0	69.4	17.9	**100**	**26.2**	91.7	**80.0**	65.3	78.0	65.3
PART	55.6	38.5	20.0	7.7	**40.0**	**15.4**	**81.8**	**69.2**	40.0	15.4
ADV	100	15.2	26.6	24.2	**42.4**	**42.4**	47.4	**54.5**	**48.4**	45.5
AUX	20.3	59.1	0	0	**18.2**	**9.1**	47.8	50	**57.1**	**54.5**
CCONJ	66.7	33.3	60.0	25.0	**71.4**	**41.7**	81.8	**75.0**	**100**	58.3
SCONJ	N/A	0	0	0	**25.0**	**20.0**	**66.7**	40.0	33.3	40.0
NUM	100	28.6	0	0	**50.0**	**57.1**	**66.7**	28.6	36.4	**57.1**

Table 2: The per-tag precision and recall for the models. For each model pair, boldface indicates the best performing model for each tag.

Table 2 shows the precision and recall for each tag for Scots only and for the zero-shot and the best cross-lingual models: the concatenated models. Comparing the GUM concatenated model to the baselines, one can see that the model shows improvements compared to both the Scots-only and zero-shot baselines, especially when it comes to nouns (NOUN), adjectives (ADJ), pronouns (PRON), particles (PART), coordinating conjunctions (CCONJ), and subordinating conjunctions (SCONJ) for which both precision and recall increased. Interjections (INTJ) were surprisingly not predicted correctly, achieving 0% for both precision and recall, despite the zero-shot model achieving 100% precision and recall. Apart from the precision for INTJ, adpositions (ADP), determiners (DET), and the recall for INTJ, and proper nouns (PROPN), the model improved for every PoS category. Some surprising errors remain, however. The verb or auxiliary verb *are* was consistently tagged as an adverb (ADV), despite occurring as such in neither the English nor the Scots data. Other (auxiliary) verbs, such as *micht* "might" and *'ve* were also tagged as adverbs. Many sentence-initial words such as *Syne* "since", *Reading* and *They* were tagged as PROPN, despite the two latter words also occurring in both languages. Other incorrect predictions are more similar to what one would expect from English PoS taggers for English, such as the labelling of VERB as auxiliary verb (AUX) and vice-versa, e.g. in *Ye jist had tae* ***be*** *maist aafa partickler* "You just had to be most awfully particular", be was labelled as an AUX instead of a VERB.

The differences between the EWT concatenated model and the EWT zero-shot baseline are much smaller, as can be seen in Table 2. While there are some improvements in both precision and recall for e.g. DET, VERB, ADV, AUX, CCONJ,and SCONJ, the difference generally not as stark as for the GUM concatenated model. Many other categories see a drop in either precision, such as INTJ, ADP, VERB, and PRON or recall, such as NOUN, PROPN, and PRON. Compared to the Scots-only baseline, the EWT concatenated model shows consistent improvement for INTJ, PRON, CCONJ and SCONJ, while also notably improving the precision for VERB and the recall for NOUN.

The EWT concatenated model also contains unexpected errors. Despite occurring in both English and Scots, auxiliary verb *can* was tagged as both an ADV and a NOUN. Another error can possibly, though not necessarily, be attributed to the quality

arated by whitespace. An option would be to separate a word like wisnae into wis+nae, according to UD guidelines (`https://universaldependencies.org/u/overview/tokenization.html`). However, this would lead to a call for a tokenizer especially adapted to Scots, which is currently not available.

of the word embeddings. *E* "he" or "the", is consistently tagged as NUM, despite it not having this tag in the training data, although this could also be due to the model parameters.

Comparing the GUM and EWT concatenated models in table 4, one can see that both models generally have comparable per-tag precision and recall, and that neither model scores consistently better than the other, with each model outperforming the other in both precision and recall in four PoS categories. The main reason for the slightly better performance of the GUM concatenated model appears to stem from better precision in PUNCT, NOUN, ADJ, and PART, all frequently occurring tags although the performance for VERB is much better for the EWT concatenated model.

7 Conclusion

We have annotated a small amount of Scots data with PoS tags, and shown how this data can be used to improve tagging for Scots. The best results were obtained by a simple concatenation model, where a large English data set was concatenated with a small amount of Scots data. We also found that while the English data EWT data set containing web data, performed better than the GUM Treebank with mostly edited data in a zero-shot setting, the GUM Treebank, trained on a mix of genres performed better in the cross-lingual setting.

While greatly improving on the zero-shot model and slightly improving on the Scots-only model, the cross-lingual models for both data sets scored lower than other studies that examine low-resource settings for PoS tagging. Longer training, higher dimensional embeddings and modifications to the model architecture such as private LSTMs and the use of adversarial training could be made. Kim et al. (2017) achieve higher accuracies for all languages using 320 tokens per language, showing the efficacy of the combination of these factors. An improvement on the model architecture can be made as well by, rather than weighting English and Scots data equally in the loss function as was done in these experiments, weighting the Scots data more heavily in the loss function of the Bi-LSTM in order to prevent underfitting on the Scots data.

Another possible cause of these results is the previously mentioned questionable quality of the word embeddings, and we think it would be interesting to train Scots word embeddings on verified Scots data, to be able to compare to the current embeddings trained on Wikipedia data with questionable quality. We also think it would be interesting to explore text normalization strategies for Scots.

Lastly and perhaps most importantly, an increase in the size of the Scots data set and an interest in developing NLP tool for minority languages is required to improve performance of the tagger. Other models that examine cross-lingual transfer, such as Yang et al. (2016) use 900 training tokens minimally, nearly double the tokens used in this paper. Yang et al. (2016) also note that improvements are smaller for cross-lingual transfer than in cross-domain training, strengthening the case for the treatment of Scots as a language in terms of the required NLP resources. Combined with the low accuracy for the zero-shot model this indicates the need for additional resources for Scots, such as dictionaries and parallel corpora.

References

Željko Agić, Dirk Hovy, and Anders Søgaard. 2015. If all you have is a bit of the Bible: Learning PoS taggers for truly low-resource languages. In *Proceedings of the 53rd Annual Meeting of the Association for Computational Linguistics and the 7th International Joint Conference on Natural Language Processing (Volume 2: Short Papers)*, pages 268–272.

Alan Akbik, Duncan Blythe, and Roland Vollgraf. 2018. Contextual string embeddings for sequence labeling. In *COLING 2018, 27th International Conference on Computational Linguistics*, pages 1638–1649.

Rami Al-Rfou, Bryan Perozzi, and Steven Skiena. 2013. Polyglot: Distributed word representations for multilingual NLP. In *Proceedings of the Seventeenth Conference on Computational Natural Language Learning*, pages 183–192, Sofia, Bulgaria. Association for Computational Linguistics.

Alasdair Allan, Andy Eagle, John Law, J Derrick McClure, George Philp, Iseabail Macleod, Liz Niven, David Purves, and John Tait. 1998. Report & recommends o the Scots spellin comatee.

Jean Anderson, Dave Beavan, and Christian Kay. 2007. Scots: Scottish corpus of texts and speech. In Joan C. Beal, Karen P. Corrigan, and Hermann L. Moisl, editors, *Creating and Digitizing Language Corpora: Volume 1: Synchronic Databases*, pages 17–34. Palgrave Macmillan UK, London.

Daniel Andor, Chris Alberti, David Weiss, Aliaksei Severyn, Alessandro Presta, Kuzman Ganchev, Slav Petrov, and Michael Collins. 2016. Globally normalized transition-based neural networks. In *Proceedings of the 54th Annual Meeting of the Association for Computational Linguistics (Volume 1: Long Papers)*, pages 2442–2452, Berlin, Germany. Association for Computational Linguistics.

Marcel Bollmann. 2013. POS tagging for historical texts with sparse training data. In *Proceedings of the 7th Linguistic Annotation Workshop and Interoperability with Discourse*, pages 11–18, Sofia, Bulgaria. Association for Computational Linguistics.

Chenhui Chu and Rui Wang. 2018. A survey of domain adaptation for neural machine translation. In *Proceedings of the 27th International Conference on Computational Linguistics*, pages 1304–1319.

Thomas Clark, Alistair Heather, James McDonald, Jamie Smith, Elizabeth Thoumire, and Antonia Uri. 2020. Mak Forrit. Blog: `https://www.makforrit.scot`.

Raj Dabre, Atsushi Fujita, and Chenhui Chu. 2019. Exploiting multilingualism through multistage fine-tuning for low-resource neural machine translation. In *Proceedings of the 2019 Conference on Empirical Methods in Natural Language Processing and the 9th International Joint Conference on Natural Language Processing (EMNLP-IJCNLP)*, pages 1410–1416.

Amitava Das. 2011. PsychoSentiWordNet. In *Proceedings of the ACL 2011 Student Session*, pages 52–57, Portland, OR, USA. Association for Computational Linguistics.

Meng Fang and Trevor Cohn. 2017. Model transfer for tagging low-resource languages using a bilingual dictionary. In *Proceedings of the 55th Annual Meeting of the Association for Computational Linguistics (Volume 2: Short Papers)*, pages 587–593.

Dan Garrette, Jason Mielens, and Jason Baldridge. 2013. Real-world semi-supervised learning of PoS-taggers for low-resource languages. In *Proceedings of the 51st Annual Meeting of the Association for Computational Linguistics (Volume 1: Long Papers)*, pages 583–592.

Tao Gui, Qi Zhang, Haoran Huang, Minlong Peng, and Xuan-Jing Huang. 2017. Part-of-Speech tagging for twitter with adversarial neural networks. In *Proceedings of the 2017 Conference on Empirical Methods in Natural Language Processing*, pages 2411–2420.

Erhard Hinrichs, Marie Hinrichs, Sandra Kübler, and Thorsten Trippel. 2019. Language technology for digital humanities: introduction to the special issue. *Language Resources & Evaluation*, 53:559–563.

Anna Jørgensen, Dirk Hovy, and Anders Søgaard. 2016. Learning a PoS tagger for AAVE-like language. In *Proceedings of the 2016 conference of the North American chapter of the association for computational linguistics: human language technologies*, pages 1115–1120.

Armand Joulin, Edouard Grave, Piotr Bojanowski, Matthijs Douze, Hérve Jégou, and Tomas Mikolov. 2016. Fasttext.zip: Compressing text classification models. *arXiv preprint arXiv:1612.03651*.

Katharina Kann, Johannes Bjerva, Isabelle Augenstein, Barbara Plank, and Anders Søgaard. 2018. Character-level supervision for low-resource PoS tagging. In *Proceedings of the Workshop on Deep Learning Approaches for Low-Resource NLP*, pages 1–11.

Billy Kay. 1988. *The mither tongue*. Grafton, London, United Kingdom.

Joo-Kyung Kim, Young-Bum Kim, Ruhi Sarikaya, and Eric Fosler-Lussier. 2017. Cross-lingual transfer learning for PoS tagging without cross-lingual resources. In *Proceedings of the 2017 conference on empirical methods in natural language processing*, pages 2832–2838.

Eleanor Lawson, Jane Stuart-Smith, and Lydia Rodger. 2019. A comparison of acoustic and articulatory parameters for the GOOSE vowel across British Isles Englishes. *The Journal of the Acoustical Society of America*, 146(6):4363–4381.

Viktoriia Lemeshchenko-Lagoda. 2019. What is Scots? In Halyna Matiukha and Maria Karpinska, editors, *Novi perspektyvy v angliys'kiy filolohiyi ta navchannya angliys'kiy movi*. TOB, Kolor Print, Melitopol.

Yu-Hsiang Lin, Chian-Yu Chen, Jean Lee, Zirui Li, Yuyan Zhang, Mengzhou Xia, Shruti Rijhwani, Junxian He, Zhisong Zhang, Xuezhe Ma, Antonios Anastasopoulos, Patrick Littell, and Graham Neubig. 2019. Choosing transfer languages for cross-lingual learning. In *Proceedings of the 57th Annual Meeting of the Association for Computational Linguistics*, pages 3125–3135, Florence, Italy. Association for Computational Linguistics.

Pierre Magistry, Anne-Laure Ligozat, and Sophie Rosset. 2019. Exploiting languages proximity for Part-of-Speech tagging of three French regional languages. *Language Resources & Evaluation*, 53:865–888.

Taesun Moon and Jason Baldridge. 2007. Part-of-Speech tagging for middle English through alignment and projection of parallel diachronic texts. In *Proceedings of the 2007 joint conference on empirical methods in Natural Language Processing and Computational Natural Language Learning (EMNLP-CoNLL)*, pages 390–399.

Barbara Plank, Anders Søgaard, and Yoav Goldberg. 2016. Multilingual Part-of-Speech tagging with bidirectional long short-term memory models and auxiliary loss. In *Proceedings of the 54th Annual Meeting of the Association for Computational Linguistics (Volume 2: Short Papers)*, pages 412–418, Berlin, Germany. Association for Computational Linguistics.

Mark Sebba. 2019. Named into being? language questions and the politics of Scots in the 2011 census in Scotland. *Language Policy*, 18(3):339–362.

Philippa Shoemark, James Kirby, and Sharon Goldwater. 2017a. Topic and audience effects on distinctively scottish vocabulary usage in twitter data. In *Proceedings of the Workshop on Stylistic Variation*, pages 59–68.

Philippa Shoemark, Debnil Sur, Luke Shrimpton, Iain Murray, and Sharon Goldwater. 2017b. Aye or naw, whit dae ye hink? Scottish independence and linguistic identity on social media. In *Proceedings of the 15th Conference of the European Chapter of the Association for Computational Linguistics: Volume 1, Long Papers*, pages 1239–1248, Valencia, Spain. Association for Computational Linguistics.

Natalia Silveira, Timothy Dozat, Marie-Catherine de Marneffe, Samuel Bowman, Miriam Connor, John Bauer, and Christopher D. Manning. 2014. A gold standard dependency corpus for English. In *Proceedings of the Ninth International Conference on Language Resources and Evaluation (LREC-2014)*.

Zhilin Yang, Ruslan Salakhutdinov, and William W Cohen. 2016. Transfer learning for sequence tagging with hierarchical recurrent networks. *arXiv preprint arXiv:* 1703.06345v1.

David Yarowsky, Grace Ngai, and Richard Wicentowski. 2001. Inducing multilingual text analysis tools via robust projection across aligned corpora. Technical report, Johns Hopkins University Baltimore, MD Dept. of Compute Science.

Amir Zeldes. 2017. The GUM corpus: Creating multilayer resources in the classroom. *Language Resources and Evaluation*, 51(3):581–612.

Daniel Zeman, Joakim Nivre, Mitchell Abrams, et al. 2019. Universal dependencies 2.5. LINDAT/CLARIAH-CZ digital library at the Institute of Formal and Applied Linguistics (ÚFAL), Faculty of Mathematics and Physics, Charles University.

Katja Zupan, Nikola Ljubešić, and Tomaž Erjavec. 2019. How to tag non-standard language: Normalisation versus domain adaptation for Slovene historical and user-generated texts. *Natural Language Engineering*, 25(5):651–674.

Efficient Unsupervised NMT for Related Languages with Cross-Lingual Language Models and Fidelity Objectives

Rami Aly[1], Andrew Caines[2], Paula Buttery[2]
[1] Computer Laboratory, University of Cambridge, U.K.
[2] Computer Laboratory & ALTA Institute, University of Cambridge, U.K.
{rami.aly|andrew.caines|paula.buttery}@cl.cam.ac.uk

Abstract

The most successful approach to Neural Machine Translation (NMT) when only monolingual training data is available, called unsupervised machine translation, is based on back-translation where noisy translations are generated to turn the task into a supervised one. However, back-translation is computationally very expensive and inefficient. This work explores a novel, efficient approach to unsupervised NMT. A transformer, initialized with cross-lingual language model weights, is fine-tuned exclusively on monolingual data of the target language by jointly learning on a paraphrasing and denoising autoencoder objective. Experiments are conducted on WMT datasets for German→English, French→English, and Romanian→English. Results are competitive to strong baseline unsupervised NMT models, especially for closely related source languages (German) compared to more distant ones (Romanian, French), while requiring about a magnitude less training time.

1 Introduction

While traditional end-to-end neural machine translation (NMT) approaches have shown highly promising results when abundant parallel data is available (Barrault et al., 2019), the task remains a considerable challenge when only monolingual training data is available, also called *unsupervised* MT (Artetxe et al., 2018a; Lample et al., 2018a). Unsupervised NMT systems tend to combine back-translation (Sennrich et al., 2016a) with cross-lingual embeddings (Artetxe et al., 2018b; Lample et al., 2018a,b) or, more recently, with weights of a pre-trained cross-lingual language model (XLM) (Conneau and Lample, 2019). Back-translation uses noisy translations, generated by a source-to-target model, as input for a target-to-source model (and vice versa). Although shown to perform well if plenty of monolingual data is available, back-translation is computationally very expensive. It is also highly inefficient as the inference performed to generate the noisy translations is of sequential nature, slowing down the training substantially.

This paper presents a novel unsupervised NMT method that does not require back-translation. Instead, it jointly fine-tunes a transformer (Vaswani et al., 2017), initialized with weights of cross-lingual language models (Conneau and Lample, 2019), on a denoising autoencoder (Vincent et al., 2008; Artetxe et al., 2018b) and paraphrasing objective exclusively on data in the target language. The alignment of the languages in the transformer's encoder means we can learn similar hidden representations for sentences of similar meaning but from different languages. The decoder, fine-tuned to generate a sentence in the target language, can thus generate a translation based on the encoder's representation of a source-language input sentence. Naturally, this method is more suitable for related languages, as the alignment of languages and hidden representations in the cross-lingual encoder is of particular importance to this approach.

Our experiments with the WMT datasets for German→English, French→English, and Romanian→English (Bojar et al., 2016) show that the proposed approach outperforms competitive models – namely Artetxe et al. (2018b), Lample et al. (2018a) and Lample et al. (2018b) – highlighting that the alignment quality achieved by the high-quality cross-lingual language model as a translation signal is superior to aligned embeddings and back-translation. Results for German are substantially higher than for French and Romanian, highlighting that our approach works particularly well for more closely related languages. While achieving competitive results, the proposed approach is substantially more efficient. It converges much quicker while requiring less than 50% time per

Proceedings of the 8th VarDial Workshop on NLP for Similar Languages, Varieties and Dialects, pages 49–59

epoch during fine-tuning which results in around a magnitude less floating point operations for the proposed approach than for an equivalent setup when using back-translation. We further show that the paraphrasing objective improves translation quality considerably compared to using the autoencoder objective in isolation.

2 Method

Given an input sequence X^s in source language s the objective is to generate a sequence Y^t in the target language t, which is semantically equivalent. A model NMT$^{s \to t}$ models the target function

$$\underset{\mathcal{Y}^t}{arg\ max} \prod_{u=1}^{m} p(y_u^t | y_{<u}^t; x_1^s, ..., x_n^s), \quad (1)$$

with $\mathcal{Y}^t$ being the set of all possible sequences in the target language. This paper focuses on the transformer model (Vaswani et al., 2017) to solve Equation 1. The transformer consists of an encoder and a decoder module: both are initialized with weights $W^{s \leftrightarrow t}$ of a cross-lingual language model and a shared subword vocabulary to align languages s and t (§ 2.3).

$$H^s = \text{ENC}_W(X^s) \quad (2)$$

$$\hat{Y}^t = \text{DEC}_W(H^s) \quad (3)$$

The encoder transforms the input into a latent space while the decoder iteratively generates the output sequence $\hat{Y}^t$.

2.1 Fine-tuning Approach

We propose a fine-tuning approach for this model that solely relies on monolingual data of the target language and the alignment W between s and t. Due to the cross-lingual weights W, the hidden representation of the encoder for both source and target language are aligned and thus expected to be similar[1]:

$$\text{ENC}_W(X^s) \sim \text{ENC}_W(Y^t) \quad (4)$$

This assumption is the essence to our approach and it applies more to closely related source and target languages than to more distant ones. Based on the assumption, our hypothesis is that it is sufficient to train the initialized encoder and decoder on sentence generation tasks in only the target language. More specifically, we explore meaning-preserving training objectives, that focus on monolingual sentence generation objectives so that the meaning of the input sequence is preserved for the generated sequence. We call these *fidelity* objectives. Thus, given a sentence P^t in the target language (specified in § 2.2) with very similar/identical meaning to a sentence Q^t of the same language in the monolingual training data, we optimize the NMT model by calculating the cross-entropy loss of the fidelity task over the shared subword vocabulary:

$$\mathcal{L}_{\text{fid}} = - \sum_{<P^t, Q^t> \in D_{\text{fid}}} log(p(Q^t | P^t)), \quad (5)$$

where D_{fid} is a fidelity training dataset. When confronted with an input sequence X^s in the source language during inference, $ENC_W(X^s)$ generates a hidden representation H^s, which is expected to be similar to the representation H^t for a semantically identical sentence in the target language due to the cross-lingual LM weights W. The similarity between H^s and H^t trains the decoder to generate a meaning-preserving sequence based on the hidden representation of the encoder and enables $\text{DEC}_W(H^s)$ to generate a sentence in the target language similar to $\text{DEC}_W(H^t)$ while preserving the meaning of the source sentence X^s.

2.2 Fidelity Objectives for Fine-tuning

We focus on two learning objectives that are solved by the model for the target language: a *denoising autoencoder* (Artetxe et al., 2018b) and *paraphrase generation* in the target language. The objectives are illustrated in Figure 1 and are learned using Eq. 5.

Denoising Autoencoder We use a straightforward autoencoder objective (Vincent et al., 2008; Artetxe et al., 2018b) to fine-tune the model so that it reconstructs the input Q^t from a noisy version P^t_{denoise} (the noise prevents the model from simply copying the input). We add noise to Q^t by either swapping, omitting or replacing words with a padding token. The number of noise operations on a sentence is a hyperparameter. The denoising autoencoder objective is used in most unsupervised NMT systems in combination with back-translation (Conneau and Lample, 2019), however, in these settings, the autoencoder objective only serves the

[1]This expectation is based on results for zero-shot classification to highlight the sentence similarity across different languages as well as the high cosine-similarity between word translation pairs shown in Conneau and Lample (2019). Languages more similar to the one the model has been trained on have higher sentence similarity and thus achieved higher scores in their experiments.

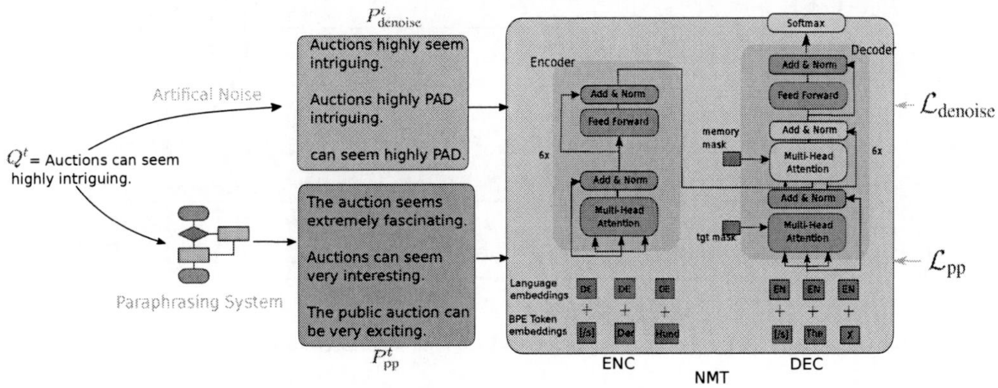

Figure 1: Illustration of the joint fine-tuning approach with denoising autoencoder and paraphrasing objectives. Note that for each sentence multiple paraphrases and noisy inputs are generated for fine-tuning the transformer.

function of making the model familiar with noise in the input that back-translated texts naturally have. Explicitly using alignment in the encoder for unsupervised translation in the way we propose has not yet been explored.

Paraphrasing In previous work the autoencoder objective has only been shown to be effective in combination with back-translation as a means to make the model familiar with noise in the input (Conneau and Lample, 2019; Artetxe et al., 2018b). This might be attributed to the limitation of the denoising autoencoder that the added noise is artificial and results in ungrammatical sentences. Thus, we additionally explore the task of reconstructing a sentence Q^t from a paraphrased version P^t_{pp} which is complemented by the denoising task. Automatically generated paraphrases are expected to be more grammatical and diverse than the simple rule-based variations used in the autoencoder objective.

2.3 Initialization

To initialize the weights W of the word embeddings, the encoder, and decoder of the transformer model we use the weights of the state-of-the-art pre-trained cross-lingual language model (XLM) of Conneau and Lample (2019). The pre-trained XLM is essentially the encoder part of the transformer model trained on the *masked language modelling* (MLM) objective on a stream of text. Furthermore, XLM uses language embeddings to assist the network in recognizing different languages. Finally, XLM and subsequently the translation model make use of subword tokenized inputs, specifically byte-pair encoding (BPE) (Sennrich et al., 2016b) to reduce the vocabulary size as it is shared by all languages in the model.

3 Evaluation

3.1 Experimental Setup

Data: Our approach uses WMT 2007-8 training data for German→English, as well as French→English (Callison-Burch et al., 2007, 2008), and the training data of WMT 2015 for Romanian→English (Bojar et al., 2015). All languages are Indo-European and therefore related to some extent, but there are differences of relatedness. French and Romanian are Italic whereas German and English are West Germanic: we therefore hold German and English to be the most closely related of our language pairs, with much that is similar in terms of lexicon and morpho-syntax and a recent shared history; followed by French and English (due to extensive lexical borrowings from language contact), and lastly Romanian→English which is the most distantly related language pair.

Note that for all language pairs, our approach converged in the first epoch, with only a few steps difference. Therefore, our approach was implicitly fine-tuned on comparable amount of data for all language pairs. Similar to previous unsupervised MT approaches, we evaluate the models on the WMT 2016 test sets for German→English and Roman→English (Bojar et al., 2016) and use the WMT 2014 test set for French→English (Bojar et al., 2014).

Implementation details: The experiments were run in Python 3.7 and Python 3.5 for the NMT model and paraphrasing system, respectively. The openly accessible repository of the work described

Model	de-en	fr-en	ro-en
(1) Lample et al. (2018a)	13.3	**14.3**	–
(2) Artetxe et al. (2018b)	–	**15.6**	–
(3) Lample et al. (2018b) Transformer	21.0	**24.2**	19.4
(4) Lample et al. (2018b) Transformer + PBSMT	25.1	**27.7**	23.9
(5) Conneau and Lample (2019)	**34.3**	33.3	31.8
(6) Transf. + autoencoder	**20.9**	18.9	18.7
(7) Transf. + autoencoder + paraphrases	**24.2**	22.1	21.2

Table 1: BLEU scores on test sets. (1)–(5) are taken from the respective papers. (6) and (7) refers to the proposed approach. **Bold** numbers indicate the language pair on which the model performs best.

in Conneau and Lample (2019)[2] was used as the basis for the implementation of this paper, and we use their provided pre-trained models [3]. The data is preprocessed into BPE tokens using FastBPE[4] with a vocabulary size of $60,000$. All models were fine-tuned on one GPU (NVIDIA Tesla P100). Since our experiments are conducted in the exact same ecosystem as Conneau and Lample (2019); Lample et al. (2018b), our results are directly comparable to theirs.

We use paraphrases created by the model proposed by Wieting et al. (2017)[5], due to its open-source access. It uses a Seq2Seq architecture to back-translate bilingual sentence pairs. For each sentence in the training data, the most probable three paraphrases are used. It would be preferable to use a fully unsupervised paraphrasing system, e.g. (Roy and Grangier, 2019). Nonetheless, we argue that the employed system does not violate the assumption of an unsupervised NMT system, since the paraphrases are only generated for the target language. Thus, while the target language must be part of at least one bilingual corpus, the source language can be arbitrary (as long as the cross-lingual language model between the source and target language exists).

Hyperparameters: Since for unsupervised NMT the assumption is made that *only* monolingual data is available, selecting the model or hyperparameters on a parallel dataset contradicts this premise. Therefore, the default hyperparameter settings from related work (Conneau and Lample, 2019) and the underlying XLM model are used[6]. The number of training epochs is based on the perplexity scores on the WMT 2013 test sets or, for Romanian, the WMT 2015 development set.

Evaluation metrics While perplexity is used as the metric during training, the performance on the test sets are reported on the commonly used BLEU metric (Papineni et al., 2002), specifically the MOSES evaluation script (Hoang and Koehn, 2008).

4 Results

Table 1 shows the BLEU scores on the test sets for source and target language. The scores for model (1) to (5) are taken from the respective papers with our re-evaluations producing almost identical results when using the respective openly accessible repository. Although the proposed model (7) uses exclusively data of the target language, it performs competitively than the sophisticated approaches in (1), (2), (3), and (4) which all use back-translation (Lample et al., 2018a,b; Artetxe et al., 2018b), especially for German→English. Since (3) uses the transformer architecture as well, the results highlight that the alignment achieved by the high-quality cross-lingual language models of XLM is superior to the gains achieved by the back-translation algorithm. When combining both back-translation and XLM, the results can, however, be further improved substantially, as shown by (5).

While previous attempts to using the denoising objective without back-translation resulted in unusable results (Artetxe et al., 2018b), we observe that our model performs reasonably well already when

[2] https://github.com/facebookresearch/XLM

[3] mlm_ende_1024, mlm_enfr_1024, and mlm_enro_1024

[4] https://github.com/glample/fastBPE

[5] https://github.com/vsuthichai/paraphraser

[6] emb_dim: 1024, #layers 6, #heads 8, dropout: 0.1, attention_dropout: 0.1, tokens_per_batch: 2000, optimizer: adam_inverse_sqrt. Denoising autoencoder parameters: word_shuffle: 3, word_dropout: 0.1, word_blank: 0.1, lr: $7 \cdot 10^{-4}$

Model	(3)	(5)	(7)
time per step (minutes)	89.55	92.24	29.54
total cost (FLOPs)	$1.78 \cdot 10^{18}$	$6.31 \cdot 10^{17}$	$8.07 \cdot 10^{16}$
cost (FLOPs) @ 100K	$5.10 \cdot 10^{17}$	$3.15 \cdot 10^{17}$	$7.47 \cdot 10^{16}$

Table 2: Comparison of average training time between different methods on a single Tesla P100 when fine-tuning for German→English. A step consists of 100K samples. Total cost reports floating-point operations for the entire training process. We use the value 9.5 TFLOP/s for the P100. Costs are shown when trained on the entire training corpus and when exclusively training on 100K sentences. The generation of paraphrases is included in (7) total cost.

training exclusively on this objective (6). Joint modelling of the paraphrasing and denoising objective (7) improves scores of the unsupervised system by about 3 BLEU points over (6).

Furthermore, our approach (7) achieves particularly high results when a source language is related (German) to the training language, compared to a more distant one (French, Romanian). While our model (7) outperforms (3) for German→English by around 3 BLEU points, it scores 2.1 points less for French→English. Moreover, scores between (7) and (3) are only comparable for German, while (3) performs much better for both the less related source languages. This observation is even amplified when the source language is Romanian. Our model appears to be more susceptible to the relatedness of the source language than (5) which uses the same cross-lingual weights, scoring 2.1 points less on French than German, compared to only 1.0 for (5). While our approach solely relies on the alignments based on these weights, the back-translation of (5) adds an important signal especially for more distant languages. This confirms the assumption made for our model: the BLEU score of our model is particularly high for the closely related German→English, compared to the more distant language pairs.

5 Efficiency

One major advantage of the proposed method over existing methods is its efficiency in terms of computational time. In Table 2 we report the average time and cost for the German→English experiments. The time to fine-tune on a full epoch is measured in the same environment under identical conditions. For our model, the measured times include the computational cost to generate the paraphrases[7]. We

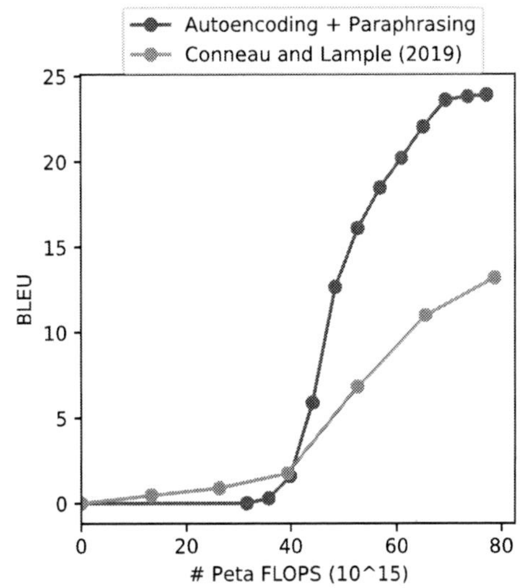

Figure 2: BLEU scores over number of FLOPs. FLOPs include the computation of the paraphrases before our model is trained.

find that by using the paraphrasing objective instead of back-translation the computational time can be reduced by a factor of three. Moreover, the entire training process requires around an order of magnitude less floating point operations due to our approach converging much quicker.

Our approach outperforms Lample et al. (2018b) while being much more efficient, however, one might suggest that the shown efficiency of the proposed model can also be achieved with the better scoring Conneau and Lample (2019) by trading off some of its performance advantages. Therefore, we explored to which extent either less training time or training data to achieve faster convergence improves its efficiency. Regarding training times, our

[7] Training the paraphrasing generator (Wieting et al., 2017) is not included in the costs as the employed paraphrasing model for English is already openly accessible. Moreover, the paraphrasing model uses a (Bi-LSTM) that was trained for 3 epochs on only 24,000 sentence pairs, which is less than 2% of the translation data used for the NMT models.

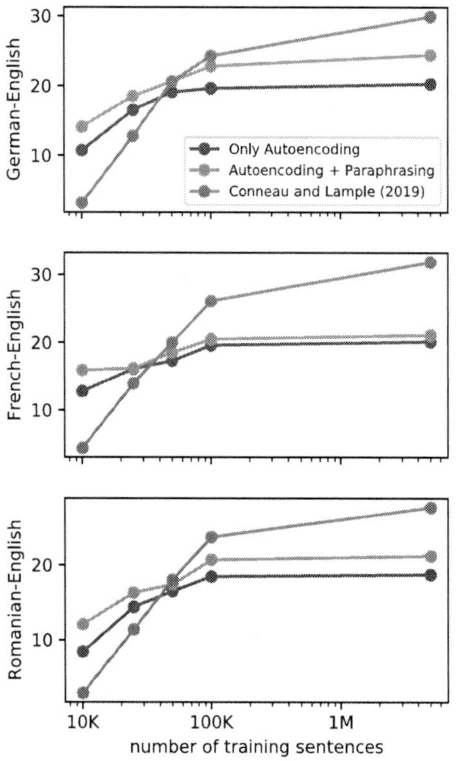

Figure 3: BLEU scores of the proposed model as well as the state-of-the-art approach of Conneau and Lample (2019) for varying number of monolingual training sentences: 10K, 25K, 50K 100K, and 5M.

proposed approach (7) scored consistently higher[8] than the other models until it's convergence, see figure 2. Only after our model converged, the model of Conneau and Lample (2019) surpasses its scores. Thus, stopping the training process earlier would not lead to better efficiency than our model. We then also analyzed the models' scores when modifying the amount of data used for fine-tuning. Results using 10K, 25K, 50K, 100K, and 5M training sentences are shown in Figure 3. As seen, when using little training data, Conneau and Lample (2019) performs much worse than the proposed model since errors and noise from translating into one direction are propagated when translating back. The less monolingual data used, the stronger the effect of this error-propagation issue. The back-translation model of Conneau and Lample (2019) starts to outperform the proposed model starting from 100K training sentences. Yet, even in this setting the proposed model remains much more efficient, as seen in the column *cost (FLOPs) @ 100K* in Table 2. The back-translation model is thus required to train on more data and ultimately longer until convergence and cannot achieve similar efficiency with scores comparable to our approach.

[8]Excluding the initial phase as our model computes the paraphrases first. Since our model catches up at a BLEU of around 1.7, we ignored this special case.

6 Model Analysis & Discussion

Alignment and translation quality: To investigate whether the alignment extends from a word-level to a phrase or even sentence level, a qualitative analysis was conducted. Example reference texts and respective translations for German→English are shown in Figure 4. It can be seen that the translation quality is high for shorter sentences but it declines with increasing sentence length. Many words and phrases are translated correctly, which generally leads to preservation of sentence meaning for simple sentences in closely-related languages like English and German. While many simple phrases are grammatical, many longer more complex structures are not.

Furthermore, the model hallucinates content, especially when confronted with numbers and named entities. For example, in sentence 5 the model generates a made-up destination *to northern Croatia* while *New Lloyd* in sentence 6 also never occurs in the source sentence. In the translation for sentence 3, the name is simply omitted and the currency, as well as the amount, is wrong. This observation can be transferred to numbers as well: in sentence 3, the number of 7.5 million was changed to 67.5 million. In an extreme example, the model hallucinates an entire clause for sentence 7. We also observed some artifacts in the output: in sentence 7, *oberflächlich* is translated into *Oberpublic*, instead of *superficial*, merging an German and English term.

Wrong translations frequently contain words that are still closely related to the correct translation. For instance, in sentence 2 the model generates the former prime minister of Israel *Olmert*, instead of *Netanyahu* and translates *meets* instead of *receives*. Or in sentence 5, the model translated into *hurdles* instead of *obstacles*. These very subtle differences are difficult for the model to capture.

Paraphrase quality Although the paraphrasing objective improves the performance of the system substantially, the generated paraphrases are still far from optimal. Figure 5 shows example paraphrases.

X-1: Die Vorbereitung lief gut.
Y: The preparation went well.
$\hat{Y}$**:** The training season went well.

X-2: Obama empfängt Netanyahu.
Y: Obama receives Netanyahu.
$\hat{Y}$**:** Obama meets Olmert.

X-3: Spaniens Nationaltorhüter Iker Casillas hat für 7,5 Millionen Euro seine Hände versichern lassen.
Y: Spain's national goalkeeper Iker Casillas insured his hands for 7.5 million euro.
$\hat{Y}$**:** Spain's King has asked for £ 67.5 million to reinsure his hands.

X-4: Wir wollten gewinnen und wir haben gewonnen, obwohl ich es bedaure, dass wir nicht noch ein oder zwei weitere Tore erzielt haben".
Y: We wanted to win and we did, although I regret that we did not score one or two goals more.
$\hat{Y}$**:** We wanted to win and we have won, although I regret it not yet that we have scored one or two more goals."

X-5: Zagreb kündigt an, die Durchreise über Slowenien nach Norden ohne Hürden zu gewähren.
Y: Zagreb has announced that they will allow passage over Slovenia towards the north without obstacles.
$\hat{Y}$**:** Zagreb has announced it will allow the migration through Slovenia to northern Croatia without hurdles.

X-6: Er könnte sich vorstellen, in Startup-Firmen der Neuen Werf zu investieren und später auch welche zu akquirieren.
Y: He can imagine investing in start-up business in Neuen Werft, and also later acquiring these.
$\hat{Y}$**:** He could also imagine investing in startup-owned companies like the New Lloyd's to invest and later in companies to quiquire.

X-7: Dieser oberflächliche Erfolg wird von dem dominiert, was Psychologen extrinsische Werte nennen; Geld ,Image, sozialer Status, alles auf Kosten intrinsischer Werte - unsere innere Sehnsucht nach persönlicher Entwicklung und Freundschaft, die sich auf unsere geistige Gesundheit viel tiefgehender auswirkt.
Y: This superficial success is dominated by what psychologists term extrinsic values; money, image, social status, all at the expense of intrinsic values - our inner yearning for personal growth and friendship - that more deeply impacts our mental health.
$\hat{Y}$**:** This OberPublic success is dominated by the things that economists call extraterrestrial values to characterize; money, image, social status all on the planet of intrinsatiable values - our inner desire for personal development and friendship, which can be felt on our mental health much deeper than it is in the physical world of human development and friendship, which is a real concern for our human health and friendship, which is in effect a greater word.

Figure 4: Example translations ($\hat{Y}$) by model (7) of sentences (X) from German to English with gold-standard translations (Y).

R: They have not been charged or formally arrested.
P1: they were not charged or officially arrested.
P2: they didn't have an arrest or official.

R: The Japanese-made tin robots have blocky heads and moveable arms and legs.
P1: the japanese robots have blocky robots, and their arms and feet.
P2: the japanese robots have blocky heads, their hands and feet.

R: The A.P. said it hoped for a resolution so it could return to full coverage of the six-week tournament before the opening match Friday between France and Argentina.
P1: the organisers said they hoped to find a resolution so he could return to full coverage of the six-week tournament before the opening - up friday between france and argentina.
P2: the panasonic said that it hoped for a resolution for an order to return to full coverage of the six-week tournament to keep an eye on friday between france and argentina.

Figure 5: Example references (R) and respective paraphrases (P) of the employed paraphrasing system (Wieting et al., 2017).

They show clear noise and are not always grammatical either. The quality of the paraphrases degrades substantially when using more paraphrases per sentence. More sophisticated paraphrasing systems (e.g. Witteveen and Andrews (2019)), might further improve results. We experimented with one, three and five extracted paraphrases per reference sentence. Using more than one paraphrase per sentence boosts performance substantially, highlighting that the paraphrasing objective also serves a data augmentation function. However, there was no noticeable difference between 3 and 5 paraphrases.

7 Literature Review

7.1 Unsupervised Machine Translation

Initial approaches for unsupervised MT focus on NMT systems in combination with back-translation, denoising autoencoding, and cross-lingual embeddings (Lample et al., 2018b; Artetxe et al., 2018b). Artetxe et al. (2018a); Lample et al. (2018b) improve over NMT approaches by focusing on phrase-based Statistical Machine Translation (PBSMT) with phrase tables from cross-lingual embedding mappings and iterative back-translation. Lample et al. (2018b) improves on these attempts by more careful initialization and language models. Lample et al. (2018b) attempt to combine both PBSMT and NMT, by tuning the NMT model on data generated by the PBSMT model and explore additional tweaks, e.g. byte-pair encodings (Sennrich et al., 2016b). Artetxe et al. (2019) also focus on PBSMT for unsupervised machine translation. They propose a more sophisticated hybridization approach and unsupervised optimization technique for the PBSMT model. Comparable performance to Artetxe et al. (2019) was achieved by Conneau and Lample (2019) by simply initializing the NMT model of Lample et al. (2018b) with the weights of a pre-trained cross-lingual transformer. An analysis on the the practicality of unsupervised machine translation systems by Kim et al. (2020) concludes that linguistic dissimilarity and a domain mismatch between source and target data pose a substantial challenge for current state-of-the-art systems. They attribute these challenges to a lack of sufficient monolingual corpora for these domains, especially if one of the languages is under-resourced. The success of unsupervised methods has led to the first WMT shared subtask on unsupervised MT in 2019 on German-Czech with system submissions being very similar to existing approaches adapted for Czech (Kvapilíková et al., 2019; Liu et al., 2019). Moreover, since 2019 WMT organizes a similar language translation task for Spanish→Portuguese, Czech→Polish, and Hindi→Nepali (Barrault et al., 2019, 2020).

7.2 Cross-lingual Learning with Transformers

The success of fine-tuning pre-trained language models, such as GPT or BERT (Radford et al., 2019; Devlin et al., 2019) has also led to various cross-lingual versions of these pre-trained models, such as M-BERT (Devlin et al., 2019) and XLM (Conneau and Lample, 2019). These cross-lingual transformers learn to align multiple languages in their latent space by concatenating the monolingual training data on a shared subword vocabulary. They have created state-of-the-art results in multiple low-resource languages. Although monolingual models still outperform these cross-lingual ones if enough training data are available (Virtanen et al., 2019), a large-scale version of XLM has been shown to produce comparable results to monolingual LMs for high-resource languages (Conneau et al., 2020).

7.3 Paraphrase Generation

Paraphrase generation is concerned with the creation of phrases/sentences that use different words to express similar information (Bhagat and Hovy, 2013). It is a heavily researched task, with recent approaches focusing on the use of deep learning treating it as a Seq2Seq problem, by either using paraphrase databases (Cao et al., 2017; Li et al., 2018; Witteveen and Andrews, 2019), exploring NMT by pivoting between languages or pairs (Mallinson et al., 2017; Wieting et al., 2017; Federmann et al., 2019), or by treating it as a sentence simplification task (Zhang and Lapata, 2017; Niu et al., 2019). Most paraphrasing systems create a list of k most probable paraphrases. While paraphrase generation focuses on English, paraphrase datasets for other languages exist (Ganitkevitch and Callison-Burch, 2014). Extremely low-resource settings for paraphrasing have also been explored using parallel corpora (Maruyama and Yamamoto, 2019) or in a fully unsupervised setting (Roy and Grangier, 2019).

8 Conclusions & Future work

This work presented a simple fine-tuning method for unsupervised NMT that solely relies on the underlying alignment of a cross-lingual language model and monolingual data in the target language. Joint learning on a denoising autoencoder and paraphrasing objective creates a competitive system to strong baselines, especially for related language pairs, while requiring much shorter training times.

While this work has explored the proposed approach on commonly used language pairs for benchmarking unsupervised MT, future work includes testing the proposed method on other language pairs. This includes i) even more closely related languages (e.g. German→Dutch or Spanish→Portuguese), ii) language pairs without any parallel data, iii) translations between dialects. Moreover, we aim to further explore to which extent the proposed method can be combined with back-translation, especially in the context of distant languages, e.g. by adding back-translation iterations on top of the proposed approach, similar to PBSMT in (Lample et al., 2018b). Other training objectives should be explored, such as sentence simplification, translating between dialects, or even abstractive summarization when scaling this approach to document-level translation. Besides higher efficiency, this approach appears promising when training data for a language pair origins from different domains (e.g. Wikipedia versus News). Since our approach only requires data in the target language, domain mismatches in the training data for the language pair do not affect the proposed method. We are further aiming for human evaluation of translation quality.

Acknowledgements

We wish to thank Dr Andreas Vlachos for his support. We also thank the anonymous reviewers for their time and effort giving us feedback on our paper. This work was supported by the Engineering and Physical Sciences Research Council Doctoral Training Partnership. The second and third authors are supported by Research England via the University of Cambridge Global Challenges Research Fund.

References

Mikel Artetxe, Gorka Labaka, and Eneko Agirre. 2018a. Unsupervised Statistical Machine Translation. In *Proceedings of the 2018 Conference on Empirical Methods in Natural Language Processing*, Brussels, Belgium.

Mikel Artetxe, Gorka Labaka, and Eneko Agirre. 2019. An effective approach to unsupervised machine translation. In *Proceedings of the 57th Annual Meeting of the Association for Computational Linguistics*, Florence, Italy.

Mikel Artetxe, Gorka Labaka, Eneko Agirre, and Kyunghyun Cho. 2018b. Unsupervised neural machine translation. In *6th International Conference on Learning Representations, ICLR 2018*, Vancouver, Canada.

Loïc Barrault, Ondřej Bojar, Marta R. Costa-jussà, Christian Federmann, Mark Fishel, Yvette Graham, Barry Haddow, Matthias Huck, Philipp Koehn, Shervin Malmasi, Christof Monz, Mathias Müller, Santanu Pal, Matt Post, and Marcos Zampieri. 2019. Findings of the 2019 Conference on Machine Translation (WMT19). In *Proceedings of the Fourth Conference on Machine Translation (Volume 2: Shared Task Papers, Day 1)*, Florence, Italy.

Loïc Barrault, Magdalena Biesialska, Ondřej Bojar, Marta R. Costa-jussà, Christian Federmann, Yvette Graham, Roman Grundkiewicz, Barry Haddow, Matthias Huck, Eric Joanis, Tom Kocmi, Philipp Koehn, Chi-kiu Lo, Nikola Ljubešić, Christof Monz, Makoto Morishita, Masaaki Nagata, Toshiaki Nakazawa, Santanu Pal, Matt Post, and Marcos Zampieri. 2020. Findings of the 2020 conference on machine translation (wmt20). In *Proceedings of the Fifth Conference on Machine Translation*, pages 1–55, Online.

Rahul Bhagat and Eduard Hovy. 2013. Squibs: What Is a Paraphrase? *Computational Linguistics*, 39(3):463–472.

Ondřej Bojar, Christian Buck, Christian Federmann, Barry Haddow, Philipp Koehn, Christof Monz, Matt Post, and Lucia Specia, editors. 2014. *Proceedings of the Ninth Workshop on Statistical Machine Translation*. Association for Computational Linguistics, Baltimore, Maryland, USA.

Ondřej Bojar, Rajen Chatterjee, Christian Federmann, Yvette Graham, Barry Haddow, Matthias Huck, Antonio Jimeno Yepes, Philipp Koehn, Varvara Logacheva, Christof Monz, Matteo Negri, Aurelie Neveol, Mariana Neves, Martin Popel, Matt Post, Raphael Rubino, Carolina Scarton, Lucia Specia, Marco Turchi, Karin Verspoor, and Marcos Zampieri. 2016. Findings of the 2016 Conference on Machine Translation. In *Proceedings of the First Conference on Machine Translation*, Berlin, Germany.

Ondřej Bojar, Rajen Chatterjee, Christian Federmann, Barry Haddow, Matthias Huck, Chris Hokamp, Philipp Koehn, Varvara Logacheva, Christof Monz, Matteo Negri, Matt Post, Carolina Scarton, Lucia Specia, and Marco Turchi. 2015. Findings of the 2015 Workshop on Statistical Machine Translation. In *Proceedings of the Tenth Workshop on Statistical Machine Translation*, Lisbon, Portugal.

Chris Callison-Burch, Philipp Koehn, Cameron Shaw Fordyce, and Christof Monz, editors. 2007. *Proceedings of the Second Workshop on Statistical Machine Translation*. Association for Computational Linguistics, Prague, Czech Republic.

Chris Callison-Burch, Philipp Koehn, Christof Monz, Josh Schroeder, and Cameron Shaw Fordyce, editors. 2008. *Proceedings of the Third Workshop on Statistical Machine Translation*. Association for Computational Linguistics, Columbus, Ohio.

Ziqiang Cao, Chuwei Luo, Wenjie Li, and Sujian Li. 2017. Joint copying and restricted generation for paraphrase. In *Thirty-First AAAI Conference on Artificial Intelligence*, San Francisco, CA, USA.

Alexis Conneau, Kartikay Khandelwal, Naman Goyal, Vishrav Chaudhary, Guillaume Wenzek, Francisco Guzmán, Edouard Grave, Myle Ott, Luke Zettlemoyer, and Veselin Stoyanov. 2020. Unsupervised cross-lingual representation learning at scale. In *Proceedings of the 58th Annual Meeting of the Association for Computational Linguistics*, Online.

Alexis Conneau and Guillaume Lample. 2019. Cross-lingual Language Model Pretraining. In *Advances in Neural Information Processing Systems 32*, Vancouver, Canada.

Jacob Devlin, Ming-Wei Chang, Kenton Lee, and Kristina Toutanova. 2019. BERT: Pre-training of Deep Bidirectional Transformers for Language Understanding. In *Proceedings of the 2019 Conference of the North American Chapter of the Association for Computational Linguistics: Human Language Technologies, Volume 1*, Minneapolis, Minnesota.

Christian Federmann, Oussama Elachqar, and Chris Quirk. 2019. Multilingual whispers: Generating paraphrases with translation. In *Proceedings of the 5th Workshop on Noisy User-generated Text (W-NUT 2019)*, Hong Kong.

Juri Ganitkevitch and Chris Callison-Burch. 2014. The Multilingual Paraphrase Database. In *Proceedings of the Ninth International Conference on Language Resources and Evaluation (LREC'14)*, Reykjavik, Iceland.

Hieu Hoang and Philipp Koehn. 2008. Design of the Moses Decoder for Statistical Machine Translation. In *Software Engineering, Testing, and Quality Assurance for Natural Language Processing*, pages 58–65, Columbus, Ohio.

Yunsu Kim, Miguel Graça, and Hermann Ney. 2020. When and why is unsupervised neural machine translation useless? In *Proceedings of the 22nd Annual Conference of the European Association for Machine Translation*, Lisboa, Portugal.

Ivana Kvapilíková, Dominik Macháček, and Ondřej Bojar. 2019. CUNI systems for the unsupervised news translation task in WMT 2019. In *Proceedings of the Fourth Conference on Machine Translation (Volume 2: Shared Task Papers, Day 1)*, Florence, Italy.

Guillaume Lample, Alexis Conneau, Ludovic Denoyer, and Marc'Aurelio Ranzato. 2018a. Unsupervised machine translation using monolingual corpora only. In *International Conference on Learning Representations*, Vancouver, Canada.

Guillaume Lample, Myle Ott, Alexis Conneau, Ludovic Denoyer, and Marc'Aurelio Ranzato. 2018b. Phrase-Based & Neural Unsupervised Machine Translation. In *Proceedings of the 2018 Conference on Empirical Methods in Natural Language Processing*, Brussels, Belgium.

Zichao Li, Xin Jiang, Lifeng Shang, and Hang Li. 2018. Paraphrase generation with deep reinforcement learning. In *Proceedings of the 2018 Conference on Empirical Methods in Natural Language Processing*, Brussels, Belgium.

Zihan Liu, Yan Xu, Genta Indra Winata, and Pascale Fung. 2019. Incorporating word and subword units in unsupervised machine translation using language model rescoring. In *Proceedings of the Fourth Conference on Machine Translation (Volume 2: Shared Task Papers, Day 1)*, Florence, Italy.

Jonathan Mallinson, Rico Sennrich, and Mirella Lapata. 2017. Paraphrasing revisited with neural machine translation. In *Proceedings of the 15th Conference of the European Chapter of the Association for Computational Linguistics: Volume 1, Long Papers*, Valencia, Spain.

T. Maruyama and K. Yamamoto. 2019. Extremely low resource text simplification with pre-trained transformer language model. In *2019 International Conference on Asian Language Processing (IALP)*, Shanghai, China.

Tong Niu, Caiming Xiong, and Richard Socher. 2019. Deleter: Leveraging BERT to perform unsupervised successive text compression. *arXiv*, 1909.03223.

Kishore Papineni, Salim Roukos, Todd Ward, and Wei-Jing Zhu. 2002. BLEU: A Method for Automatic Evaluation of Machine Translation. In *Proceedings of the 40th Annual Meeting of the Association for Computational Linguistics*, Philadelphia, Pennsylvania, USA.

Alec Radford, Jeffrey Wu, Rewon Child, David Luan, Dario Amodei, and Ilya Sutskever. 2019. Language Models are Unsupervised Multitask Learners. *OpenAI Blog*, 1(8).

Aurko Roy and David Grangier. 2019. Unsupervised paraphrasing without translation. In *Proceedings of the 57th Annual Meeting of the Association for Computational Linguistics*, Florence, Italy.

Rico Sennrich, Barry Haddow, and Alexandra Birch. 2016a. Improving Neural Machine Translation Models with Monolingual Data. In *Proceedings of the 54th Annual Meeting of the Association for Computational Linguistics (Volume 1: Long Papers)*, Berlin, Germany.

Rico Sennrich, Barry Haddow, and Alexandra Birch. 2016b. Neural Machine Translation of Rare Words with Subword Units. In *Proceedings of the 54th Annual Meeting of the Association for Computational Linguistics (Volume 1: Long Papers)*, Berlin, Germany.

Ashish Vaswani, Noam Shazeer, Niki Parmar, Jakob Uszkoreit, Llion Jones, Aidan N Gomez, Łukasz Kaiser, and Illia Polosukhin. 2017. Attention is All you Need. In *Advances in Neural Information Processing Systems 30*, Vancouver, Canada.

Pascal Vincent, Hugo Larochelle, Yoshua Bengio, and Pierre-Antoine Manzagol. 2008. Extracting and composing robust features with denoising autoencoders. In *Proceedings of the 25th International Conference on Machine Learning*, ICML '08, Helsinki, Finland.

Antti Virtanen, Jenna Kanerva, Rami Ilo, Jouni Luoma, Juhani Luotolahti, Tapio Salakoski, Filip Ginter, and Sampo Pyysalo. 2019. Multilingual is not enough: BERT for Finnish. *arXiv:1912.07076 [cs]*.

John Wieting, Jonathan Mallinson, and Kevin Gimpel. 2017. Learning Paraphrastic Sentence Embeddings from Back-Translated Bitext. In *Proceedings of the 2017 Conference on Empirical Methods in Natural Language Processing*, Copenhagen, Denmark.

Sam Witteveen and Martin Andrews. 2019. Paraphrasing with Large Language Models. In *Proceedings of the 3rd Workshop on Neural Generation and Translation*, Hong Kong.

Xingxing Zhang and Mirella Lapata. 2017. Sentence simplification with deep reinforcement learning. In *Proceedings of the 2017 Conference on Empirical Methods in Natural Language Processing*, Copenhagen, Denmark.

Fine-tuning Distributional Semantic Models for Closely-Related Languages

Kushagra Bhatia
Macquarie Group Limited, Gurugram
kushagra.bhatia@macquarie.com

Divyanshu Aggarwal
Dept of Biotechnology, DTU Delhi
divyanshuggrwl@gmail.com

Ashwini Vaidya
Dept of Humanities and Social Sciences, IIT Delhi
avaidya@hss.iitd.ac.in

Abstract

In this paper we compare the performance of three models: SGNS (skip-gram negative sampling) and augmented versions of SVD (singular value decomposition) and PPMI (Positive Pointwise Mutual Information) on a word similarity task. We particularly focus on the role of hyperparameter tuning for Hindi based on recommendations made in previous work (on English). Our results show that there are language specific preferences for these hyperparameters. We extend the best settings for Hindi to a set of related languages: Punjabi, Gujarati and Marathi with favourable results. We also find that a suitably tuned SVD model outperforms SGNS for most of our languages and is also more robust in a low-resource setting.

1 Introduction

The development of word embedding models in NLP has led to improved performance on a range of lexical semantic tasks (Baroni et al., 2014). The SGNS (skip-gram negative sampling) training method has been shown to outperform previously used count-based models such as PPMI (Positive Point based Mutual Information) and SVD (truncated Singular Value Decomposition).

In this paper, we look at the task of word similarity in Hindi and related languages Punjabi, Gujarati and Marathi. Specifically, we experiment with hyperparameter tuning for SGNS, SVD and PPMI for Hindi and then ask whether the same hyperparameters can be extended and applied to typol related languages. We make use of the hyperparameters formulated in Levy et al. (2015) to tune all three models. We find that a suitably tuned SVD model *outperforms* SGNS. This result differs from Levy et al. (2015) which shows that fine-tuned SGNS and SVD models perform at par. We find that our Hindi SVD results are better than multilingual fastText (Grave et al., 2018) and the recently released IndicNLP Suite (Kakwani et al., 2020).

We hypothesize that hyperparameters are sensitive to linguistic properties. If this is true, then we should find similar results in languages that are typologically related to Hindi. Our results suggest that these hyperparameter settings for Hindi can be extended to typologically-related languages. Indeed, the results show that adapting the hyperparameters from Hindi is more advantageous as compared to the default settings or the settings recommended for English in Levy et al. (2015).

While reasonably large resources and datasets exist for the major Indian languages, Joshi et al. (2020) have shown that more than half of the Indo-Aryan languages represented in Wikipedia can be classified as having 'poor resource availability'. Given these limitations, a model that is able to generate representations that are robust in the face of less data can be advantageous. In our experiments, we take successively smaller corpus slices from our Hindi, Marathi, Gujarati and Punjabi corpora in order to test our models' performance. We find that SVD is more robust compared to other models in a low-resource setting. Sahlgren and Lenci (2016) have investigated the effects of data size on distributional semantic models and their results on the robustness of SVD correspond with our findings for Hindi and related languages.

In this paper, we first describe the creation of a new word similarity dataset for Hindi, which addresses some of the limitations of existing evaluation datasets. We then discuss the hyperparameter settings suggested in Levy et al. (2015) and describe our results for Hindi and related languages on the entire corpus as well as on smaller corpus sizes. We conclude with a summary of our findings.

Proceedings of the 8th VarDial Workshop on NLP for Similar Languages, Varieties and Dialects, pages 60–66
April 20, 2021 ©2021 Association for Computational Linguistics

2 Word Similarity Dataset

In order to evaluate our distributed semantic models, we carry out an intrinsic evaluation of the models based on word similarity. For the languages in our study, the currently available word similarity datasets include translated versions of English WordSim-353 (WS-353) (Akhtar et al., 2017).

However, we note that WordSim-353 (Finkelstein et al., 2001) has been criticized for conflating association and similarity in its word-pair annotation guidelines (Hill et al., 2015). As a consequence, WS-353 measures association rather than similarity. In addition to this, we observe that the Hindi version of WS-353 consists of numerous transliterations from English. In order to develop a more robust evaluation dataset for our word experiments, we created Hin-RG63, the Hindi version for English RG-65 (Rubenstein and Goodenough, 1965). This dataset carefully dissociates similarity and relatedness in its annotation guidelines and has been used as a benchmark for SemEval tasks (Camacho-Collados et al., 2015). While we were unable to create RG-65 translations for the other languages included in this paper, we plan to extend the work done for Hindi to more languages in the future.

Two native speakers of Hindi, who were also bilinguals provided the translation of words in English RG-65 to Hindi. A third translator moderated any disagreements. It is noteworthy that two of the word pairs from English RG-65 did not have any suitable distinct translation and hence were not included in the final dataset. 16 Hindi native speakers were presented with the similarity scoring guidelines given in Jurgens et al. (2014). The annotators were presented with a practice session consisting of sample word pairs before rating the actual Hindi word pairs in the dataset. Next, the annotators were asked to score each pair on a scale of 0 to 4. To present more flexibility, scoring with a step of 0.5 was permitted.

We computed inter-annotator agreement using pairwise correlation between individual annotators' ratings. Pearson and Spearman correlation coefficients are used to assess the linear correlation and monotonic relationship respectively. We report an average pairwise Pearson correlation of 0.814, and average pairwise Spearman correlation of 0.805 for Hin RG-63, our version of English RG-65. We make the dataset available for public use.[1]

3 Comparing SVD, PPMI and SGNS

Baroni et al. (2014)'s paper compared word embedding models or 'context-predicting models' like SGNS with 'context-counting' models like SVD on various lexical semantic benchmarks. Their results showed the superiority of context-predicting models. In a follow-up to this result, Levy et al. (2015) demonstrated that suitably augmented and tuned PMI (Pointwise Mutual Information) and SVD (Singular Value Decomposition) i.e context-counting models can perform at par with word embedding models. In fact, insights from word embeddings can be used to *augment* count-based models, resulting in only very small differences in performance.

These system design changes formulated as a set of transferable hyperparameters in Levy et al. (2015) were applied either at the pre-processing or post-processing stage, modifying the word vectors generated from these methods. The following section expands upon these hyperparameters

3.1 Hyperparameters

A major contribution of the Levy et al. (2015) study was the formulation of hyperparameters for context-counting models that are inspired by context predicting models. Such adaptations are feasible due to an overlap between the mathematical objectives of the two, which improve the performance of the traditional methods. The authors used a large English corpus with 1.5 billion tokens for their experiments and inferred that the differences between the two families of models are trivial.

All three methods, viz. SGNS, SVD and PPMI output the word vector representation. Following the same nomenclature for hyperparameters as Levy et al. (2015), we summarize the hyperparameters used in our experiments in Table 1.

For context-predicting models, cds is the smoothing factor to which the context count is raised in the unigram distribution for negative sampling. In Levy et al. (2015) cds has been adapted for PPMI and SVD. We examine values for cds= 0.75, otherwise the standard unigram sampling distribution is followed ($cds = 1$).

The hyperparameter neg denotes the number of negative samples for context-predicting models.

[1] https://github.com/ashwinivd/similarity_hindi

Hyperparameter	Abreviation	Search Space
Context Distribution Smoothing	cds	0.75, 1†
Eigenvalue Weighting	eig	0, 0.5, 1†
Shifted PPMI	neg	1†, 5, 15
Context Vector Addition	$w + c$	only w†, w+c
Window Size	win	2†, 3, 5

Table 1: Hyperparameter search space studied in our work.† Default settings. The hyperparameter $w + c$ is used for SVD and SGNS, not PPMI. eig is only used for SVD.

This translates to the amount that the PPMI matrix is shifted for context-counting (PPMI and SVD) models.

Eigenvalue weighting (eig) represents the exponent to the eigenvalue matrix in the word vector representation equation, obtained after factorization of the PPMI matrix. The values $eig = 0\ and\ 0.5$ lead to the symmetric versions of SVD, with the prior version completely removing the eigenvalue matrix from the representation.

Pennington et al. (2014) introduce the concept of context vector addition ($w + c$) to the word vector output by the model. Following the same idea, we check whether such an addition at post processing is beneficial for SGNS and SVD methods. The window size (win) is the range in which the context words are chosen on both sides of the analyzed word.

4 Experiments

4.1 Datasets

The model training was performed using publicly available monolingual corpora. For Hindi we used HindMonoCorp (Bojar et al., 2014) and for the other languages viz. Marathi, Gujarati and Punjabi, IndicCorp (Kakwani et al., 2020) is used. The text is pre-processed by removing punctuation, followed by normalization using the Indic NLP Library[2]. The statistics for each corpora is shown in Table 2 with the vocabulary size calculated after ignoring words appearing less than 100 times. We vary the size of corpus used for training the methods. For the experiments in a low-resource setting, corpus slices are created by randomly sampling a fraction of sentences from the entire corpus (4.3.2).

Language	Tokens	Sentences	Vocabulary
Hindi	786M	44M	100,667
Gujarati	719M	41.1M	158,445
Punjabi	773M	29.2M	82,512
Marathi	551M	34M	155,113

Table 2: Statistics of corpora used for model training. Values in million (M)

Evaluation of models trained on different languages is performed on WS235, annotated by Akhtar et al. (2017). We further evaluate the Hindi models on our very own Hin-RG65. The average Spearman correlation between the vector cosine similarity and the human rating of the word-pairs is used to rank the word representations.

4.2 Hyperparameter tuning

We study the impact of different hyperparameters on the performance, by evaluating the models trained on the complete HindMonoCorp with different configrations. A few pre-processing hyperparameters viz. deletion of rare words prior to creation of context window, dynamic context weighting and subsampling were only analyzed in the preliminary stage of experiments. These hyperparameters did not have much impact on the performance, and were not investigated further. We summarize the advantageous configurations of the hyperparameters shown in Table 1, along with the observed differences from Levy et al. (2015)'s recommendations for English.

Levy et al. (2015) advocated the use of $cds = 0.75$ for all 3 models: SGNS, PPMI and SVD. However, we do not observe a persistent trend for context distribution smoothing (cds). Although PPMI shows slight improvement with $cds = 0.75$, SVD and SGNS do not show any preferences.

For English it was observed that SVD performed better with a shorter window ($win = 2$), whereas SGNS did not show any preferences for win. In contrast, we observe a tendency of both the methods towards a larger window size ($win = 5$). Such a trend may be attributed to the difference in linguistic properties and morphology of the two languages. PPMI however performed best with $win = 2$.

Levy et al. (2015)'s results for English, show that a value of neg as 5 or 15 was equally beneficial for SGNS. For our work on Hindi, it showed a clear

[2]https://pypi.org/project/indic-nlp-library/

preference for $neg = 15$. Any value below this was not beneficial. We think this may be due to the relatively higher vocabulary-to-token ratio of the Hindi training corpus (as compared to English). Similarly, in the case of the context vector $w + c$, Levy et al. (2015) are equivocal about its impact, but we found that addition of a context vector ($w + c$) always yielded an improvement in performance of SGNS.

In concordance with Levy et al. (2015), we observe substantial gains for SVD when the eigenvalue matrix is removed from the word vector equation (i.e. $eig = 0$), over $eig = 1$ (the default value) or 0.5.

After filtering out the top performing set of hyperparameters on the Hindi corpus, we validate whether our inferences hold on the other three inspected Indo-Aryan languages.

4.3 Training and Evaluation

For all four languages, we trained a 500-dimensional representation for all the models.

We investigate the performance gains when training with optimal configuration. With this aim, we evaluate our techniques trained on the complete corpus. Finally, in order to analyse the trends for low-resource scenarios, we report the performance of the fine-tuned models when trained with varying corpus sizes.

It should be noted that the hyperparameter search is independently carried out on the evaluation set for Hindi. This gives us an upper limit on the method's performance and highlights the importance of suitable hyperparameters. In a real setting however, we would require a dedicated development set for tuning the models. For Gujarati, Marathi and Punjabi, we are not tuning the hyperparameters over the evaluation set and are simply adapting to the recommended configurations obtained from Hindi.

Language	PPMI	SVD	SGNS
WS-235			
Hindi	0.541	0.578	0.575
Gujarati	0.359	0.417	0.446
Punjabi	0.264	0.337	0.198
Marathi	0.379	0.383	0.390
Hin-RG63			
Hindi	0.685	0.696	0.624

Table 3: Performance (*Spearman correlation*) of models trained on the complete monolingual corpus with default hyperparameters.

Language	PPMI	SVD	SGNS
WS-235			
Hindi	0.566	0.609	0.550
Gujarati	0.343	0.483	0.461
Punjabi	0.259	0.342	0.210
Marathi	0.361	0.421	0.369
Hin-RG63			
Hindi	0.703	0.704	0.548

Table 4: Performance (*Spearman correlation*) of models trained on the complete monolingual corpus with hyperparameters as recommended in (Levy et al., 2015)

4.3.1 Full Corpus

We train the investigated distributional semantic methods on the complete corpora for each language. Table 3 and Table 4 report the performance of models trained with default hyperparameters and configuration recommended for English respectively. On comparing the performance with models trained on optimal hyperparameters for Hindi, we see a superior performance for each model across all the Indo-Aryan languages (Table 5). This result demonstrates that hyperparameter configurations can be adapted well for closely-related languages.

We further compare our fine-tuned models with two pre-trained word embedding models, namely fastText (FT-WC), trained on Common Crawl and Wikipedia (Grave et al., 2018) and IndicFastText (I-FT) (Kakwani et al., 2020). We note that for Hindi, IndicFastText is trained on a *larger* dataset than

Language	PPMI	SVD	SGNS	FT-WC	I-FT
WS-235					
Hindi	0.642	**0.656**	0.645	0.550	0.598
Gujarati	0.453	0.542	0.536	0.477	**0.567**
Punjabi	0.267	**0.385**	0.247	0.350	0.357
Marathi	0.372	0.446	0.427	**0.464**	0.459
Hin-RG63					
Hindi	0.722	**0.809**	0.724	0.758	0.632

Table 5: Performance (*Spearman correlation*) of models trained on the complete monolingual corpus with optimal hyperparameters for Hindi. FT-WC is fastText trained on Wikipedia and Common Crawl; I-FT is IndicFastText.

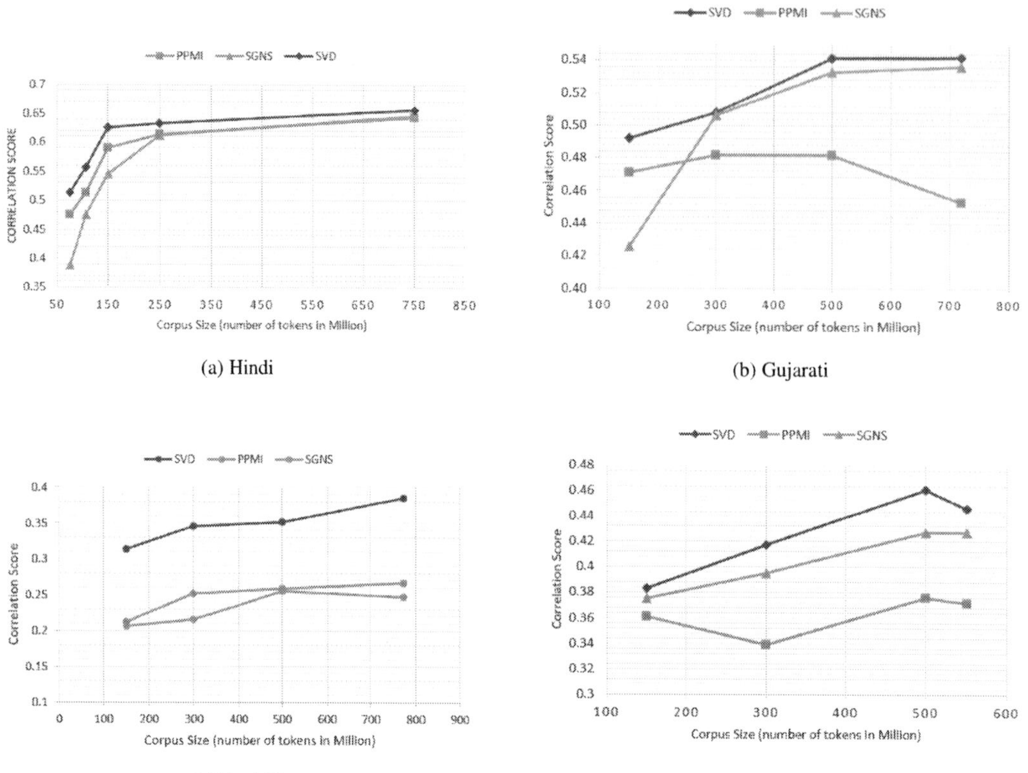

(a) Hindi

(b) Gujarati

(c) Punjabi

(d) Marathi

Figure 1: Performance of PPMI, SVD and SGNS on WS-235 for Hindi,Gujarati, Punjabi and Marathi. Performance for each model is reported for varying sizes of the corpus.

the previously released fastText. Table 5 shows the evaluation results for all five models. Out of the three studied models, SVD consistently shows superior performance over all four languages. On comparison with FastText and IndicFastText, our modified SVD either outperforms both or is on par. For Hindi, since the tuning is exhaustive we observe the three tuned models to achieve a higher score than the FastText models on both Hin-WS235 and Hin-RG63. Here, it should also be noted that the training corpus used to achieve this score was almost half the size of the one used by IndicFastText, further supporting our rationale of fine-tuning. Our SVD model with adapted hyperparameters for the other Indo-Aryan languages performs on par with the fastText models, even outperforms IndicFastText for Punjabi. We also confirmed that the current dimensionality settings did not affect our results for SGNS, as experiments with lower dimensionalities of 200 and 300 showed negligible gains for SGNS.

4.3.2 Low-resource setting

We analyze the performance of all three models with varying data sizes for each language. We would like to experiment with other Indo-Aryan languages which are truly low-resource, but evaluation datasets only exist for a fraction of available languages. Hence, we decided to experiment with the same languages using different sizes.

The best correlation score of each method after training on different slices of corpora is shown in Figure 1. We infer from the graphs that SVD is quite robust with respect to data size and even with a fraction of data i.e. in case of low-resource scenario, does not show a considerable dip in performance. For Punjabi, there is a substantial gain in performance when using SVD across all data sizes. On the other hand, SGNS and SVD are almost similar for Gujarati, and SGNS may improve with more data.

For Hindi, careful tuning of SVD and PPMI even on a fifth of the complete corpus attains a performance on par with FastText and IndicFastText.

5 Summary

Our work shows that careful hyperparameter tuning can go a long way in improving the performance of distributed semantic models. Interestingly, we find that the general recommendations in Levy et al. (2015) for hyperparameter settings work well only for English word representations. For Hindi, some of their recommendations hold, whereas others do not. Moreover, the hyperparameter settings for Hindi carry over well to related languages and there is performance improvement compared to the default or English-specific settings. This seems to suggest that language specific differences are playing a role with respect to hyperparameter settings.

Perhaps the most interesting result is that modified SVD is more robust than SGNS, both across languages and data sizes. This contrasts with the idea that the differences between the architectures of particular distributional semantic models are trivial so long as they are trained in a similar fashion (Levy et al., 2015).

We also note that the problem of building word embeddings for low-resource languages has been addressed using cross-lingual representations (Ruder et al., 2019). These rely on alignments between low-resource and better-resourced languages. Techniques such as cognate detection have been used to improve these alignments (Sharoff, 2020). Newer contextualized word embedding models can make these alignments internally, allowing for cross lingual transfer (Conneau et al., 2020). In this paper we have chosen to focus on monolingual word embeddings and leave the exploration of cross-lingual representations for future work.

Acknowledgements

The authors acknowledge the Summer Fellowship Research programme (SFRP-2020) of CEP, IIT Delhi, which enabled Kushagra Bhatia and Divyanshu Aggarwal to pursue research in IIT Delhi.

References

Syed Sarfaraz Akhtar, Arihant Gupta, Avijit Vajpayee, Arjit Srivastava, and Manish Shrivastava. 2017. Unsupervised morphological expansion of small datasets for improving word embeddings. In *Proceedings of the 18th International Conference on Computational Linguistics and Intelligent Text Processing (CICLING)*.

Marco Baroni, Georgiana Dinu, and Germán Kruszewski. 2014. Don't count, predict! a systematic comparison of context-counting vs. context-predicting semantic vectors. In *Proceedings of the 52nd Annual Meeting of the Association for Computational Linguistics (Volume 1: Long Papers)*, pages 238–247, Baltimore, Maryland. Association for Computational Linguistics.

Ondrej Bojar, Vojtech Diatka, Pavel Rychlý, Pavel Stranák, Vít Suchomel, Ales Tamchyna, and Daniel Zeman. 2014. Hindencorp-hindi-english and hindi-only corpus for machine translation. In *LREC*, pages 3550–3555.

José Camacho-Collados, Mohammad Taher Pilehvar, and Roberto Navigli. 2015. A framework for the construction of monolingual and cross-lingual word similarity datasets. In *Proceedings of the 53rd annual meeting of the association for computational linguistics and the 7th international joint conference on natural language processing (volume 2: Short papers)*, pages 1–7.

Alexis Conneau, Shijie Wu, Haoran Li, Luke Zettlemoyer, and Veselin Stoyanov. 2020. Emerging cross-lingual structure in pretrained language models. In *Proceedings of the 58th Annual Meeting of the Association for Computational Linguistics*, pages 6022–6034, Online. Association for Computational Linguistics.

Lev Finkelstein, Evgeniy Gabrilovich, Yossi Matias, Ehud Rivlin, Zach Solan, Gadi Wolfman, and Eytan Ruppin. 2001. Placing search in context: The concept revisited. In *Proceedings of the 10th international conference on World Wide Web*, pages 406–414.

Edouard Grave, Piotr Bojanowski, Prakhar Gupta, Armand Joulin, and Tomas Mikolov. 2018. Learning word vectors for 157 languages. In *Proceedings of the International Conference on Language Resources and Evaluation (LREC 2018)*.

Felix Hill, Roi Reichart, and Anna Korhonen. 2015. Simlex-999: Evaluating semantic models with (genuine) similarity estimation. *Computational Linguistics*, 41(4):665–695.

Pratik Joshi, Sebastin Santy, Amar Budhiraja, Kalika Bali, and Monojit Choudhury. 2020. The state and fate of linguistic diversity and inclusion in the nlp world. In *Proceedings of the 58th Annual Meeting of the Association for Computational Linguistics*.

David Jurgens, Mohammad Taher Pilehvar, and Roberto Navigli. 2014. Semeval-2014 task 3: Cross-level semantic similarity. In *SemEval@ COLING*, pages 17–26.

Divyanshu Kakwani, Anoop Kunchukuttan, Satish Golla, Gokul N.C., Avik Bhattacharyya, Mitesh M. Khapra, and Pratyush Kumar. 2020. IndicNLPSuite: Monolingual Corpora, Evaluation Benchmarks and Pre-trained Multilingual Language Models for Indian Languages. In *Findings of EMNLP*.

Omer Levy, Yoav Goldberg, and Ido Dagan. 2015. Improving distributional similarity with lessons learned from word embeddings. *Transactions of the Association for Computational Linguistics*, 3:211–225.

Jeffrey Pennington, Richard Socher, and Christopher D Manning. 2014. Glove: Global vectors for word representation. In *Proceedings of the 2014 conference on empirical methods in natural language processing (EMNLP)*, pages 1532–1543.

Herbert Rubenstein and John B Goodenough. 1965. Contextual correlates of synonymy. *Communications of the ACM*, 8(10):627–633.

Sebastian Ruder, Ivan Vulić, and Anders Søgaard. 2019. A survey of cross-lingual word embedding models. *J. Artif. Int. Res.*, 65(1):569–630.

Magnus Sahlgren and Alessandro Lenci. 2016. The effects of data size and frequency range on distributional semantic models. In *Proceedings of the 2016 Conference on Empirical Methods in Natural Language Processing*, pages 975–980, Austin, Texas. Association for Computational Linguistics.

Serge Sharoff. 2020. Finding next of kin: Cross-lingual embedding spaces for related languages. *Natural Language Engineering*, 26(2):163–182.

Discriminating Between Similar Nordic Languages

René Haas
IT University of Copenhagen
renha@itu.dk

Leon Derczynski
IT University of Copenhagen
leod@itu.dk

Abstract

Automatic language identification is a challenging problem. Discriminating between closely related languages is especially difficult. This paper presents a machine learning approach for automatic language identification for the Nordic languages, which often suffer miscategorisation by existing state-of-the-art tools. Concretely we will focus on discrimination between six Nordic languages: Danish, Swedish, Norwegian (Nynorsk), Norwegian (Bokmål), Faroese and Icelandic.

1 Introduction

Automatic language identification is a core problem in NLP but remains a difficult task (Caswell et al., 2020), especially across domains (Lui and Baldwin, 2012; Derczynski et al., 2013). Discriminating between closely related languages is often a particularly difficult subtask of this problem (Zampieri et al., 2014).

Language technology for Scandinavian languages is in a nascent phase (e.g. Kirkedal et al. (2019)). One problem is acquiring enough text with which to train e.g. large language models. Good quality language ID is critical to this data sourcing, though leading models often confuse similar Nordic languages.

This paper presents data and baselines for automatic language identification between six closely-related Nordic languages: Danish, Swedish, Norwegian (Nynorsk), Norwegian (Bokmål), Faroese and Icelandic.

Further, we investigate feature extraction methods for Nordic language identification and evaluates the performance of a selection of baseline models.

Finally, we test the models on a data set from a different domain in order to investigate how well the models generalize in distinguishing similar Nordic languages when classifying sentences across domains.

2 Related Work

The problem of discriminating between similar languages has been investigated in recent work (Goutte et al., 2016; Zampieri et al., 2015) which discuss the results from two editions of the "Discriminating between Similar Languages (DSL) shared task". Over the two editions of the DSL shared task different teams competed to develop the best machine learning algorithms to discriminate between the languages in a corpus consisting of 20K sentences in each of the languages: Bosnian, Croatian, Serbian, Indonesian, Malaysian, Czech, Slovak, Brazil Portuguese, European Portuguese, Argentine Spanish, Peninsular Spanish, Bulgarian and Macedonian.

Similar work has included (Toftrup et al., 2021), who include Nordic languages in a larger exercise in reproducing a commercial language ID system; and (Rangel et al., 2018), who attempt native language extraction, a task complex in the Nordic context which is rich in cognates and shared etymologies.

However, no prior work has focused specifically on the group of Nordic languages, leaving users of those languages without high quality automatically-extracted single language corpora (Derczynski et al., 2020). This is particularly disadvantageous for some Nordic language pairs, such as Danish/Norwegian and Faroese/Icelandic, where general-purpose many-language systems fall down (Toftrup et al., 2021). Thus, we focus specifically on data for this language and baseline methods.

3 The Nordic DSL data set

This section describes the construction of the Nordic DSL (Distinguishing Similar Lanugages)

Proceedings of the 8th VarDial Workshop on NLP for Similar Languages, Varieties and Dialects, pages 67–75
April 20, 2021 ©2021 Association for Computational Linguistics

data set.

Data was scraped from Wikipedia. We downloaded summaries for randomly chosen Wikipedia articles in each of the languages, saved as raw text to six `.txt` files of about 10MB each. While Bornholmsk would be a welcome addition (Derczynski and Kjeldsen, 2019), exhibiting some similarity to Faroese and Danish, there is not yet enough digital text.

After the initial cleaning (described in the next section) the data set contained just over 50K sentences in each of the language categories. From this, two data sets with exactly 10K and 50K sentences respectively were drawn from the raw data set. In this way the data sets are stratified, containing the same number of sentences for each language.

We split these data sets, reserving 80% for the training set and 20% for the test set.

3.1 Data Cleaning and encoding.

This section describes how the data set is initially cleaned and how sentences are extracted from the raw data.

Extracting Sentences The first pass in sentence tokenisation is splitting by line breaks. We then extract shorter sentences with the sentence tokenizer (`sent_tokenize`) function from NLTK (Loper and Bird, 2002). This does a better job than just splitting by `'.'` due to the fact that abbreviations, which can appear in a legitimate sentence, typically include a period symbol.

Cleaning characters The initial data set has many characters that do not belong to the alphabets of the languages we work with. Often the Wikipedia pages for people or places contain names in foreign languages. For example a summary might contain Chinese or Russian characters which are not strong signals for the purpose of discriminating between the target languages.

Further, it can be that some characters in the target languages are mis-encoded. These mis-encodings are also not likely to be intrinsically strong or stable signals.

To simplify feature extraction, and to reduce the size of the vocabulary, the raw data is converted to lowercase and stripped of all characters which are not part of the standard alphabet of the six languages.

In this way we only accept the characters:

```
'abcdefghijklmnopqr
stuvwxyzáäåæéíðóöøúýþ '
```

and replace everything else with white space before continuing to extract the features. For example the raw sentence

```
'Hesbjerg er dannet ved
sammenlægning af de 2 gårde
Store Hesbjerg
og Lille Hesbjerg i 1822.'
```

will be reduced to

```
'hesbjerg er dannet ved
sammenlægning af de gårde store
hesbjerg og lille hesbjerg i ',
```

We thus make the assumption that capitalisation, numbers and characters outside this character set do not contribute much information relevant for language classification.

Feature encoding After the initial cleaning of the data we consider two methods for feature encoding: 1) Character level n-grams and 2) Skipgram and CBOW encodings created by training an unsupervised fasttext model on the dataset.

The Skipgram and CBOW methods encode sentences into fixed-length vectors by considering world level n-grams which are augmented with character level n-gram information (Bojanowski et al., 2016).

In the experiments presented in this paper, the CBOW and Skipgram encodings have the following settings: We use individual words (uni-grams) augmented with character level n-grams of size 2-5 with a context window of 5. The encoding result in fixed-length vectors in $\mathbb{R}^{100}$.

4 Baselines

4.1 langid.py

We compare with an off-the-shelf language identification system, `langid.py` (Lui and Baldwin, 2012). `langid.py` comes with a pretrained model which covers 97 languages. The data for langid.py comes from five different domains: government documents, software documentation, newswire, online encyclopedia and an internet crawl. Features are selected for cross-domain stability using the LD heuristic (Lui and Baldwin, 2011).

We evaluated how well langid.py performed on the Nordic DSL data set. It is a peculiar feature of the Norwegian language that there exist two different written languages but three different language codes. Since langid.py also returned the language id "no" (Norwegian) on some of the data points we restrict langid.py to only be able to return either "nn" (Nynorsk) or "nb" (Bokmål) as predictions.

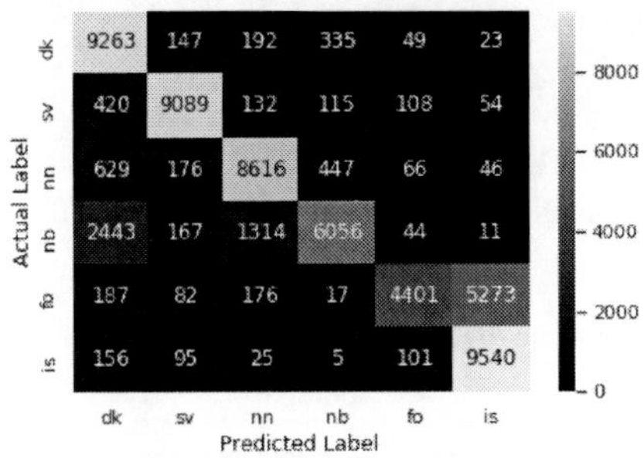

Figure 1: Confusion matrix with results from langid.py on the full Wikipedia data set

Figure 1 shows the confusion matrix for the langid.py classifier which achieved an accuracy of 78.3% on the data set. The largest confusions were between Danish and Bokmål, and between Faroese and Icelandic. `langid.py` was able to correctly classify most of the Danish instances; however, approximately a quarter of the instance in Bokmål were incorrectly classified as Danish and just under an eighth was misclassified as Nynorsk.

Furthermore, langid.py correctly classified most of the Icelandic data points; however, over half of the data points in Faroese were incorrectly classified as Icelandic.

4.2 Baseline with linear models

Table 1 shows results for running the models on a data set with 10K sentences in each language category. Models tend to perform better if we use character bi-grams instead of single characters. Logistic regression and SVM outperform Naive Bayes and K-nearest neighbors in all cases. Furthermore, for all models, we get the best performance if we use the skipgram model from FastText.

Comparing the CBOW mode from FastText with character bi-grams, the CBOW model is on par with bi-grams for the KNN and Naive Bayes classifiers, while bi-grams outperform CBOW for Logistic Regression and support vector machines.

Model	Encoding	Accuracy
Knn	cbow	0.780
Log-Reg	cbow	0.819
Naive Bayes	cbow	0.660
SVM	cbow	0.843
Knn	skipgram	0.918
Log-Reg	skipgram	**0.929**
Naive Bayes	skipgram	0.840
SVM	skipgram	**0.928**
Knn	char bi-gram	0.745
Log-Reg	char bi-gram	0.907
Naive Bayes	char bi-gram	0.653
SVM	char bi-gram	0.905
Knn	char uni-gram	0.620
Log-Reg	char uni-gram	0.755
Naive Bayes	char uni-gram	0.614
SVM	char uni-gram	0.707

Table 1: Overview of results for the data set with 10K data points in each language.

5 Our Approach

5.1 Using FastText

The methods described above are quite simple. We also compared the above method with FastText, which is a library for creating word embeddings developed by Facebook (Joulin et al., 2016).

Bojanowski et al. (2016) explain how FastText extracts feature vectors from raw text data. FastText makes word embeddings using one of two model architectures: continuous bag of words (CBOW) or the continuous skipgram model.

The skipgram and CBOW models are first proposed in (Mikolov et al., 2013) which is the paper introducing the word2vec model for word embeddings. FastText builds upon this work by proposing an extension to the skipgram model which takes into account sub-word information.

Both models use a neural network to learn word embedding from using a context windows consisting of the words surrounding the current target word. The CBOW architecture predicts the current word based on the context, and the skipgram predicts surrounding words given the current word (Mikolov et al., 2013).

5.2 Using A Convolutional Neural Network

While every layer in a classic multilayer perceptron is densely connected, such that each of the nodes in a layer are connected to all nodes in the next layer, in a convolutional neural network we use one or more convolutional layers. Convolutional Neural Networks have an established use for text classification (Jacovi et al., 2018).

Our CNN is implemented with keras. We use an embedding layer followed by two blocks with a 1D convolutional layer and dropout. The first block has 128 filters while the second has 64. Both convolutional blocks use a kernel size of 5 and stride of 1. The two blocks are followed by a dense layer with 32 hidden nodes before the output layer which has 6 nodes. We use ReLu activation in the convolutional and fully connected layers and SoftMax in the output layer.

6 Results

6.1 Results with neural networks

Results for the neural network architectures are in Table 2. Here we compare the result of doing character level uni- and bi-grams using Multilayer Perceptron and Convolutional neural networks. The CNN performs the best, achieving an accuracy of 95.6% when using character bi-grams. Both models perform better using bi-grams than individual characters as features while the relative increase in performance is greater for the MLP model.

Model	Encoding	Accuracy
MLP	char bi-gram	0.898
CNN	char bi-gram	**0.956**
MLP	char uni-gram	0.697
CNN	char uni-gram	0.942

Table 2: Overview of results for the neural network models for the data set with 10K data points in each language.

6.2 Increasing the size of the data set

Often the performance of supervised classification models increases with more training data. To measure this effect we increase the amount of training data to 50K sentences in each of the language categories. Due to longer training times only the baseline models were included, with the skipgram encoding from FastText which we saw achieved the highest accuracy.

Table 3 shows that the performance of the logistic regression model and the K-nearest-neighbors algorithm improved slightly by including more data. Unexpectedly, performance of the support vector machine and Naïve Bayes dropped slightly with extra data.

Model	Encoding	Accuracy
Knn	skipgram	0.931
Logistic Regression	skipgram	**0.933**
Naive Bayes	skipgram	0.806
SVM	skipgram	0.925

Table 3: Overview of results for the "classical" ML models on the Wikipedia data set with 50K data points in each language.

Model	Encoding	Accuracy
MLP	char bi-gram	0.918
CNN	char bi-gram	**0.970**

Table 4: Overview of results for the MLP and CNN on the Wikipedia data set with 50K data points in each language.

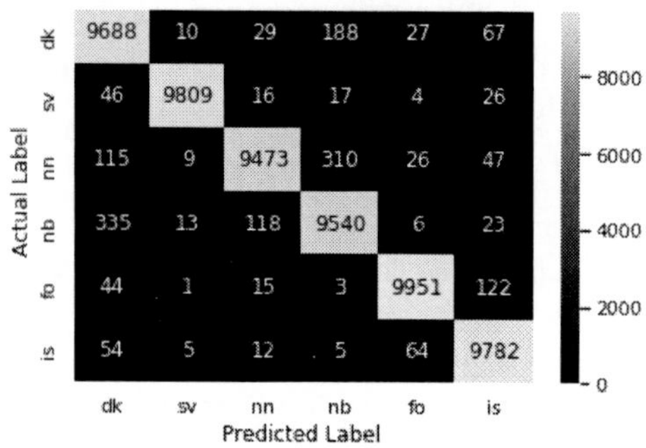

Figure 2: Confusion matrix with results from the CNN on the full Wikipedia data set.

Even when including five times the amount of data, the best result, logistic regression with an accuracy of 93.3%, is still worse than for the Convolutional Neural Network trained on 10K data points in each language.

Table 4 shows results for running the neural networks on the larger data set. Both models improve by increasing the amount of data and the Convolutional Neural Network reached an accuracy of 97% which is the best so far.

Figure 2 shows performance of the CNN trained on the Wikipedia data set with 50K data points per language. The model achieved an accuracy of 97% on the data set. The largest classification errors are between Danish, Bokmål and Nynorsk as well as between Icelandic and Faroese.

6.3 Using FastText supervised

FastText can also be used for supervised classification. In Joulin et al. (2016) the authors show that FastText can obtain performance on par with meth-

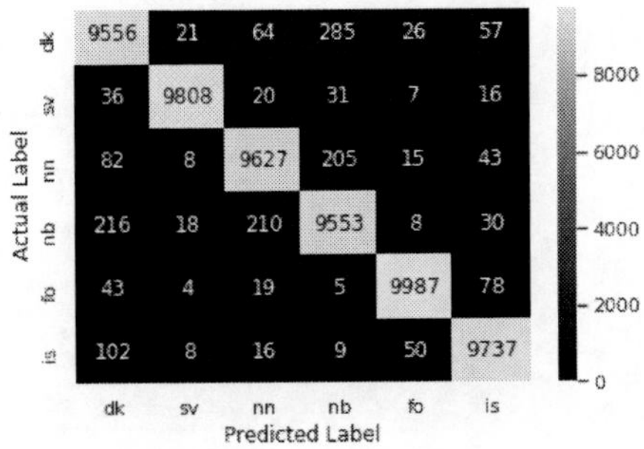

Figure 3: Confusion matrix with results from a supervised FastText model on the full Wikipedia data set.

ods inspired by deep learning, while being much faster on a selection of different tasks, e.g. tag prediction and sentiment analysis. We apply FastText classification to the Nordic DSL task. The confusion matrix from running the FastText supervised classifier can be seen in Figure 3. The supervised FastText model achieved an accuracy of 97.1% and thus the performance is similar to that of the CNN.

6.4 Cross-domain evaluation

Training on single-domain data can lead to classifiers that only work well on a single domain. To see how the two best performing models generalize, we tested on a non-Wikipedia data set.

For this, we used Tatoeba,[1] a large database of user-provided sentences and translations.

The language style used in the Tatoeba data set is different from the language used in Wikipedia. The Tatoeba data set mainly consists of sentences written in everyday language. Below are some examples from the Danish part of Tatoeba.

> Hvordan har du det? (How are you?)
>
> På trods af al sin rigdom og berømmelse, er han ulykkelig. (Despite all his riches and renown, he is unlucky.)
>
> Vi fløj over Atlanterhavet. (We flew over the Atlantic Ocean.)
>
> Jeg kan ikke lide æg. (I don't like eggs.)
>
> Folk som ikke synes at latin er det smukkeste sprog, har intet forstået. (People who don't think Latin is the most beautiful language have understood nothing.)

[1] `tatoeba.org/`

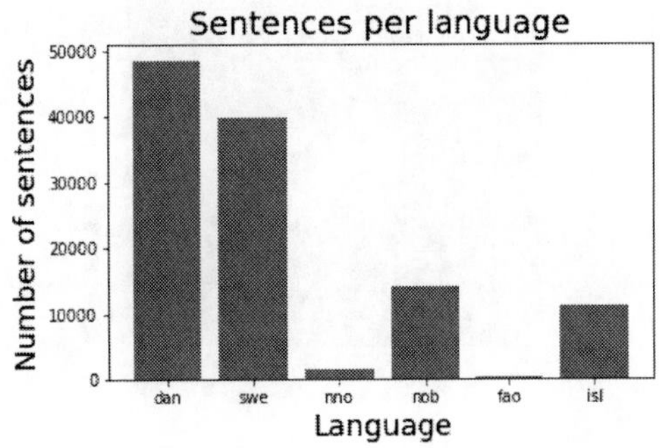

(a) Distribution of the number of sentences in each language in the Tatoeba data set.

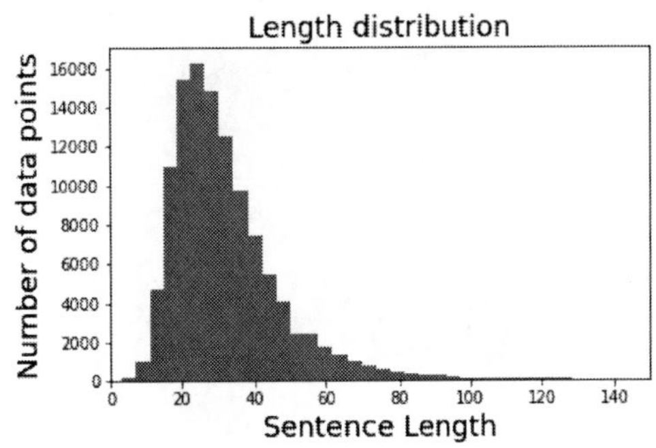

(b) Distribution of the length of sentences in the Tatoeba data set.

Figure 4: Distribution of the lengths and language classes of Tatoeba sentences.

Figure 4a shows the number of sentences in each language in the Tatoeba data set.

Performance drops when shifting to Tatoeba conversations. For reference the accuracy of langid.py on this data set is 80.9% so FastText actually performs worse than the baseline with an accuracy of 75.5% while the CNN is better than the baseline with an accuracy of 83.8%.

One explanation for the drop in performance is that the sentences in the Tatoeba data are significantly shorter than the sentences in the Wikipedia data set as seen in Figure 4b. Both models tend to mis-classify shorter sentences more often than longer sentences. This and the fact that the text genre is different might explain why the models trained on the Wikipedia data set does not generalise to the Tatoeba data set without a drop on performance.

The CNN uses character bi-grams as features while, with the standard settings, FastText uses only individual words to train. The better performance of the CNN might indicate that character

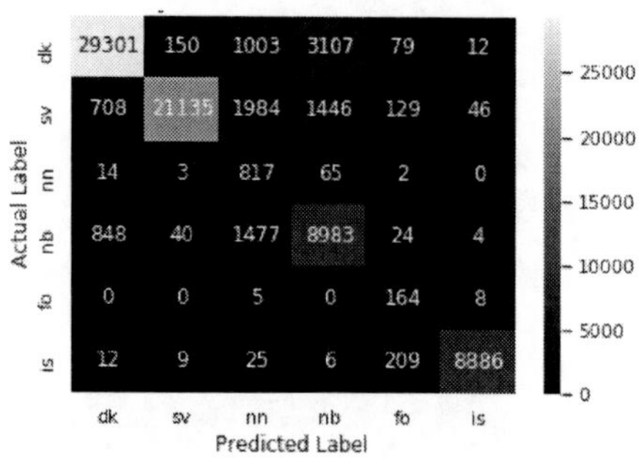

Figure 5: Confusion matrix for FastText trained using only character level n-grams on the Wikipedia data set and evaluated on the Tatoeba data set.

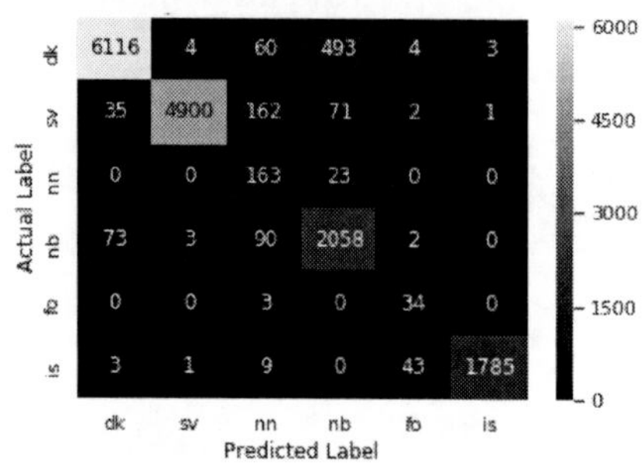

Figure 6: Results for FastText trained w. char n-grams on Wikipedia+Tatoeba and evaluated on Tatoeba.

level n-grams are more useful features for language identification than words alone.

To test this we changed the setting of FastText to train using only character level n-grams in the range 1-5 instead of individual words. Figure 5 shows the confusion matrix for this version of the FastText model. This version still achieved 97.8% on the Wikipedia test set while improving the accuracy on the Tatoeba data set from 75.4% to 85.8% which is a substantial increase.

Thus, using character-level features seems to improve the FastText models' ability to generalize to sentences belonging to a domain different from the one they have been trained on, supporting findings in prior work (Lui and Baldwin, 2011).

6.5 Retraining on the combined data set

To improve the accuracy over the Tatoeba data set, we retrained the FastText model on a combined data set consisting of data points from both Wikipedia and Tatoeba data.

The FastText model achieved an accuracy of 97.2% on this combined data set and an accuracy of 93.2% when evaluating this model on the Tatoeba test set alone - the confusion matrix is Figure 6.

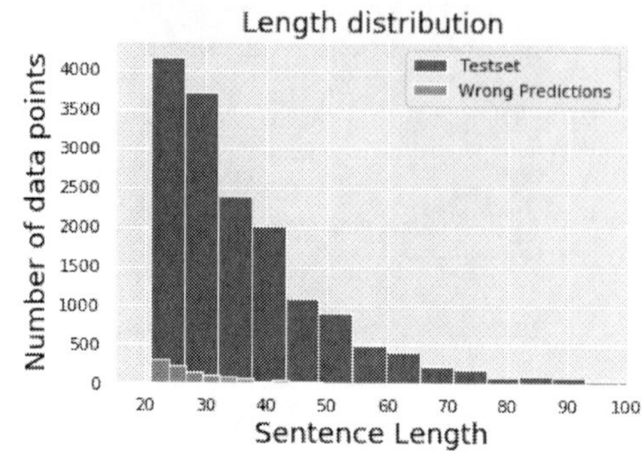

Figure 7: Distribution of sentence lengths Tatoeba test set along with the mis-classified sentences.

As was the case with the Wikipedia data set the mis-classified sentences tend to be shorter than the average sentence in the data set. Figure 7 shows the distribution of sentence lengths for the Tatoeba test set along with the mis-classified sentences. In the Tatoeba test set the mean length of sentences is 37.66 characters with a standard deviation of 17.91 while the mean length is only 29.70 characters for the mis-classified sentences with a standard deviation of 9.65. This again indicates that shorter sentences are harder to classify.

7 Analysis

7.1 Visualisation

To gain additional insight on how the different word embedding capture important information about each of the language classes, we visualized the embeddings using two different techniques for dimensionality reduction.

We used two different methods: Principal Component Analysis (PCA) and T-distributed Stochastic Neighbor Embedding (t-SNE). We begin with a brief explanation of the two techniques and proceed with an analysis of the results.

Principal Component Analysis The first step is to calculate the covariance matrix of the data set, with components:

$$K_{X_i,X_j} = E[(X_i - \mu_i)(X_j - \mu_j)] \quad (1)$$

where X_i is the ith component of the feature vector and μ_i is the mean of that component.

The next step is to calculate the eigenvectors and eigenvalues of the covariance matrix by solving the eigenvalue equation. The eigenvalues are the variances along the direction of the eigenvectors

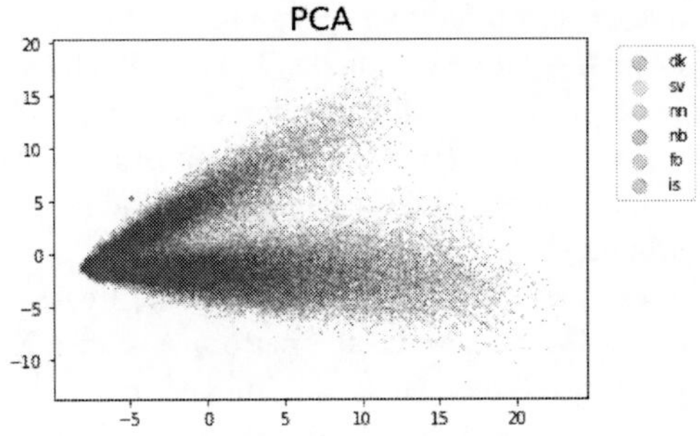

(a) Character bigram

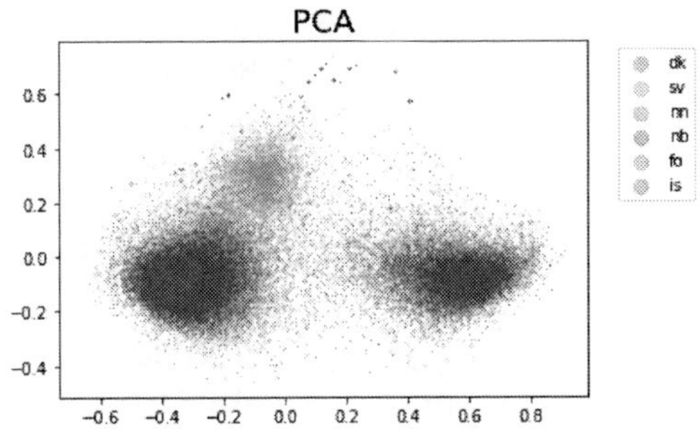

(b) Fasttext cbow

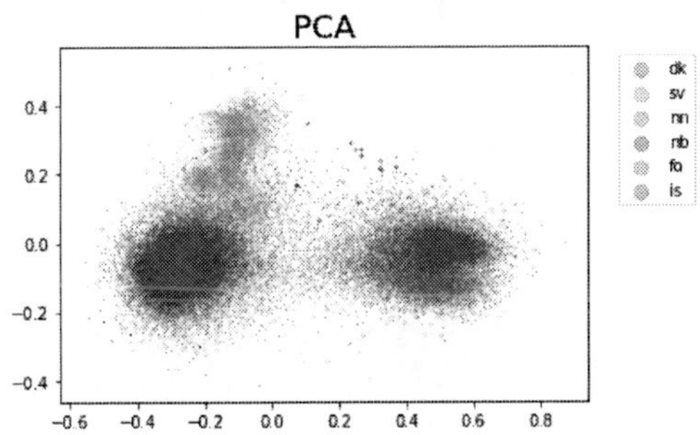

(c) Fasttext skipgram

Figure 8: Dimensionality reduction using PCA

or "Principal Components". To project our data set onto 2D space we select the two eigenvectors' largest associated eigenvalue and project our data set onto this subspace.

In Figure 8 we see the result of running PCA on the wikipedia data set where we have used character level bi-grams as features, as well as the CBOW and skipgram models from FastText.

In the figure for encoding with character level bi-grams, the PCA algorithm resulted in two elongated clusters. Without giving any prior information about the language of each sentences, PCA is apparently able to discriminate between Danish, Swedish, Nynorsk and Bokmål on one side, and Faroese and Icelandic on the other, since the majority of the sentences in each language belong to either of these two clusters.

With the FastText implementations we observe three clusters. For both CBOW and skipgram we see a distinct cluster of Swedish sentences. When comparing the two FastText models we see that the t-SNE algorithm with skipgrams seems to be able to separate Faroese and Icelandic data points to a high degree compared with the CBOW model. For the cluster of Danish, Bokmål, and Nynorsk sentences the skipgram models seem to give a better separation.

t-SNE The T-distributed Stochastic Neighbor Embedding method (van der Maaten and Hinton, 2008) favours retaining local relationships over remote ones.

In t-SNE, for a given data point x_i, the probability of picking another data point x_j as a neighbor to x_i is given by:

$$p_{ji} = \frac{\exp(||x_i - x_j||^2/2\sigma_i^2)}{\sum_{k \neq i} \exp(||x_i - x_k||^2/2\sigma_i^2)} \qquad (2)$$

Given this probability distribution the goal is to find the low-dimensional mapping of the data points x_i which we denote y_i follow a similar distribution. To solve what is referred to as the "crowding problem", t-SNE uses the Student t-distribution which is given by:

$$q_{ij} = \frac{(1 + ||y_i - y_j||^2)^{-1}}{\sum_{k \neq l}(1 + ||y_k - y_l||^2)^{-1}} \qquad (3)$$

Optimization of this distribution is done using gradient decent on the Kullback-Leibler divergence which is given by:

$$\frac{\delta C}{\delta y_i} = 4 \sum_j (p_{ij} - q_{ij})(y_i - y_j)(1 + ||y_i - y_j||^2)^{-1} \qquad (4)$$

t-SNE results over the Wikipedia data sets can be seen in Figure 9. As was the case with PCA, it appears that the encoding with FastText seem to capture the most relevant information to discriminate between the languages; especially the skipgram mode does well at capturing information relevant to this task.

Here we recover some interesting information about the similarity of the languages. The data points in Bokmål lie between those in Danish and

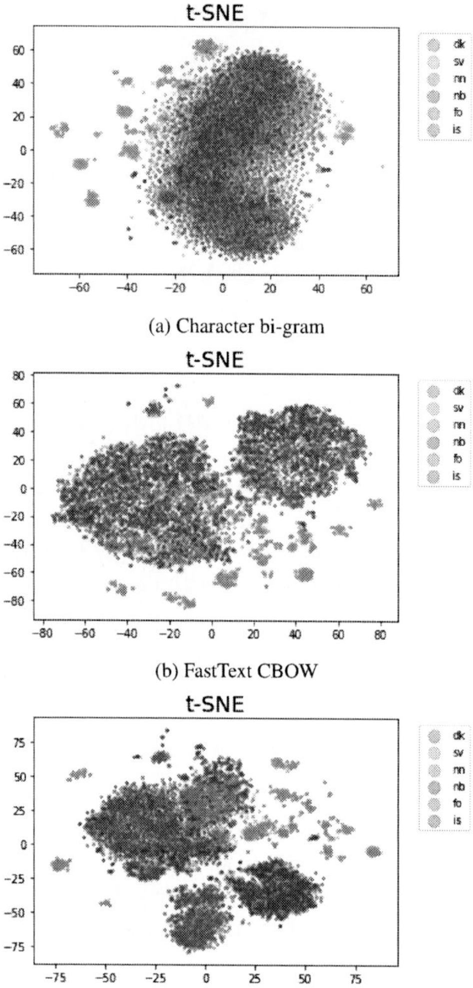

(a) Character bi-gram

(b) FastText CBOW

(c) FastText skip-gram

Figure 9: Dimensionality reduction using t-SNE

Nynorsk, while Icelandic and Faroese have their own two separate clusters.

This fits speaker intuitions about these languages. Interestingly the Swedish data points and quite scattered, and t-SNE does not make a coherent Swedish cluster.

This does not however mean that the Swedish data points are not close in the original space. Some care is needed when interpreting the plot since t-SNE groups together data points such that neighboring points in the input space will tend to be neighbors in the low dimensional space.

7.2 Discussion

The dimensionality reduction techniques applied, PCA and t-SNE, were able to cluster the input sentences into three main language categories: (1) Danish-Nynorsk-Bokmål; (2) Faroese-Icelandic; (3) Swedish. Generally the supervised models made the most errors when discriminating between languages belonging to either of these language groups.

For the "classical" models, Logistic Regression and SVMs achieved better performance than KNN and Naive Bayes, where the latter performed worst. This was true in all cases irrespective of the method of feature extraction.

Additionally we saw that when we used feature vectors from the FastText skipgram model the classification models achieved better results than when using either FastText CBOW or character n-grams.

Generally we saw that increasing the number of data points lead to better performance. When comparing the CNN with the "classical" models however the CNN performed better than any of the other models even when trained on less data points. In this way it seems that the CNN achieves higher sample efficiency compared to the other models.

8 Conclusion

This paper presented dataset, baseline approaches, and analyses on automatically distinguishing similar Nordic languages. We visualized embeddings produced by character level bi-grams, CBOW and skipgram. We argue that, of these, FastText's skipgram embeddings capture most information for discriminating between languages.

Data and code are available at `https://github.com/renhaa/NordicDSL`.

As baselines, we compared four different classical models: KNN, Logistic regression, Naive Bayes and a linear SVM with two neural network architectures: Multilayer perceptron and a convolutional neural network. The two best performing models, FastText supervised and CNN, saw reduced performance when going off-domain. Using character n-grams as features instead of words increased the performance for the FastText supervised classifier. Training on multiple domains resulted in an expected performance increase.

References

Piotr Bojanowski, Edouard Grave, Armand Joulin, and Tomas Mikolov. 2016. Enriching word vectors with subword information. *arXiv preprint arXiv:1607.04606*.

Isaac Caswell, Theresa Breiner, Daan van Esch, and Ankur Bapna. 2020. Language id in the wild: Unexpected challenges on the path to a thousand-language web text corpus. *arXiv preprint arXiv:2010.14571*.

Leon Derczynski, Rebekah Baglini, Morten H Christiansen, Manuel R Ciosici, Jacob Aarup Dalsgaard, Riccardo Fusaroli, Peter Juel Henrichsen, Rasmus Hvingelby, Andreas Kirkedal, Alex Speed Kjeldsen, et al. 2020. The Danish Gigaword Project. *arXiv preprint arXiv:2005.03521*.

Leon Derczynski and Alex Speed Kjeldsen. 2019. Bornholmsk natural language processing: Resources and tools. In *Proceedings of the 22nd Nordic Conference on Computational Linguistics*, pages 338–344.

Leon Derczynski, Diana Maynard, Niraj Aswani, and Kalina Bontcheva. 2013. Microblog-genre noise and impact on semantic annotation accuracy. In *Proceedings of the 24th ACM Conference on Hypertext and Social Media*, pages 21–30.

Cyril Goutte, Serge Léger, Shervin Malmasi, and Marcos Zampieri. 2016. Discriminating similar languages: Evaluations and explorations. In *Proceedings of Language Resources and Evaluation (LREC). Portoroz, Slovenia. pp 1800-1807 (2016)*.

Alon Jacovi, Oren Sar Shalom, and Yoav Goldberg. 2018. Understanding convolutional neural networks for text classification. In *Proceedings of the 2018 EMNLP Workshop BlackboxNLP: Analyzing and Interpreting Neural Networks for NLP*, pages 56–65, Brussels, Belgium. Association for Computational Linguistics.

Armand Joulin, Edouard Grave, Piotr Bojanowski, and Tomas Mikolov. 2016. Bag of tricks for efficient text classification. *arXiv preprint arXiv:1607.01759*.

Andreas Kirkedal, Barbara Plank, Leon Derczynski, and Natalie Schluter. 2019. The lacunae of danish natural language processing. In *Proceedings of the 22nd Nordic Conference on Computational Linguistics*, pages 356–362.

Edward Loper and Steven Bird. 2002. Nltk: The natural language toolkit. In *In Proceedings of the ACL Workshop on Effective Tools and Methodologies for Teaching Natural Language Processing and Computational Linguistics. Philadelphia: Association for Computational Linguistics*.

Marco Lui and Timothy Baldwin. 2011. Cross-domain feature selection for language identification. In *Proceedings of 5th international joint conference on natural language processing*, pages 553–561.

Marco Lui and Timothy Baldwin. 2012. Langid.py: An off-the-shelf language identification tool. In *Proceedings of the ACL 2012 System Demonstrations*, ACL '12, pages 25–30, Stroudsburg, PA, USA. Association for Computational Linguistics.

Laurens van der Maaten and Geoffrey Hinton. 2008. Visualizing data using t-SNE. *Journal of Machine Learning Research*, 9:2579–2605.

Tomas Mikolov, Kai Chen, Greg Corrado, and Jeffrey Dean. 2013. Efficient estimation of word representations in vector space. *arXiv preprint arXiv:1301.3781*.

Francisco Rangel, Paolo Rosso, Julian Brooke, and Alexandra L Uitdenbogerd. 2018. Cross-corpus native language identification via statistical embedding. In *Proceedings of the Second Workshop on Stylistic Variation*, pages 39–43.

Mads Toftrup, Søren Asger Sørensen, Manuel R. Ciosici, and Ira Assent. 2021. A reproduction of Apple's bi-directional LSTM models for language identification in short strings. In *Proceedings of the EACL Student Research Workshop*.

Marcos Zampieri, Liling Tan, Nikola Ljubesic, and Jörg Tiedemann. 2014. A report on the dsl shared task 2014. In *VarDial@COLING*.

Marcos Zampieri, Liling Tan, Nikola Ljubešic, Jörg Tiedemann, and Preslav Nakov. 2015. Overview of the dsl shared task 2015. In *Joint Workshop on Language Technology for Closely Related Languages, Varieties and Dialects*, page 1.

Naive Bayes-based Experiments in Romanian Dialect Identification

Tommi Jauhiainen[1,2], **Heidi Jauhiainen**[1], **Krister Lindén**[1]
[1]Department of Digital Humanities, University of Helsinki, Finland
[2]Department of English, Rochester Institute of Technology, USA
tommi.jauhiainen@helsinki.fi

Abstract

This article describes the experiments and systems developed by the SUKI team for the second edition of the Romanian Dialect Identification (RDI) shared task which was organized as part of the 2021 VarDial Evaluation Campaign. We submitted two runs to the shared task and our second submission was the overall best submission by a noticeable margin. Our best submission used a character n-gram based naive Bayes classifier with adaptive language models. We describe our experiments on the development set leading to both submissions.

1 Introduction

Romanian Dialect Identification (RDI) 2021 was a shared task focusing on discriminating between two written language varieties, Romanian and Moldavian. These are considered dialects of the Romanian language (ron) by the ISO-639-3 standard.[1] Together with the Uralic Language Identification (ULI) shared task it was one of the newest additions to a series of shared tasks in language or dialect identification organized as parts of the VarDial workshop series (Zampieri et al., 2014, 2015; Malmasi et al., 2016; Zampieri et al., 2017, 2018, 2019; Gaman et al., 2020; Chakravarthi et al., 2021).

Since the 2015 edition of VarDial, we have participated in many of the language identification shared tasks as the SUKI team. In the beginning, we were developing the original HeLI method (Jauhiainen, 2010; Jauhiainen et al., 2016), then we added language model adaptation to it (Jauhiainen et al., 2018a), and in this article we aim to improve on the results of our implementation of a naive Bayes based classifier (Jauhiainen et al., 2020) using character n-grams with and without language model adaptation (Jauhiainen et al., 2019a).

[1]https://iso639-3.sil.org/code/ron

In this article, we first give a quick overview of the related work on language identification, romanian dialect identification in particular, blacklist classifiers, and language model adaptation in Section 2. In Section 3, we provide information about the data set and the evaluation measures used in the RDI shared task. Then, in Section 4, we proceed to describe our experiments in building a competitive Romanian dialect identification system using the provided training data. In the experiment section, we also describe the methods used in sufficient detail for the reader to reproduce the systems. Sections 5 and 6 provide the results we attained in the shared task and the conclusions we were able to make from them and from our experiments on the training data.

2 Related Work

Dialect identification is part of a broader task of language identification. Automatic language identification of digital texts has been investigated for over 50 years. The first published experiments where a computer program has identified languages were conducted by Mustonen (1965). Identification of a long, monolingual, text is very simple if the languages to be identified are clearly different from one another. However, the task of language identification includes many challenges which increase its difficulty. For example, the texts can be very short, the languages to be discriminated can be very similar, or the amount of training data can be very small. When these challanges occur together, they can make language identification extremely difficult. The methods used and the challenges faced so far in language identification research were compiled in an extensive survey by Jauhiainen et al. (2019b).

Proceedings of the 8th VarDial Workshop on NLP for Similar Languages, Varieties and Dialects, pages 76–83
April 20, 2021 ©2021 Association for Computational Linguistics

2.1 Romanian Dialect Identification

RDI 2021 is the third shared task focusing on discriminating between the Moldavian and Romanian dialects of the Romanian language (ron). It appeared for the first time as one of the tracks of the Moldavian vs. Romanian Cross-dialect Topic identification shared task (MRC) in 2019 (Zampieri et al., 2019) and as a separate task in 2020 (Gaman et al., 2020).

We participated in the RDI 2020 shared task with a naive Bayes based dialect identifier. In our system description article for RDI 2020 (Jauhiainen et al., 2020), we provide an extensive listing of previous dialect identification experiments using the MOROCO dataset (Butnaru and Ionescu, 2019), which also functions as the training set for the shared task at hand. The highest F_1 score so far presented for the MOROCO dataset, 0.962, was provided by Wu et al. (2019) using a linear SVM classifier with language model adaptation.

Next we will shortly introduce some of the systems used in the RDI 2020 edition (Gaman et al., 2020). The RDI 2020 shared task was won by Çöltekin (2020). Her winning system, which obtained a Macro F_1 score of 0.7876, was based on a linear SVM classifier and used a language model adaptation scheme identical to the one used by Wu et al. (2019) a year earlier. In the winning system, she used only the provided target-development data for training the SVM. The best submission of the second ranked team, Anumiti (Popa and Ştefănescu, 2020), achieved an F_1 score of 0.7752. Their best system was an ensemble of five transformer-based classifiers combined using an SVM. The classifiers used in the ensemble were multilingual BERT, XLM, XLM-R, cased Romanian BERT, and uncased Romanian BERT. Ceolin and Zhang (2020) achieved a score of 0.6661 with a multinomial naive Bayes classifier using character n-grams from five to eight. We used a naive Bayes classifier with character n-grams from four to five, obtaining a Macro F_1 score of 0.6584 (Jauhiainen et al., 2020). Zaharia et al. (2020) used pre-trained Romanian BERT models and achieved an F_1 score of 0.6576. The UAIC team used an ensemble of TF-IDF encoders and a convolutional neural network attaining a score of 0.5553 (Rebeja and Cristea, 2020).

2.2 Blacklist Classifiers

Blacklists are lists of words or any other character sequences which if found, rule out the language. Blacklist classifiers have been previously used in language identification by Ljubešić et al. (2007) and Tiedemann and Ljubešić (2012). They used a blacklist of words with frequency cut-offs to distinguish between Bosnian, Croatian, and Serbian. Later, Barbaresi (2016) and Kroon et al. (2018) experimented with blacklisting when preparing for shared task submissions, but their experiments did not improve results and were not used in the final systems.

2.3 Language Model Adaptation

In language model adaptation, the language models are dynamically modified during the identification phase using the information in the mystery text (or collection of texts) itself. Using adaptive models in language identification shared tasks has proved to be important since we introduced the first language model adaptation experiments in language identification of texts during the VarDial Evaluation Campaign 2018 (Jauhiainen et al., 2018a,b; Zampieri et al., 2018).

As previously mentioned the winning submission of RDI 2020 used language model adaptation with SVMs (Çöltekin, 2020). The method used was identical to the one used by Wu et al. (2019) a year earlier in the shared tasks of the VarDial Evaluation Campaign 2019 (Zampieri et al., 2019). Using these systems, Wu et al. (2019) won the German Dialect Identification (GDI) 2019 shared task and the simplified track of the Discriminating between Mainland and Taiwan variation of Mandarin Chinese (DMT). In the method, the SVM was adapted once after the initial identification of all the test lines. The lines with a distance of 0.50 or higher from the SVM decision boundary were added to the training data of the identified language. The SVM was then re-trained with the additional data and re-run on the test set.

3 Shared Task Setup

The task of the RDI 2021 was to identify the dialect, either Romanian or Moldavian from a line of text.

The participants were provided with two sets of data, one for training and one for development. An augmented MOROCO data set (Butnaru and Ionescu, 2019) was used as the training data. The provided *train.txt* file included a total of 39,487 samples of texts from the news domain, which is 5,923 samples more than the MOROCO data set currently available on GitHub.[2]

The development data provided were tweets which in the RDI 2020 were used as the target development data (215 tweets) and the test data (5,022 tweets). The data set was published by Găman and Ionescu (2020) as MOROCO-Tweets and are available on GitHub.[3]

The participants were informed that the test set would also consist of tweets making the development set in-domain and the training set out-of-domain in relation to the test set. The task was closed, so only the data provided by the organizers was to be used in preparation of the participating systems. One of the motivations of the task was to evaluate cross-domain language identification systems but, nevertheless, the use of the development data for training the classifiers was not prohibited. The task description was very similar to the one in 2020. However, last year there were only 215 tweets available for development as opposed to the 5,237 tweets available for the 2021 edition.

In both the training and the development data, the named entities had been replaced with *NE* tags. The participants were informed that this would also be the case with the forthcoming test data. The development data included 2,612 lines of Moldavian and 2,625 lines of Romanian.

The test set was provided in the beginning of the general evaluation period of the VarDial Evaluation Campaign. The exact division of the samples between the two dialects in the test set was not a priori known to the participants. The test set contained 2,665 samples of Moldavian and 2,617 samples of Romanian which means that there was slightly larger difference between the two dialects than in the development set. As in RDI 2020, the evaluation measure used was the macro F_1 score. It gives both dialects equal value despite the possibility of there being an unequal number of samples in each dialect.

4 Experiments on the Development Data

When planning to participate in the RDI shared task, we contemplated evaluating two new additional methods combined with our existing language identifiers. The first additional method considered was active language model adaptation based on the length of the text to be identified (mystery text). However, the initial experiments did not produce any meaningful results with the data set at hand and consequently we did not use the adaptation to the text length in the submissions and are not reporting the experiments here. The other additional method under investigation was the use of so called blacklists in language identification to which we return in Section 4.2. For all the experiments, as well as for the submission runs, we removed the *NE*.

From the beginning, we suspected that using the in-domain development set would most probably be far more beneficial than using the out-of-domain training set. The language identification methods we were using have a number of parameters which are set using a development set. In light of this, we divided the development set in two parts. We used the first 1,306 lines of Moldavian and the first 1,313 lines of Romanian for the *dev-dev* and the rest was used for *dev-test*.

As the task was very similar to the RDI 2020 task, we continued our experiments from the conclusions we had arrived in 2020 (Jauhiainen et al., 2020). We had experimented with three types of generative classifiers using character *n*-grams: the simple scoring, the sum of relative frequencies and the product of relative frequencies. As the results with the two former were clearly inferior to the product of relative frequencies, we begun our experiments using this naive Bayesian classifier.

4.1 Product of Relative Frequencies

As it had proven to be beneficial on many occasions in the past (Jauhiainen, 2019), we started with a classifier which modified the training and the test data so that all non-alphabetic characters were removed and the remaining alphabetic characters lowercased.

The product of relative frequencies classifier is basically a naive Bayes style generative classifier using the relative frequencies of character *n*-grams as probabilities and is defined as follows in Equation 1:

$$p(g,M) = \begin{cases} \sum_i^{l_{M^F}} -lg_{10}\left(\frac{c(C_g,f_i)}{l_{C_g^F}}\right), \textit{if}\; c(C_g,f_i) > 0 \\ \sum_i^{l_{M^F}} -lg_{10}\left(\frac{1}{l_{C_g^F}}\right) pm, \textit{otherwise} \end{cases} \tag{1}$$

where l_{M^F} is the number of individual features in the mystery text M to be identified and $c(C_g, f_i)$

[2]https://github.com/butnaruandrei/MOROCO

[3]https://github.com/raduionescu/MOROCO-Tweets

is the count of M's ith feature f_i in the training corpus C_g of a dialect g. $l_{C_g^F}$ is the total number of the features of the same type (in this case the same length character n-grams) in C_g.

In case the feature f_i was not found in C_g, a smoothing value was used. As the smoothing value we used the relative frequency of a feature found only once in the training corpus. Instead of multiplying relative frequencies, the sum of their negative logarithms was used. If the smoothing value was was used, the resulting logarithm was multiplied by a penalty modifier, pm, determined using the development set.

First, we set out to optimize the length range of the character n-grams to be used as features as well as the penalty modifier applied to unseen features. In RDI 2020, we ended up using four to five characters as the length with a penalty modifier of 1.40 (Jauhiainen et al., 2020) and these were the parameters we started our experiments with in RDI 2021.

We used the provided training data for training the classifier and the *dev-dev* set to optimize the parameters with a greedy algorithm. Using the greedy algorithm, we found at least a local maximum macro F_1 score of 0.6614 using character n-grams from five to six in length and a penalty modifier of 1.62. This score was very well in line with our best result of 0.6584 in RDI 2020. When evaluated with the *dev-test* set, the same classifier gave a score of **0.6678** which was even better than the one on the data it was optimized for. These results clearly indicated that the first half of the development set was very similar to the second half. Table 1 lists the results of these and some of the following experiments using the training and the development sets.

The second experiment was to combine the training data with the *dev-dev* data, retrain the classifier and test evaluate it using *dev-test*. We used the same parameters and arrived at a macro F_1 score of **0.7203**. This was in line with our suspicions that using the development data itself in this shared task would be crucial in order to obtain high end results.

In the third experiment, we completely left out the training data and used merely the *dev-dev* data to train the classifier. This resulted in a score of **0.7889**, which was again a huge increase on the previous results. This results was now already slightly higher than the winning 0.7876 result of RDI 2020 by Çöltekin (2020). In anticipation of the submission run, we optimized the parameters for the *dev-test* set, ending up using character n-grams from two to six with a penalty modifier of 1.31. Those parameters gave an F_1 score of **0.8072**.

4.2 Blacklist Classifier

The success of using blacklists in language identification of very close languages by Ljubešić et al. (2007) and Tiedemann and Ljubešić (2012) had given us an idea to experiment with combining a blacklist identifier with the generative classifier. We created separate character n-gram lists for each dialect from the training data as well as the *dev-dev* set with the *createmodels.java* program which is part of the HeLI package on GitHub (Jauhiainen et al., 2016).[4]

In the first experiment with blacklist, we used lowercased character n-grams from 4 to 11 in length. We created a blacklist for each of the dialects to be identified. We first populated the blacklist for dialect 1 with those n-grams which were found from the *dev-dev* of dialect 2, but not of the dialect 1. Then, we pruned the list so, that only the n-grams found in the training data of dialect 2 but not in dialect 1 were kept.

We incorporated the blacklists as a preprocessing step on the product of relative frequencies classifier so that the blacklists would judge the mystery text if a blacklisted n-gram would be found from the mystery text.

We continued our practical experiments using the *dev-test* optimized parameters with the NB classifier from the previous experiments in Section 4.1. Adding the blacklists improved the resulting F_1 score slightly to **0.8118**. If the blacklists generated from the *dev-dev* set were not pruned using the training set, the score was merely 0.5719 using the complete blacklist and 0.8076 if only those n-grams that occurred more than 16 times were used.

In the second experiment, we simply combined the *dev-dev* and the training data and used an unpruned blacklist with a frequency cut-off. We evaluated the blacklists with the minimum frequencies from 1 to 10, and the best result of **0.8140** was achieved with the minimum frequency of 7. As the absolute frequency is tightly related to the size of the data set and we were about to use also the *dev-test* set with a submission, we calculated corresponding relative frequencies for each n-gram size.

[4]https://github.com/tosaja/HeLI

Training data	Development data	Testing data	Method	Macro F_1
train	dev-dev	dev-test	NB	0.6678
train + dev-dev	dev-dev	dev-test	NB	0.7203
dev-dev	dev-dev	dev-test	NB	0.7889
dev-dev	dev-test	dev-test	NB	0.8072
dev-dev	dev-test	dev-test	NB + blacklist 1	0.8118
dev-dev	dev-test	dev-test	NB + blacklist 2	0.8140
dev-dev	dev-test	dev-test	NB + blacklist 3	0.8144
dev-dev	dev-test	dev-test	NB + blacklist 3 (all characters)	0.8411
dev-dev	dev-test	dev-test	NB (all characters)	0.8380
dev-dev	dev-test	dev-test	NB + adaptation (all characters)	0.8186

Table 1: Results of the experiments with the training and the development data.

Due to rounding differences, using the relative frequencies gave a score of **0.8144**.

For the third experiment, we extracted the character sets for both dialects from the *dev-dev* set. After some manual inspection, it seemed that there were notable differences in the usage of non-alphabetic characters. In light of this, we modified the identifier to not remove the non-alphabetic characters and we left off the lowercasing as well. We run a new search for the best parameters and received a Macro F_1 score of **0.8411** using character n-grams from two to five, with a penalty modifier 1.61. We decided to use this system for our first submission.

4.3 Language Model Adaptation

For the second submission, we had decided to prepare a version of the naive Bayes classifier using adaptive language models. As our starting point, we reused the system which was used to win the first track of the DMT shared task in 2019 (Jauhiainen et al., 2019a). Combining the blacklist classifier with adaptive language models did not seem straightforward, so we left it for future work.

We first calculated the baseline for the identifier using the same parameters as for the blacklist classifier (character n-grams from 2 to 5 and penalty modifier 1.61) without removing the non-alphabetic characters and conserving the case differences. Using the *dev-dev* for training, the classifier achieved a Macro F_1 score of **0.8380** when tested on *dev-test* without language model adaptation.

In the adaptive version, the classifier keeps a separate record of the lines of the mystery text which have been finally identified. First, every line of the mystery text is identified and the resulting identifications are stored in a temporary table together with the probability differences between the best and the second best language. A larger probability difference corresponds to the identifier having a greater confidence in the identification and are thus called confidence scores. A fixed size fraction of the temporarily identified mystery lines with the highest confidence scores are then processed and their information added to the corresponding language models as well as their identification recorded as finally identified. Then all those lines not yet finally identified are re-identified with the newly adapted language models. This is repeated until all the fractions are processed. The number of fractions the mystery file is divided in is a tunable parameter.

We experimented with several fraction sizes and none really improved the scores when evaluated on the *dev-test* set. This was not totally surprising as we had noted earlier that the *dev-dev* and the *dev-test* sets were very similar. Nevertheless, we decided to submit a run using the adaptive models, as we had no idea how different the actual test set would be from the development set. As a fraction size, we decided to use full division, so that the information from only the most confident line would be added to the language models. This was possible due to the relatively small size of the test set. With the test set size of 5,282 lines the non-adaptive version does 5,282 identifications and the adaptive version with a maximum split 13,949,762 identifications.[5] For the *dev-test* the full split gave a Macro F_1 score of **0.8186**.

5 Submissions and Results

We ended up making two submissions to the shared task. Since it might not be obvious from Section 4 which systems were finally used to generate the

[5] $5,282 * 5,282/2$

submitted results, we will now give short descriptions of these systems.

5.1 Run 1

The results for the first run were produced by using a custom coded language identifier using the product of relative frequencies of character n-grams. Basically it is a naive Bayes classifier using the relative frequencies as probabilities as in Equation 1 (Jauhiainen et al., 2019a). The lengths of the character n-grams used were from 2 to 5. Instead of multiplying the relative frequencies, we summed up their negative logarithms. As a smoothing value, we used the negative logarithm of an n-gram appearing only once multiplied by a penalty modifier. In this case, the penalty modifier was 1.61.

Only the development data was used as training material in this run. All characters were used and not lowercased. The named entity tags were removed in preprocessing from both training and testing data.

In addition to the basic classifier, we used a blacklist of lowercase character n-grams generated from the training and the development data.

5.2 Run 2

The results for the second run were also produced by a language identifier using the product of relative frequencies of character n-grams. The lengths of the character n-grams used were from 2 to 5. Instead of multiplying the relative frequencies we summed up their negative logarithms. As a smoothing value, we used the negative logarithm of an n-gram appearing only once multiplied by a penalty modifier. In this case, the penalty modifier was 1.61.

In addition, we used the same language model adaptation technique as we used with the HeLI method in GDI 2018 (Jauhiainen et al., 2018a). We used one epoch of language model adaptation to the test data.

Only the development data was used as training material in this run. All characters were used and not lowercased. The named entity tags were removed in preprocessing from both training and testing data.

5.3 Results

Table 2 shows the results of the shared task. Our second run won by a considerable margin.

As of this writing, we have no knowledge of the systems used by the other two teams.

Rank	Team	Run	Macro F_1
1	**SUKI**	**2**	**0.7772**
2	UPB	2	0.7325
3	UPB	1	0.7319
4	**SUKI**	**1**	**0.7266**
5	UPB	3	0.6743
6	Phlyers	1	0.6532
7	Phlyers	2	0.5133

Table 2: The results of each team participating on the RDI 2021 shared task.

6 Conclusions

The results would seem to indicate that the tweets in the actual test data were clearly more out-of-domain when compared with the development data than our *dev-dev* set was from the *dev-test* set. The adaptive version, which gave lower scores between *dev-dev* and *dev-test* than the blacklist classifier was clearly superior with the actual test data.

We believe, that if the shared task instructions would have explicitly prohibited using the development data as training material, the results would have been even more interesting. As the development data was available for actually training the classifier as well, it proved to be useful to just forget the actual training data and train the classifier using only the smaller development data available. The best submission of the 2020 edition managed to point this out as it used a far smaller development set as training material, still winning the shared task.

Unfortunately, the two top teams from the RDI 2020 (Çöltekin, 2020; Popa and Ştefănescu, 2020) were not participating in RDI 2021 and the scores of their systems remain a mystery this time. If we compare our RDI 2021 results with the results of the best two teams from 2020, we notice that they are very close.

Acknowledgments

We would like to thank the RDI organizers for organizing the shared task. The research presented in this article has been partly funded by The Finnish Research Impact Foundation, the Kone Foundation, the Academy of Finland, and the University of Helsinki in cooperation with Lingsoft.

References

Adrien Barbaresi. 2016. An unsupervised morphological criterion for discriminating similar languages. In *Proceedings of the Third Workshop on NLP for Similar Languages, Varieties and Dialects (VarDial3)*, pages 212–220, Osaka, Japan. The COLING 2016 Organizing Committee.

Andrei Butnaru and Radu Tudor Ionescu. 2019. MOROCO: The Moldavian and Romanian dialectal corpus. In *Proceedings of the 57th Annual Meeting of the Association for Computational Linguistics*, pages 688–698, Florence, Italy. Association for Computational Linguistics.

Andrea Ceolin and Hong Zhang. 2020. Discriminating between standard Romanian and Moldavian tweets using filtered character ngrams. In *Proceedings of the 7th Workshop on NLP for Similar Languages, Varieties and Dialects*, pages 265–272, Barcelona, Spain (Online). International Committee on Computational Linguistics (ICCL).

Bharathi Raja Chakravarthi, Mihaela Găman, Radu Tudor Ionescu, Heidi Jauhiainen, Tommi Jauhiainen, Krister Lindén, Nikola Ljubešić, Niko Partanen, Ruba Priyadharshini, Christoph Purschke, Eswari Rajagopal, Yves Scherrer, and Marcos Zampieri. 2021. Findings of the VarDial Evaluation Campaign 2021. In *Proceedings of the Eighth Workshop on NLP for Similar Languages, Varieties and Dialects (VarDial)*.

Çağrı Çöltekin. 2020. Dialect identification under domain shift: Experiments with discriminating Romanian and Moldavian. In *Proceedings of the 7th Workshop on NLP for Similar Languages, Varieties and Dialects*, pages 186–192, Barcelona, Spain (Online). International Committee on Computational Linguistics (ICCL).

Mihaela Gaman, Dirk Hovy, Radu Tudor Ionescu, Heidi Jauhiainen, Tommi Jauhiainen, Krister Lindén, Nikola Ljubešić, Niko Partanen, Christoph Purschke, Yves Scherrer, and Marcos Zampieri. 2020. A report on the VarDial evaluation campaign 2020. In *Proceedings of the 7th Workshop on NLP for Similar Languages, Varieties and Dialects*, pages 1–14, Barcelona, Spain (Online). International Committee on Computational Linguistics (ICCL).

Mihaela Găman and Radu Tudor Ionescu. 2020. The unreasonable effectiveness of machine learning in moldavian versus romanian dialect identification. *arXiv preprint arXiv:2007.15700*.

Tommi Jauhiainen. 2010. Tekstin kielen automaattinen tunnistaminen. Master's thesis, University of Helsinki, Helsinki.

Tommi Jauhiainen. 2019. *Language identification in texts*. Ph.D. thesis, University of Helsinki, Finland.

Tommi Jauhiainen, Heidi Jauhiainen, and Krister Lindén. 2018a. HeLI-based experiments in Swiss German dialect identification. In *Proceedings of the Fifth Workshop on NLP for Similar Languages, Varieties and Dialects (VarDial 2018)*, pages 254–262, Santa Fe, New Mexico, USA. Association for Computational Linguistics.

Tommi Jauhiainen, Heidi Jauhiainen, and Krister Lindén. 2018b. Iterative language model adaptation for Indo-Aryan language identification. In *Proceedings of the Fifth Workshop on NLP for Similar Languages, Varieties and Dialects (VarDial 2018)*, pages 66–75, Santa Fe, New Mexico, USA. Association for Computational Linguistics.

Tommi Jauhiainen, Heidi Jauhiainen, and Krister Lindén. 2019a. Discriminating between Mandarin Chinese and Swiss-German varieties using adaptive language models. In *Proceedings of the Sixth Workshop on NLP for Similar Languages, Varieties and Dialects*, pages 178–187, Ann Arbor, Michigan. Association for Computational Linguistics.

Tommi Jauhiainen, Heidi Jauhiainen, and Krister Lindén. 2020. Experiments in language variety geolocation and dialect identification. In *Proceedings of the 7th Workshop on NLP for Similar Languages, Varieties and Dialects*, pages 220–231, Barcelona, Spain (Online). International Committee on Computational Linguistics (ICCL).

Tommi Jauhiainen, Krister Lindén, and Heidi Jauhiainen. 2016. HeLI, a word-based backoff method for language identification. In *Proceedings of the Third Workshop on NLP for Similar Languages, Varieties and Dialects (VarDial3)*, pages 153–162, Osaka, Japan. The COLING 2016 Organizing Committee.

Tommi Jauhiainen, Marco Lui, Marcos Zampieri, Timothy Baldwin, and Krister Lindén. 2019b. Automatic Language Identification in Texts: A Survey. *Journal of Artificial Intelligence Research*, 65:675–782.

Martin Kroon, Masha Medvedeva, and Barbara Plank. 2018. When simple n-gram models outperform syntactic approaches: Discriminating between Dutch and Flemish. In *Proceedings of the Fifth Workshop on NLP for Similar Languages, Varieties and Dialects (VarDial 2018)*, pages 244–253, Santa Fe, New Mexico, USA. Association for Computational Linguistics.

Nikola Ljubešić, Nives Mikelić, and Damir Boras. 2007. Language Identification: How to Distinguish Similar Languages? In *Proceedings of the 29th International Conference on Information Technology Interfaces (ITI 2007)*, pages 541–546, Cavtat/Dubrovnik, Croatia.

Shervin Malmasi, Marcos Zampieri, Nikola Ljubešić, Preslav Nakov, Ahmed Ali, and Jörg Tiedemann. 2016. Discriminating between similar languages and Arabic dialect identification: A report on the third DSL shared task. In *Proceedings of the Third*

Workshop on NLP for Similar Languages, Varieties and Dialects (VarDial3), pages 1–14, Osaka, Japan. The COLING 2016 Organizing Committee.

Seppo Mustonen. 1965. Multiple Discriminant Analysis in Linguistic Problems. *Statistical Methods in Linguistics*, 4:37–44.

Cristian Popa and Vlad Ştefănescu. 2020. Applying multilingual and monolingual transformer-based models for dialect identification. In *Proceedings of the 7th Workshop on NLP for Similar Languages, Varieties and Dialects*, pages 193–201, Barcelona, Spain (Online). International Committee on Computational Linguistics (ICCL).

Petru Rebeja and Dan Cristea. 2020. A dual-encoding system for dialect classification. In *Proceedings of the 7th Workshop on NLP for Similar Languages, Varieties and Dialects*, pages 212–219, Barcelona, Spain (Online). International Committee on Computational Linguistics (ICCL).

Jörg Tiedemann and Nikola Ljubešić. 2012. Efficient discrimination between closely related languages. In *Proceedings of COLING 2012*, pages 2619–2634, Mumbai, India. The COLING 2012 Organizing Committee.

Nianheng Wu, Eric DeMattos, Kwok Him So, Pin-zhen Chen, and Çağrı Çöltekin. 2019. Language discrimination and transfer learning for similar languages: Experiments with feature combinations and adaptation. In *Proceedings of the Sixth Workshop on NLP for Similar Languages, Varieties and Dialects*, pages 54–63, Ann Arbor, Michigan. Association for Computational Linguistics.

George-Eduard Zaharia, Andrei-Marius Avram, Dumitru-Clementin Cercel, and Traian Rebedea. 2020. Exploring the power of Romanian BERT for dialect identification. In *Proceedings of the 7th Workshop on NLP for Similar Languages, Varieties and Dialects*, pages 232–241, Barcelona, Spain (Online). International Committee on Computational Linguistics (ICCL).

Marcos Zampieri, Shervin Malmasi, Nikola Ljubešić, Preslav Nakov, Ahmed Ali, Jörg Tiedemann, Yves Scherrer, and Noëmi Aepli. 2017. Findings of the VarDial evaluation campaign 2017. In *Proceedings of the Fourth Workshop on NLP for Similar Languages, Varieties and Dialects (VarDial)*, pages 1–15, Valencia, Spain. Association for Computational Linguistics.

Marcos Zampieri, Shervin Malmasi, Preslav Nakov, Ahmed Ali, Suwon Shon, James Glass, Yves Scherrer, Tanja Samardžić, Nikola Ljubešić, Jörg Tiedemann, Chris van der Lee, Stefan Grondelaers, Nelleke Oostdijk, Dirk Speelman, Antal van den Bosch, Ritesh Kumar, Bornini Lahiri, and Mayank Jain. 2018. Language identification and morphosyntactic tagging: The second VarDial evaluation campaign. In *Proceedings of the Fifth Workshop on NLP for Similar Languages, Varieties and Dialects (VarDial 2018)*, pages 1–17, Santa Fe, New Mexico, USA. Association for Computational Linguistics.

Marcos Zampieri, Shervin Malmasi, Yves Scherrer, Tanja Samardžić, Francis Tyers, Miikka Silfverberg, Natalia Klyueva, Tung-Le Pan, Chu-Ren Huang, Radu Tudor Ionescu, Andrei M. Butnaru, and Tommi Jauhiainen. 2019. A report on the third VarDial evaluation campaign. In *Proceedings of the Sixth Workshop on NLP for Similar Languages, Varieties and Dialects*, pages 1–16, Ann Arbor, Michigan. Association for Computational Linguistics.

Marcos Zampieri, Liling Tan, Nikola Ljubešić, and Jörg Tiedemann. 2014. A report on the DSL shared task 2014. In *Proceedings of the First Workshop on Applying NLP Tools to Similar Languages, Varieties and Dialects*, pages 58–67, Dublin, Ireland. Association for Computational Linguistics and Dublin City University.

Marcos Zampieri, Liling Tan, Nikola Ljubešić, Jörg Tiedemann, and Preslav Nakov. 2015. Overview of the DSL shared task 2015. In *Proceedings of the Joint Workshop on Language Technology for Closely Related Languages, Varieties and Dialects*, pages 1–9, Hissar, Bulgaria. Association for Computational Linguistics.

UnibucKernel: Geolocating Swiss German Jodels Using Ensemble Learning

Mihaela Găman[1], **Sebastian Cojocariu**[1], **Radu Tudor Ionescu**[1,2,*]
[1]Department of Computer Science, [2]Romanian Young Academy
University of Bucharest
14 Academiei, Bucharest, Romania
*raducu.ionescu@gmail.com

Abstract

In this work, we describe our approach addressing the Social Media Variety Geolocation task featured in the 2021 VarDial Evaluation Campaign. We focus on the second subtask, which is based on a data set formed of approximately 30 thousand Swiss German Jodels. The dialect identification task is about accurately predicting the latitude and longitude of test samples. We frame the task as a double regression problem, employing an XGBoost meta-learner with the combined power of a variety of machine learning approaches to predict both latitude and longitude. The models included in our ensemble range from simple regression techniques, such as Support Vector Regression, to deep neural models, such as a hybrid neural network and a neural transformer. To minimize the prediction error, we approach the problem from a few different perspectives and consider various types of features, from low-level character n-grams to high-level BERT embeddings. The XGBoost ensemble resulted from combining the power of the aforementioned methods achieves a median distance of 23.6 km on the test data, which places us on the third place in the ranking, at a difference of 6.05 km and 2.9 km from the submissions on the first and second places, respectively.

1 Introduction

The Social Media Variety Geolocation (SMG) task was proposed, for the second year consecutively, in the 2021 edition of the VarDial Evaluation Campaign (Chakravarthi et al., 2021). This task is aimed at geolocation prediction based on short text messages exchanged by the users of social media platforms such as Twitter or Jodel. The location from where a short text was posted on a certain social media platform is expressed by two components: the latitude and the longitude. Naturally, the geolocation task is formulated as a double regression problem. Twitter and Jodel are the platforms used for data collection, and similar to the previous spin of SMG at VarDial 2020 (Găman et al., 2020), the task is divided into three subtasks, by language area, namely:

- Standard German Jodels (DE-AT) - which targets conversations initiated in Germany and Austria in regional dialectal forms (Hovy and Purschke, 2018).
- Swiss German Jodels (CH) - containing a smaller number of Jodel conversations from the German speaking half of Switzerland (Hovy and Purschke, 2018).
- BCMS Tweets - from the area of Bosnia and Herzegovina, Croatia, Montenegro and Serbia where the macro-language is BCMS, with both similarities and a fair share of variation among the component languages (Ljubešić et al., 2016).

The focus of our work falls only on the second subtask, SMG-CH, tackled via a variety of handcrafted and deep learning models. We propose a single ensemble model joining the power of several individual models through meta-learning based on Extreme Gradient Boosting (XGBoost) (Chen and Guestrin, 2016). We trained two independent ensemble models, each predicting one of the components that form the geographical coordinates (latitude and longitude).

The first model plugged into our meta-learner is a Support Vector Regression (SVR) model (Chang and Lin, 2002) based on string kernels. Previous usage in dialect identification has proved the efficiency of this technique in the task of interest (Butnaru and Ionescu, 2018b; Găman and Ionescu, 2020; Ionescu and Butnaru, 2017; Ionescu and Popescu, 2016).

Proceedings of the 8th VarDial Workshop on NLP for Similar Languages, Varieties and Dialects, pages 84–95
April 20, 2021 ©2021 Association for Computational Linguistics

The second model included in the ensemble is a hybrid convolutional neural network (CNN) (Liang et al., 2017) that combines, in the same architecture, character-level (Zhang et al., 2015) and word-level representations. The ability of capturing morphological relationships at the character level and using them as features for CNNs is also known to give promising results in dialect identification (Butnaru and Ionescu, 2019; Tudoreanu, 2019). Different from works using solely character-level CNNs for dialect identification (Butnaru and Ionescu, 2019; Tudoreanu, 2019), we believe that the addition of words might bring the benefit of learning dialect-specific multi-word expressions that are hard to capture at the character level (Dhingra et al., 2016; Ling et al., 2015).

Bidirectional Encoder Representations from Transformers (BERT) (Devlin et al., 2019) is a top performing technique used in recent years for solving mainstream NLP problems. Thus, it seems fit to also include the outputs of a fine-tuned German version of BERT in our XGBoost meta-learner.

We conducted experiments on the development set provided by the shared task organizers (Hovy and Purschke, 2018) in order to decide which model to choose as our submission for the SMG-CH subtask. Our results indicate that the ensemble model attains the best performance. With median distances that are 5-6 km higher, all the other models, tested individually on the development set, provide slightly worse predictions.

The remainder of this paper is organized as follows. We present related work on dialect identification and geolocation of short texts in Section 2. Our approach is described in detail in Section 3. We present the experiments and empirical results in Section 4. Finally, our conclusions are drawn in Section 5.

2 Related Work

Our study of the related work starts with a brief overview of geotagging based on text. Then, we look at more specific methods studying geotagging in social media and we also investigate the amount of research done, from a computational linguistics perspective, in geotagging by dialect, with focus on last year's approaches for the same subtask, namely SMG-CH at VarDial 2020.

Text-based geotagging. The works based on text to perform geotagging can be divided into three generic categories by the approaches taken in order to predict location. The first type of approach relies mainly on gazetteers as the source of the location mappings. This tool is adopted in a number of works (Cheng et al., 2010; Lieberman et al., 2010; Quercini et al., 2010), from ruled-based methods (Bilhaut et al., 2003) to various machine learning techniques that rely on named entity recognition (Ding et al., 2000; Gelernter and Mushegian, 2011; Qin et al., 2010). This category of methods brings the disadvantage of relying on specific mentions of locations in text, rather than inferring them in a less straightforward manner. These direct mentions of places are not a safe assumption, especially when it comes to social media platforms which represent the data source in some of these studies (Cheng et al., 2010). The other two main categories of approaches for text-based geolocation rely on either supervised (Kinsella et al., 2011; Wing and Baldridge, 2011) or unsupervised (Ahmed et al., 2013; Eisenstein et al., 2010; Hong et al., 2012) learning. The latter methods usually employ clustering techniques based on topic models.

Geolocation in social media. A number of works (Rout et al., 2013) look at this task from a supervised learning perspective. However, in these studies, other details (e.g. social ties) in the users profile are considered rather than their written content. Other works in this area are related to our current interest in studying language variation for the geolocation of social media posts (Doyle, 2014; Eisenstein et al., 2010; Han et al., 2014; Rahimi et al., 2017; Roller et al., 2012). Among these, various machine learning techniques are employed in location prediction, ranging from probabilistic graphical models (Eisenstein et al., 2010) and adaptive grid search (Roller et al., 2012) to Bayesian methods (Doyle, 2014) and neural networks (Rahimi et al., 2017).

Dialect-based geolocation. Many dialects are covered in the text-based geotagging research to date, including Dutch (Wieling et al., 2011), British (Szmrecsanyi, 2008), American (Eisenstein et al., 2010; Huang et al., 2016) and African American Vernacular English (Jones, 2015). Out of all the languages that were subject to location detection by dialect, we are interested in German. In this direction, the study that is the most relevant to our work is that of Hovy and Purschke (2018) which targets the German language and its variations. Approximately 16.8 million online posts from the German-speaking area of Europe are employed in this study with the aim of learning document representations of cities. A small fraction of these posts are Jodels collected from the German speaking side of Switzerland, and these are also used in the SMG-CH subtask that we are addressing in this paper. The assumption here is that the methods should manage to capture enough regional variations in the written language, which can serve as the means to automatically distinguish the geographical region of social media posts. The verification performed in this direction in the original paper (Hovy and Purschke, 2018) used clustering to determine larger regions covering a given dialect. However, given the shared task formulation, we take a different approach and use the provided data in a double regression setup, addressing the problem both from a shallow and a deep learning perspective.

As previously mentioned, this is the second consecutive year in which SMG-CH is featured at VarDial (Chakravarthi et al., 2021), with a similar format, although an updated data set. The participants of the 2020 SMG-CH shared task (Găman et al., 2020) studied this task from a variety of angles. Some techniques are based on deep neural networks such as the popular BERT architecture (Găman and Ionescu, 2020; Scherrer and Ljubešić, 2020), bidirectional Long Short-Term Memory (LSTM) networks applied on FastText embeddings (Mishra, 2020) or character-level CNNs (Găman and Ionescu, 2020). Other techniques are based on shallow or handcrafted features such as a grid-based prediction using an n-gram language model (Jauhiainen et al., 2020) or a clustering technique that shifts the problem into a discrete space, then uses an SVM for the classification of posts into regions. Our best submission (Găman and Ionescu, 2020) in last year's campaign was an ensemble based on XGBoost as meta-learner over the predictions of three different models: ν-SVR with string kernels, a character-level CNN and an LSTM based on BERT embeddings. This year, we acknowledge that our deep learning models had sub-optimal results in our previous participation at SMG-CH. Consequently, for this year, we bring stronger neural networks into the XGBoost ensemble. Instead of using an LSTM with BERT embeddings, we fine-tune the cased version of German BERT and use it directly for double regression in a setup that is more suitable to the data set size, compared to our previous endeavour. Instead of a character-level CNN, we use a hybrid CNN which learns end-to-end representations for both words and characters. The aforementioned deep learning models are plugged into an XGBoost ensemble alongside a retrained version of the ν-SVR model employed in our past participation (Găman and Ionescu, 2020). Our current changes introduce a significant improvement in median distance compared to our previous results, on a similar (and perhaps more challenging) data set.

3 Method

The only system that our team submitted for the SMG-CH subtask is an ensemble model based on the XGBoost meta-learner, as illustrated in Figure 1. In this section, we describe the three machine learning techniques that provide their predictions as input for the meta-learner, as well as the gradient boosting method that combines the independent models.

3.1 Support Vector Regression with String Kernels

String Kernels (Lodhi et al., 2001) provide a way of comparing two documents, based on the inner product generated by all substrings of length n, typically known as character n-grams. Being relatively simple to use and implement, this technique has many applications according to the literature (Cozma et al., 2018; Giménez-Pérez et al., 2017; Masala et al., 2017; Ionescu and Butnaru, 2018; Ionescu et al., 2014, 2016; Popescu and Ionescu, 2013), with emphasis on dialect identification and the good results obtained for this task in previous VarDial evaluation campaigns (Butnaru and Ionescu, 2018b; Ionescu and Butnaru, 2017; Ionescu and Popescu, 2016).

Similar to our last year's submission for the SMG-CH subtask (Găman and Ionescu, 2020), we employ the string kernels computed by the efficient algorithm introduced by Popescu et al. (2017). This gives us a dual representation of the data, through a kernel matrix where the cell on row i and column j represents the similarity between two text samples x_i and x_j. In our experiments, we consider the presence bits string kernel (Popescu and Ionescu, 2013) as the similarity function. For two strings x_i and x_j over a set of characters S, the presence bits string kernel is defined as follows:

$$k^{0/1}(x_i, x_j) = \sum_{g \in S^n} \#(x_i, g) \cdot \#(x_j, g), \quad (1)$$

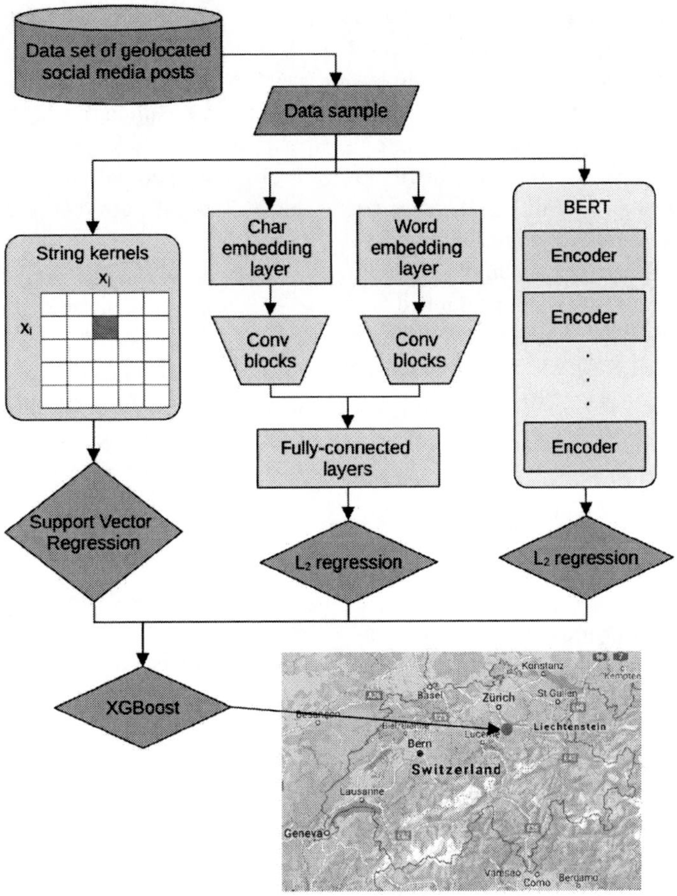

Figure 1: Ensemble proposed by UnibucKernel for the SMG-CH shared task. Best viewed in color.

where n is the length of n-grams and $\#(x, g)$ is a function that returns 1 when the number of occurrences of n-gram g in x is greater than 1, and 0 otherwise.

The resulting kernel matrix is plugged into a ν-Support Vector Regression (ν-SVR) model. SVR (Drucker et al., 1997) is a modified Support Vector Machines (SVM) (Cortes and Vapnik, 1995) model that is repurposed for regression. Similar to SVM, SVR uses the notion of support vectors and margin in order to find an optimal estimator. However, instead of a separating hyperplane, SVR aims to find a hyperplane that estimates the data points (support vectors) within the margin with minimal error. In our experiments, we employ an equivalent SVR formulation known as ν-SVR (Chang and Lin, 2002), where ν is the configurable proportion of support vectors to keep with respect to the number of samples in the data set. Using ν-SVR, the optimal solution can converge to a sparse model, with only a few support vectors. This is especially useful in our case, as the data set provided for the SMG-CH subtask does not contain too many samples. Another reason to employ ν-SVR in our regression task is that it was found to surpass other regression methods for other use cases, such as complex word identification (Butnaru and Ionescu, 2018a).

3.2 Hybrid Convolutional Neural Network

Characters are the base units in building words that exist in the vocabulary of most languages. Among the advantages of working at the character level, we enumerate (i) the neutrality with respect to language theory (independence of word boundaries, semantic structure or syntax) and (ii) the robustness to spelling errors and words that are outside the vocabulary (Ballesteros et al., 2015). These explain the growing interest in using characters as features in various language modeling setups (Al-Rfou et al., 2019; Ballesteros et al., 2015; Sutskever et al., 2011; Wood et al., 2009; Zhang et al., 2015).

Word embeddings are vectorial word representations that associate similar vectors to semantically related words, allowing us to express semantic relations mathematically in the generated embedding space. From the initial works of Bengio et al. (2003) and Schütze (1993) to the recent improvements in the quality of the embedding and the training time (Collobert and Weston, 2008; Mikolov et al., 2013a,b; Pennington et al., 2014), generating meaningful representations of words became a hot topic in the NLP research community. These improvements, and many others not mentioned here, have been extensively used in various NLP tasks (Garg et al., 2018; Glorot et al., 2011; Ionescu and Butnaru, 2019; Musto et al., 2016).

Considering the sometimes orthogonal benefits of character and word embeddings, an intuitive idea has emerged, namely that of combining the character and word representations, which should complement each other in various aspects and provide better meaningful cues in the learning process of hybrid neural architectures (Liang et al., 2017). Thus, throughout the experiments performed in this work, we choose to employ a hybrid convolutional neural network working at both the character level (Zhang et al., 2015) and the word level (Kim, 2014). The hybrid architecture concatenates two CNNs, out of which one is equipped with a character embedding layer and the other has an analogous word embeddings layer. The networks are able to automatically learn a 2D representation of text formed of either character or word embedding vectors, that are further processed by convolutional and fully-connected layers.

The last convolutional activation maps of our two CNNs sharing similar architectural choices are concatenated in what we call a hybrid network (Liang et al., 2017), with the aim of accurately and simultaneously predicting the two location components required for the geolocation task. The first component of the hybrid network is a character-level CNN, which takes the first and last 250 characters in the input and encodes each character with its position in the alphabet, then learns end-to-end embeddings for each character, as vectors of 128 components. The second CNN used as part of the hybrid network operates at the word level and it receives as input each sample encoded, initially, as an array of 100 indexes, corresponding to the position of each word in the vocabulary. As part of the pre-processing for the word-level CNN, we split the initial text into words, keeping the first 50 words and the last 50 words in the sample. In the end, we employ the German Snowball Stemmer (Weissweiler and Fraser, 2018) to reduce each word to its stem, in an effort to reduce the vocabulary size by mapping variations of the same word to a single vocabulary entry. The word-level CNN is also equipped with an embedding layer, learning end-to-end word representations as vectors of length 128.

Each of the two CNNs has three convolutional (conv) layers placed after the initial embedding layer. The number of filters decreases from 1024 for the first conv layer to 728 for the second conv layer and to 512 for the third conv layer. Each conv layer is equipped with Rectified Linear Units (ReLU) (Nair and Hinton, 2010) as the activation function. The convolutional filter sizes differ across the two convolutional architectures. Hence, we use kernels of sizes 9, 7 and 7 for the char CNN. In the same time, we choose 7, 5 and 3 as appropriate filter sizes for the conv layers of the word CNN. In the char CNN, each conv layer is followed by a max-pooling layer with filters of size 3. In the word CNN, we add max-pooling layers only after the first two conv layers. The pooling filter sizes are 3 for the first pooling layer and 2 for the second pooling layer. The activation maps resulting after the last conv blocks of the char and the word CNNs are concatenated and the hybrid network continues with four fully-connected (fc) layers with ReLU activations. The fc layers are formed of 512, 256, 128 and 64 individual neural units, respectively.

3.3 Fine-Tuned German BERT

Transformers (Vaswani et al., 2017) represent an important advance in NLP, with many benefits over the traditional sequential neural architectures. Based on an encoder-decoder architecture with attention, transformers proved to be better at modeling long-term dependencies in sequences, while being effectively trained as the sequential dependency of previous tokens is removed. Unlike other contemporary attempts at using transformers in language modeling (Radford et al., 2018), BERT (Devlin et al., 2019) builds deep language representations in a self-supervised fashion and incorporates context from both directions. The masked language modeling technique enables BERT to pretrain these deep bidirectional representations, that can be further fine-tuned and adapted for a variety of downstream tasks, without significant architectural updates. We also make use of this property in the current work, employing the Hugging Face (Wolf et al., 2020) version of the cased German BERT model[1]. The model was initially trained on the latest German Wikipedia dump, the OpenLegalData dump and a collection of news articles, summing up to a total of 12 GB of text files. We fine-tune this pre-trained German BERT model for the geolocation of Swiss German short texts, in a regression setup. The choice of hyperparameters is, in part, inspired by the winning system in the last year's SMG-CH subtask at VarDial (Scherrer and Ljubešić, 2020).

3.4 Ensemble Learning

Gradient tree boosting (Friedman, 2001) is based on training a tree ensemble model in an additive fashion. This technique has been successfully used in classification (Li, 2010) and ranking (Burges, 2010) problems, obtaining notable results in reputed competitions such as the Netflix Challenge (Bennett and Lanning, 2007). Furthermore, gradient tree boosting is the ensemble method of choice in some real-world pipelines running in production (He et al., 2014). XGBoost (Chen and Guestrin, 2016) is a tree boosting model targeted at solving large-scale tasks with limited computational resources. This approach aims at parallelizing tree learning while also trying to handle various sparsity patterns. Overfitting is addressed through shrinkage and column subsampling. Shrinkage acts as a learning rate, reducing the influence of each individual tree. Column subsampling is borrowed from Random Forests (Breiman, 2001), bearing the advantage of speeding up the computations. In the experiments, we employ XGBoost as a meta-learner over the individual predictions of each of the models described above. We opted for XGBoost in detriment of average voting and a ν-SVR meta-learner, both providing comparatively lower performance levels in a set of preliminary ensemble experiments.

4 Experiments

4.1 Data Set

The SMG-CH subtask (Hovy and Purschke, 2018) offers, as support, a training set of 25,261 Jodel posts, provided in plain text format. Each textual input is associated with a pair of coordinates, i.e. latitude and longitude, representing the position on Earth from where the text was posted. The development set is provided in an identical format and it is composed of 2,416 samples that we use to perform hyperparameter tuning and validate the results of our models. The test set has 2,438 samples without the corresponding coordinates, in order to avoid cheating or overfitting. Additionally, the proposed evaluation metric is the median distance between the predicted and the reference coordinates. A baseline median distance of 53.13 km is also included in the specifications.

4.2 Parameter Tuning

SVR based on string kernels. We compute the presence bits string kernel using the efficient algorithm proposed by Popescu et al. (2017). In order to find the optimal range of n-grams, we experiment with multiple blended spectrum string kernels based on various n-gram ranges that include n-grams from 3 to 7 characters long. The best performance in terms of both mean absolute error (MAE) and mean squared error (MSE) was attained by a string kernel based on the blended spectrum of 3 to 5 character n-grams. These results are consistent with those reported by Ionescu and Butnaru (2017) and Găman and Ionescu (2020), suggesting that the 3-5 n-gram range is optimal for German dialect identification. The resulting kernel matrix is used as input for two ν-SVR models, optimized for predicting the latitude and longitude (in degrees), respectively. For each of the two regressors, we tune the regularization penalty C, in a range of values from 10^{-4} to 10^{4}. Similarly, for the proportion of support vectors ν, we consider 10 values uniformly covering the interval $(0, 1]$ with a step of 0.1. To search for the optimal combination of hyperparameters, we apply grid search. Consistent with our previous study that inspired this choice of model and features (Găman and Ionescu, 2020), for both regression models, the best hyperparameter combination is $C = 10$ and $\nu = 0.5$.

Hybrid CNN. As regularization for each conv block of the two CNNs, we introduce Gaussian noise and spatial dropout. We try many different magnitudes in the two regularization techniques, obtaining a few slightly different variations of the same model. These are compared against each other using grid search, selecting the best model to be included in our final ensemble. The rates used for the spatial dropout (Tompson et al., 2015) are in the range $[0.001, 0.2]$, with a step of 0.001, with

[1] `https://huggingface.co/bert-base-german-cased`

Table 1: The preliminary results of our team (UnibucKernel) obtained on the development set of the SMG-CH subtask.

Method	Median (km)	Mean (km)
Hybrid CNN	30.05	35.75
ν-SVR with string kernels	30.31	34.82
BERT #1 (L_2)	30.63	35.78
BERT #2 (L_1, truncated)	33.86	38.85
BERT #3 (L_1)	30.17	36.16
XGBoost ensemble	25.11	30.75

the best dropout rate deemed to be 0.007. For the Gaussian noise, we consider standard deviations in the range $[0.0001, 0.01]$, with the best results obtained with a standard deviation of 0.001. After each of the four fully-connected layers, we employ plain dropout (Srivastava et al., 2014) with a rate of 0.005, deemed the best choice in the range $[0.001, 0.5]$.

In the optimization phase, common evaluation metrics such as the mean squared error (MSE) and the mean absolute error (MAE) are typically used to measure performance. In addition to these two metrics, we consider another error function as candidate for the loss to be minimized, namely the Huber loss. Although minimizing the Huber loss tends to give optimal values for the classical evaluation metrics, we finally use MSE as loss, given that it seems to converge to better results in terms of the median distance, which is the official evaluation metric in the SMG shared task. We optimize the hybrid CNN using the Adam optimization algorithm (Kingma and Ba, 2015) with an initial learning rate of 10^{-3}, chosen from the range $[10^{-5}, 10^{-2}]$, a weight decay of 10^{-7}, selected in the initial range $[10^{-9}, 10^{-6}]$, and the learning rate decay of 0.999. We train the hybrid architecture on mini-batches of 96 samples for 1000 epochs with early stopping. The network included in the final ensemble converged in 136 epochs.

Fine-Tuned German BERT. We fine-tune three BERT models in slightly different setups. The pre-trained base model used as starting point is the cased German BERT (Wolf et al., 2020). We set the maximum sequence length to 128, applying zero-padding to reach the fixed length for the samples that are shorter. The batch size, unanimously used, is 32, with a training that goes on for a maximum of 50 epochs. We optimize the models using Adam, with an initial learning rate $\alpha = 5 \cdot 10^{-5}$. The division by zero is prevented by the introduction of $\epsilon = 10^{-8}$. Moving to the particularities of each of the three fine-tuned BERT models, we note a difference in the choice of the loss function, such that the first model employs the L_2 loss (MSE), while the other two models use the L_1 loss (MAE). Another variation is introduced by the text truncation choices, such that for the first and third models, we do not enforce truncation, while for the second model, all the samples are enforced to align to the provided maximum sequence length. These differences are reflected in the number epochs required for complete convergence: 20, 18 and 33, respectively. We monitor the median distance for early stopping and observe that the best performance upon convergence is obtained by the third model, with a median distance of 30.17 km on the validation set, followed by the results of the first (30.63 km) and second (33.86 km) models, respectively. In the ensemble, we include only the top scoring BERT model.

Extreme Gradient Boosting. We employed XGBoost as a meta-learner, training it over the predictions of all the other models described in Section 3. We selected XGBoost as the submission candidate, as it provided the best results. The XGBoost regressor, deemed optimal by the hyperparameter tuning, has default values for most parameters[2], except for the number of estimators and the maximum tree depth. We set the number of estimators to 100 for the latitude regressor and to 1000 for the longitude regressor. Similarly, the maximum depth of the trees is 10 for the latitude model and 20 for the longitude one.

4.3 Preliminary Results

We train three different models which rely on different learning methods and types of features to perform the required double regression. Thus, we have the hybrid CNN relying on both words and characters as features, the shallow ν-SVR based on

[2] `https://xgboost.readthedocs.io/en/latest/`

Table 2: The final results obtained on the test set of the SMG-CH subtask by our ensemble model against the baseline and the top scoring methods.

Method	Rank	Median (km)	Mean (km)	AUC
HeLju_uc	1st	17.55	25.84	74907.5
HeLju_c	2nd	20.70	29.62	67237.5
UnibucKernel	3rd	23.60	29.75	63347.0
baseline	-	53.13	51.50	28637.0

string kernels and three fine-tuned German BERT models looking at higher-level features and understanding dependencies in a bidirectional manner.

Table 1 shows the preliminary results obtained on the development set by each individual model as well as the results of the submitted XGBoost ensemble. The individual models provide quite similar results in terms of the median distance between the predicted and ground-truth locations. These results stay around a value of 30 km for the median distance and 35 km for the mean distance. Among the independent models, the hybrid CNN obtains slightly better results in terms of the median distance (30.05 km), whereas the second attempt at fine-tuning BERT gives the worst distances, namely 33.86 km for the median distance and 38.85 km for the mean distance. ν-SVR surpasses all the other models, by a small margin, in terms of the mean distance (34.82 km). The results of the submitted XGBoost ensemble model stand proof that our intuition was correct, namely that all these individual models have the potential to complement each other if put together in an ensemble. Indeed, the submitted system clearly surpasses the best individual model by approximately 5 km in terms of both the median and the mean distance metrics.

4.4 Final Results

For our final submission, we trained all the individual models on both the provided training and development data sets. Then, we also retrained the submitted ensemble model, in a hope that this will give an even smaller median distance on the test set, compared to what we have obtained in the preliminary validation phase.

Table 2 shows an improvement in terms of the median distance on the test set compared to the one obtain on the development data. We cannot be sure that this improvement is solely due to the retraining that involves the development set. However, we conjecture that this endeavour played its part in the slightly better results. We outperform the baseline model by 29.53 km in terms of the median distance and by 21.75 km in terms of the mean distance, obtaining the third place in the competition. The constrained submission proposed by the organizers of the SMG-CH shared task surpasses our model by 2.9 km in terms of the median distance and by 0.13 km in terms of the mean distance. The unconstrained system on the first place, which was also proposed by the organizers of the SMG-CH shared task, distances itself by larger margins, with a difference of 6.05 km for the median distance and a difference of 3.91 km for the mean distance.

5 Conclusion

In this paper, we proposed an ensemble learning model for the geolocation of Swiss German social media posts. The ensemble is based on an XGBoost meta-learner applied on top of three individual models: a hybrid CNN, an approach based on string kernels and a fine-tuned German BERT model. Given the final results obtained in the SMG-CH subtask, we conclude that predicting the location of Swiss German social media posts is a challenging task, the median distance being higher than 20 km. Using external data sources to build a language model seems to be a more promising path towards success, as shown by the final standings of the VarDial 2020 (Găman et al., 2020) and 2021 (Chakravarthi et al., 2021) SMG shared tasks.

In future work, we aim to study the applicability of our ensemble on other geolocation tasks, perhaps taking into consideration future VarDial challenges.

Acknowledgments

The authors thank reviewers for their useful remarks. This work was supported by a grant of the Romanian Ministry of Education and Research, CNCS - UEFISCDI, project number PN-III-P1-1.1-TE-2019-0235, within PNCDI III. This article has also benefited from the support of the Romanian Young Academy, which is funded by Stiftung Mercator and the Alexander von Humboldt Foundation for the period 2020-2022.

References

Amr Ahmed, Liangjie Hong, and Alex J. Smola. 2013. Hierarchical geographical modeling of user locations from social media posts. In *Proceedings of WWW*, pages 25–36.

Rami Al-Rfou, Dokook Choe, Noah Constant, Mandy Guo, and Llion Jones. 2019. Character-Level Language Modeling with Deeper Self-Attention. In *Proceedings of AAAI*, pages 3159–3166.

Miguel Ballesteros, Chris Dyer, and Noah A. Smith. 2015. Improved Transition-Based Parsing by Modeling Characters instead of Words with LSTMs. In *Proceedings of EMNLP 2015*, pages 349–59.

Yoshua Bengio, Réjean Ducharme, Pascal Vincent, and Christian Janvin. 2003. A Neural Probabilistic Language Model. *Journal of Machine Learning Research*, 3:1137–1155.

James Bennett and Stan Lanning. 2007. The Netflix Prize. In *Proceedings of KDD*, page 35.

Frédérik Bilhaut, Thierry Charnois, Patrice Enjalbert, and Yann Mathet. 2003. Geographic reference analysis for geographic document querying. In *Proceedings of GEOREF*, pages 55–62.

Leo Breiman. 2001. Random Forests. *Machine Learning*, 45(1):5–32.

Christopher J.C. Burges. 2010. From RankNet to LambdaRank to LambdaMART: An Overview. Technical Report MSR-TR-2010-82, Microsoft.

Andrei Butnaru and Radu Tudor Ionescu. 2018a. UnibucKernel: A kernel-based learning method for complex word identification. In *Proceedings of BEA-13*, pages 175–183.

Andrei Butnaru and Radu Tudor Ionescu. 2018b. UnibucKernel Reloaded: First Place in Arabic Dialect Identification for the Second Year in a Row. In *Proceedings of VarDial*, pages 77–87.

Andrei Butnaru and Radu Tudor Ionescu. 2019. MOROCO: The Moldavian and Romanian Dialectal Corpus. In *Proceedings of ACL*, pages 688–698.

Bharathi Raja Chakravarthi, Mihaela Găman, Radu Tudor Ionescu, Heidi Jauhiainen, Tommi Jauhiainen, Krister Lindén, Nikola Ljubešić, Niko Partanen, Ruba Priyadharshini, Christoph Purschke, Eswari Rajagopal, Yves Scherrer, and Marcos Zampieri. 2021. Findings of the VarDial Evaluation Campaign 2021. In *Proceedings of the Eighth Workshop on NLP for Similar Languages, Varieties and Dialects (VarDial)*.

Chih-Chung Chang and Chih-Jen Lin. 2002. Training ν-Support Vector Regression: Theory and Algorithms. *Neural Computation*, 14:1959–1977.

Tianqi Chen and Carlos Guestrin. 2016. XGBoost: A scalable tree boosting system. In *Proceedings of KDD*, pages 785–794.

Zhiyuan Cheng, James Caverlee, and Kyumin Lee. 2010. You are where you tweet: a content-based approach to geo-locating Twitter users. In *Proceedings of CIKM*, pages 759–768.

Ronan Collobert and Jason Weston. 2008. A Unified Architecture for Natural Language Processing: Deep Neural Networks with Multitask Learning. In *Proceedings of ICML*, pages 160–167.

Corinna Cortes and Vladimir Vapnik. 1995. Support-vector networks. *Machine Learning*, 20(3):273–297.

Mădălina Cozma, Andrei Butnaru, and Radu Tudor Ionescu. 2018. Automated essay scoring with string kernels and word embeddings. In *Proceedings of ACL*, pages 503–509.

Jacob Devlin, Ming-Wei Chang, Kenton Lee, and Kristina Toutanova. 2019. BERT: Pre-training of Deep Bidirectional Transformers for Language Understanding. In *Proceedings of NAACL*, pages 4171–4186.

Bhuwan Dhingra, Zhong Zhou, Dylan Fitzpatrick, Michael Muehl, and William W. Cohen. 2016. Tweet2Vec: Character-Based Distributed Representations for Social Media. In *Proceedings of ACL*, pages 269–274.

Junyan Ding, Luis Gravano, and Narayanan Shivakumar. 2000. Computing geographical scopes of web resources. In *Proceedings of VLDV*.

Gabriel Doyle. 2014. Mapping dialectal variation by querying social media. In *Proceedings of EACL 2014*, pages 98–106.

Harris Drucker, Christopher J.C. Burges, Linda Kaufman, Alex J. Smola, and Vladimir Vapnik. 1997. Support vector regression machines. In *Proceedings of NIPS*, pages 155–161.

Jacob Eisenstein, Brendan O'Connor, Noah A. Smith, and Eric Xing. 2010. A latent variable model for geographic lexical variation. In *Proceedings of EMNLP*, pages 1277–1287.

Jerome H. Friedman. 2001. Greedy function approximation: a gradient boosting machine. *Annals of statistics*, pages 1189–1232.

Nikhil Garg, Londa Schiebinger, Dan Jurafsky, and James Zou. 2018. Word embeddings quantify 100 years of gender and ethnic stereotypes. *Proceedings of the National Academy of Sciences*, 115:E3635–E3644.

Judith Gelernter and Nikolai Mushegian. 2011. Geo-parsing messages from microtext. *Transactions in GIS*, 15(6):753–773.

Rosa M. Giménez-Pérez, Marc Franco-Salvador, and Paolo Rosso. 2017. Single and Cross-domain Polarity Classification using String Kernels. In *Proceedings of EACL*, pages 558–563.

Xavier Glorot, Antoine Bordes, and Yoshua Bengio. 2011. Domain Adaptation for Large-Scale Sentiment Classification: A Deep Learning Approach. In *Proceedings of ICML*, pages 513–520.

Mihaela Găman, Dirk Hovy, Radu Tudor Ionescu, Heidi Jauhiainen, Tommi Jauhiainen, Krister Lindén, Nikola Ljubešić, Niko Partanen, Christoph Purschke, Yves Scherrer, and Marcos Zampieri. 2020. A Report on the VarDial Evaluation Campaign 2020. In *Proceedings of VarDial*, pages 1–14.

Mihaela Găman and Radu Tudor Ionescu. 2020. Combining Deep Learning and String Kernels for the Localization of Swiss German Tweets. In *Proceedings of VarDial*, pages 242–253.

Bo Han, Paul Cook, and Timothy Baldwin. 2014. Text-Based Twitter User Geolocation Prediction. *Journal of Artificial Intelligence Research*, 49:451–500.

Xinran He, Junfeng Pan, Ou Jin, Tianbing Xu, Bo Liu, Tao Xu, Yanxin Shi, Antoine Atallah, Ralf Herbrich, Stuart Bowers, and Joaquin Q. Candela. 2014. Practical Lessons from Predicting Clicks on Ads at Facebook. In *Proceedings of ADKDD*, pages 1–9.

Liangjie Hong, Amr Ahmed, Siva Gurumurthy, Alex J. Smola, and Kostas Tsioutsiouliklis. 2012. Discovering Geographical Topics in the Twitter Stream. In *Proceedings of WWW*, pages 769–778.

Dirk Hovy and Christoph Purschke. 2018. Capturing Regional Variation with Distributed Place Representations and Geographic Retrofitting. In *Proceedings of EMNLP*, pages 4383–4394.

Yuan Huang, Diansheng Guo, Alice Kasakoff, and Jack Grieve. 2016. Understanding US regional linguistic variation with Twitter data analysis. *Computers, Environment and Urban Systems*, 59:244–255.

Radu Tudor Ionescu and Andrei Butnaru. 2017. Learning to Identify Arabic and German Dialects using Multiple Kernels. In *Proceedings of VarDial*, pages 200–209.

Radu Tudor Ionescu and Andrei Butnaru. 2018. Improving the results of string kernels in sentiment analysis and Arabic dialect identification by adapting them to your test set. In *Proceedings of EMNLP*, pages 1084–1090.

Radu Tudor Ionescu and Andrei Butnaru. 2019. Vector of Locally-Aggregated Word Embeddings (VLAWE): A Novel Document-level Representation. In *Proceedings of NAACL*, pages 363–369.

Radu Tudor Ionescu and Marius Popescu. 2016. UnibucKernel: An Approach for Arabic Dialect Identification based on Multiple String Kernels. In *Proceedings of VarDial*, pages 135–144.

Radu Tudor Ionescu, Marius Popescu, and Aoife Cahill. 2014. Can characters reveal your native language? A language-independent approach to native language identification. In *Proceedings of EMNLP*, pages 1363–1373.

Radu Tudor Ionescu, Marius Popescu, and Aoife Cahill. 2016. String kernels for native language identification: Insights from behind the curtains. *Computational Linguistics*, 42(3):491–525.

Tommi Jauhiainen, Heidi Jauhiainen, and Krister Lindén. 2020. Experiments in language variety geolocation and dialect identification. In *Proceedings of VarDial*, pages 220–231.

Taylor Jones. 2015. Toward a description of African American Vernacular English dialect regions using "Black Twitter". *American Speech*, 90(4):403–440.

Yoon Kim. 2014. Convolutional Neural Networks for Sentence Classification. In *Proceedings of EMNLP*, pages 1746–1751.

Diederik P. Kingma and Jimmy Ba. 2015. Adam: A method for stochastic optimization. In *Proceedings of ICLR*.

Sheila Kinsella, Vanessa Murdock, and Neil O'Hare. 2011. "I'm eating a sandwich in Glasgow" modeling locations with tweets. In *Proceedings of SMUC*, pages 61–68.

Ping Li. 2010. Robust Logitboost and Adaptive Base Class (ABC) Logitboost. In *Proceedings of UAI*, pages 302–311.

Dongyun Liang, Weiran Xu, and Yinge Zhao. 2017. Combining Word-Level and Character-Level Representations for Relation Classification of Informal Text. In *Proceedings of RepL4NLP*, pages 43–47.

Michael D. Lieberman, Hanan Samet, and Jagan Sankaranarayanan. 2010. Geotagging with local lexicons to build indexes for textually-specified spatial data. In *Proceedings of ICDE*, pages 201–212.

Wang Ling, Tiago Luís, Luís Marujo, Ramón Fernandez Astudillo, Silvio Amir, Chris Dyer, Alan W. Black, and Isabel Trancoso. 2015. Finding Function in Form: Compositional Character Models for Open Vocabulary Word Representation. In *Proceedings of EMNLP*, pages 1520–1530.

Nikola Ljubešić, Tanja Samardžić, and Curdin Derungs. 2016. TweetGeo - A Tool for Collecting, Processing and Analysing Geo-encoded Linguistic Data. In *Proceedings of COLING*, pages 3412–3421.

Huma Lodhi, John Shawe-Taylor, Nello Cristianini, and Christopher J.C.H. Watkins. 2001. Text Classification Using String Kernels. In *Proceedings of NIPS*, pages 563–569.

Mihai Masala, Stefan Ruseti, and Traian Rebedea. 2017. Sentence selection with neural networks using string kernels. In *Proceedings of KES*, pages 1774–1782.

Tomas Mikolov, Kai Chen, Greg Corrado, and Jeffrey Dean. 2013a. Efficient Estimation of Word Representations in Vector Space. In *Proceedings of ICLR Workshops*.

Tomas Mikolov, Ilya Sutskever, Kai Chen, Greg S. Corrado, and Jeff Dean. 2013b. Distributed Representations of Words and Phrases and their Compositionality. In *Proceedings of NIPS*, pages 3111–3119.

Piyush Mishra. 2020. Geolocation of Tweets with a BiLSTM Regression Model. In *Proceedings of VarDial*, pages 283–289.

Cataldo Musto, Giovanni Semeraro, Marco Degemmis, and Pasquale Lops. 2016. Learning Word Embeddings from Wikipedia for Content-Based Recommender Systems. In *Proceedings of ECIR*, pages 729–734.

Vinod Nair and Geoffrey E. Hinton. 2010. Rectified Linear Units Improve Restricted Boltzmann Machines. In *Proceedings of ICML*, pages 807–814.

Jeffrey Pennington, Richard Socher, and Christopher D. Manning. 2014. GloVe: Global Vectors for Word Representation. In *Proceedings of EMNLP*, pages 1532–1543.

Marius Popescu, Cristian Grozea, and Radu Tudor Ionescu. 2017. HASKER: An efficient algorithm for string kernels. Application to polarity classification in various languages. In *Proceedings of KES*, pages 1755–1763.

Marius Popescu and Radu Tudor Ionescu. 2013. The Story of the Characters, the DNA and the Native Language. In *Proceedings of BEA-8*, pages 270–278.

Teng Qin, Rong Xiao, Lei Fang, Xing Xie, and Lei Zhang. 2010. An efficient location extraction algorithm by leveraging web contextual information. In *Proceedings of GIS*, pages 53–60.

Gianluca Quercini, Hanan Samet, Jagan Sankaranarayanan, and Michael D. Lieberman. 2010. Determining the spatial reader scopes of news sources using local lexicons. In *Proceedings of GIS*, pages 43–52.

Alec Radford, Karthik Narasimhan, Tim Salimans, and Ilya Sutskever. 2018. Improving language understanding with unsupervised learning. Technical report, OpenAI.

Afshin Rahimi, Trevor Cohn, and Timothy Baldwin. 2017. A Neural Model for User Geolocation and Lexical Dialectology. In *Proceedings of ACL*, pages 209–216.

Stephen Roller, Michael Speriosu, Sarat Rallapalli, Benjamin Wing, and Jason Baldridge. 2012. Supervised Text-based Geolocation Using Language Models on an Adaptive Grid. In *Proceedings of EMNLP*, pages 1500–1510.

Dominic Rout, Kalina Bontcheva, Daniel Preoţiuc-Pietro, and Trevor Cohn. 2013. Where's @wally? A Classification Approach to Geolocating Users Based on their Social Ties. In *Proceedings of HT*, pages 11–20.

Yves Scherrer and Nikola Ljubešić. 2020. HeLju@VarDial 2020: Social Media Variety Geolocation with BERT Models. In *Proceedings of VarDial*, pages 202–211.

Hinrich Schütze. 1993. Word Space. In *Proceedings of NIPS*, pages 895–902.

Nitish Srivastava, Geoffrey E. Hinton, Alex Krizhevsky, Ilya Sutskever, and Ruslan Salakhutdinov. 2014. Dropout: A Simple Way to Prevent Neural Networks from Overfitting. *Journal of Machine Learning Research*, 15(1):1929–1958.

Ilya Sutskever, James Martens, and Geoffrey E. Hinton. 2011. Generating Text with Recurrent Neural Networks. In *Proceedings of ICML*, pages 1017–1024.

Benedikt Szmrecsanyi. 2008. Corpus-based dialectometry: Aggregate morphosyntactic variability in british english dialects. *International Journal of Humanities and Arts Computing*, 2(1-2):279–296.

Jonathan Tompson, Ross Goroshin, Arjun Jain, Yann LeCun, and Christoph Bregler. 2015. Efficient object localization using convolutional networks. In *Proceedings of CVPR*, pages 648–656.

Diana Tudoreanu. 2019. DTeam@VarDial 2019: Ensemble based on skip-gram and triplet loss neural networks for Moldavian vs. Romanian cross-dialect topic identification. In *Proceedings of VarDial*, pages 202–208.

Ashish Vaswani, Noam Shazeer, Niki Parmar, Jakob Uszkoreit, Llion Jones, Aidan N. Gomez, Łukasz Kaiser, and Illia Polosukhin. 2017. Attention is all you need. In *Proceedings of NIPS*, pages 5998–6008.

Leonie Weissweiler and Alexander Fraser. 2018. Developing a Stemmer for German Based on a Comparative Analysis of Publicly Available Stemmers. In *Proceedings of GSCL*, pages 81–94.

Martijn Wieling, John Nerbonne, and R. Harald Baayen. 2011. Quantitative social dialectology: Explaining linguistic variation geographically and socially. *PloS One*, 6(9):e23613.

Benjamin Wing and Jason Baldridge. 2011. Simple supervised document geolocation with geodesic grids. In *Proceedings of ACL*, pages 955–964.

Thomas Wolf, Lysandre Debut, Victor Sanh, Julien Chaumond, Clement Delangue, Anthony Moi, Pierric Cistac, Tim Rault, Remi Louf, Morgan Funtowicz, Joe Davison, Sam Shleifer, Patrick von Platen, Clara Ma, Yacine Jernite, Julien Plu, Canwen Xu, Teven Le Scao, Sylvain Gugger, Mariama Drame, Quentin Lhoest, and Alexander Rush. 2020. Transformers: State-of-the-Art Natural Language Processing. In *Proceedings of EMNLP: System Demonstrations*, pages 38–45.

Frank Wood, Cédric Archambeau, Jan Gasthaus, Lancelot James, and Yee Whye Teh. 2009. A Stochastic Memoizer for Sequence Data. In *Proceedings of ICML*, pages 1129–1136.

Xiang Zhang, Junbo Zhao, and Yann LeCun. 2015. Character-level Convolutional Networks for Text Classification. In *Proceedings of NIPS*, pages 649–657.

Optimizing a Supervised Classifier for a Difficult Language Identification Problem

Yves Bestgen
Laboratoire d'analyse statistique des textes - LAST
Institut de recherche en sciences psychologiques
Université catholique de Louvain
Place Cardinal Mercier, 10 1348 Louvain-la-Neuve, Belgium
yves.bestgen@uclouvain.be

Abstract

This paper describes the system developed by the Laboratoire d'analyse statistique des textes for the Dravidian Language Identification (DLI) shared task of VarDial 2021. This task is particularly difficult because the materials consists of short YouTube comments, written in Roman script, from three closely related Dravidian languages, and a fourth category consisting of several other languages in varying proportions, all mixed with English. The proposed system is made up of a logistic regression model which uses as only features n-grams of characters with a maximum length of 5. After its optimization both in terms of the feature weighting and the classifier parameters, it ranked first in the challenge. The additional analyses carried out underline the importance of optimization, especially when the measure of effectiveness is the Macro-F1.

1 Introduction

Identifying the language in which something is written is a prerequisite for many NLP systems, for example in information retrieval and machine translation, but also for applications as common as spell checkers. This task therefore captured the attention of researchers many years ago and, as highlighted by Jauhiainen et al. (2019), it was quickly considered to be very largely solved. This conclusion, obtained in ideal situations (only one language per text, reduced number of potential languages, relatively long documents) was far too optimistic as shown by the series of VarDial evaluation campaigns (Zampieri et al., 2020). The Dravidian Language Identification (DLI) shared task of VarDial 2021 (Chakravarthi et al., 2021) is undoubtedly a perfect example of a particularly complex situation even if the number of languages to be distinguished is small since it focuses on three Dravidian languages. The major problems it poses are:

- As stated by the task organizers, the three target Dravidian languages are closely related and some of the words are common in all these languages.
- The material includes a fourth category labeled *Other-language* which appears to contain several other languages in varying proportions.
- The material consists of short YouTube comments, written in Roman script and not in native script, which can make different languages more similar, but also standardize the way authors write. A significant number of them contain only one or two words like *Neerali* (Malayalam), *BGM chindi* (Kannada) or even a series of letters such as *A S U R A N* (Tamil).
- If two languages are represented by a large number of comments (almost 11,000 instances for Tamil and 4,000 for Malayalam), the learning material contains only 493 comments in Kannada and 1,008 in Other-language.
- Above all, these comments are one of the most extreme instances of code-mixed sentences, including inter-sentential and intra-sentential switches between a Dravidian (or other) language and English (Chakravarthi et al., 2020b,a). Both the syntax and the lexicon of the two languages are mixed and often in several points of a comment as in the following examples: *But ore oru varutham ennana Sunday release pannirukkalam yesterday aavathu announcement pannirukkalam* (Tamil) and *lalettan marana mass..intha movie bayangara hit adikkum...love from tamilnadu* (other-language).

Proceedings of the 8th VarDial Workshop on NLP for Similar Languages, Varieties and Dialects, pages 96–101
April 20, 2021 ©2021 Association for Computational Linguistics

Another difficulty is that all the instances to be classified are YouTube comments. They are therefore very similar in nature, structure and by the author's aims regardless of the language in which they are expressed. For example, many of them relate only to the number of views (*326K likes in 1 HOUR*, Tamil) or to a portion of the video that is considered by the author to be particularly interesting (*2.08 to 2.10 gun rotating style semma super*, Tamil).

In a previous edition of VarDial (Zampieri et al., 2017), I obtained good results with a relatively simple system, based mainly on character n-grams and a supervised classifier (Bestgen, 2017). The present study was aimed at determining whether this approach could be competitive in the DLI shared task. This report describes the system proposed by the Laboratoire d'analyse statistique des textes (LAST), simpler than the one used for VarDial 2017, but better optimized. It ranked first out of four systems, but it should be noted that the differences between the systems were small.

The remainder of this report first presents the data provided by the task organizers and describes the proposed system. The following section analyzes the performance obtained by comparing it to other participating systems and assesses the importance of each component and parameter of the system to its efficiency.

It must be mentioned that the LAST also participated in this year extension of the ULI 2020 task (Jauhiainen et al., 2020). I decided to not discuss this participation here partly because the system used is the same as that proposed for the DLI 2021 task and because it was not able to end up with better scores than the organizers' baseline. This is a classic criterion for eliminating underperforming systems.

2 Data provided for the challenge

The learning materials for this shared task consist of 16,674 YouTube comments from three South Dravidian subgroup language: Tamil (ISO 639-3: tam), Malayalam (ISO 639-3: mal), and Kannada (ISO 639-3: kan). All these comments were written in Roman script and most of them contain some code switching: Dravidian languages grammar with English lexicon or English grammar with Dravidian languages lexicons. The task was made even more complex by adding a fourth category of comments, also in Roman script, labeled *Other-language*, whose contains was not made clear to the participants. The average length of the comments is 8.5 tokens and 58 characters. A quarter of the comments contain 6 tokens or less. An important feature of the materials is the presence of a strong imbalance in class frequencies, with two thirds of the instances belonging to the Tamil category and one quarter belonging to the Malayalam category (see Table 1).

	Learn		Test	
Language	Freq.	%	Freq.	%
Kannada	493	3.0	63	1.4
Malayalam	4,204	25.2	1,171	25.5
Tamil	10,969	65.8	3,049	66.5
Other-language	1,008	6.0	305	6.6
Total	16,674	100	4,588	100

Table 1: Frequency distribution of the languages according to the material sets.

The test materials consisted of 4,588 comments in one of these four categories. As shown in Table 1, the imbalance between categories is even greater in the test material, an observation confirmed by a chi-square test for a contingency table ($chi^2(3) = 37.0, p < .0001$). The difference is mainly observed in the Kannada category which represents 3% of the learning set, but only 1.37% of test set.

3 Developed System

In the *Closed* submission type in which I participated, only materials provided by the organizers could be used. The main consequence was to make the automatic identification of words written in English more or less difficult and any syntactic analysis impossible. I thus chose to base the proposed system on character n-grams alone, an approach frequently used for this kind of task (Zampieri et al., 2020). The system was optimized during the training phase by means of a 5-fold cross-validation procedure, the folds of which being stratified according to the categories. During this phase, the official measure to rank the challenge participants was unknown. Due to the strong imbalance of the categories (see Table 1), I assumed that the Macro-F1 would be chosen (Opitz and Burst, 2021) and therefore used it during optimization.

This cross-validation step led to design the system as described below.

- The character n-grams of length 1 to 5 were extracted from the lowercased comments, keeping every character including spaces between tokens and punctuation marks. The n-grams located at the beginning or at the end of a comment were distinguished from the others by the presence of a specific symbol. All n-grams observed less than twice in the materials were discarded.

- Each n-gram character was weighted by BM25 (Robertson and Zaragoza, 2009; Bestgen, 2017), which is considered as one of the most effective weighting schema (Manning et al., 2008). It is a kind of TF-IDF that takes into account the length of the document. The formula is provided in Bestgen (2017).

- For each instance, the features thus formed were normalized by the L2 norm.

- The supervised classifier used was the LIBLINEAR L2-regularized logistic regression (dual) model (Fan et al., 2008). Two parameters were optimized: the regularization parameter C, which was set at 9, and the -wi options for adjusting the parameter C of different categories, which was set at 300 for Kannada, 24 for Malayalam, 1 for Tamil and 310 for Other-language.

4 Analyses and Results

The organizers of the challenge decided to use as performance measure the weighted average F1-score (WA-F1), which weights the F1-score for each class by its support and is very close to the Micro-F1. When it is important that the systems be the most effective in the most populated categories, the choice of the WA-F1 is evident. Its main weakness is to give very little importance to rare categories, as it is the case with Kannada and, to a lesser extent, with "Other-language". As the proposed system has been optimized for the Macro-F1, the results will be presented by means of both measures as did the task organizers in another study on these same languages (Chakravarthi et al., 2020a). It is important to note, however, that when some classes are very rare, a small change in effectiveness on them can have a big impact on the Macro-F1 while it will hardly change the WA-F1.

Team	WA-F1	Macro-F1
LAST	0.928	0.810
HWR	0.923	0.793
Nayel	0.915	0.765
Phlyers	0.896	0.728

Table 2: Results of the four participating teams on the test set.

4.1 Shared Task Results

As shown in Table 2, the proposed system ranked first of the four participating teams for both metrics. Looking at the system performance for the different languages, Table 3 shows that the Other-language and Kannada categories are the most difficult to identify. The performance on the Other-language category is even very poor and this is the case for all the systems submitted. On the other hand, the effectiveness for the two most frequent categories is excellent.

Language	Prec.	Recall	F1
Kannada	0.857	0.659	0.745
Malayalam	0.939	0.947	0.943
Tamil	0.961	0.959	0.960
Other-language	0.577	0.605	0.591

Table 3: Results for the four languages.

	Kan	Mal	Tam	Oth	Total
Kan	54	2	4	3	63
Mal	1	1,100	38	32	1,171
Tam	12	28	2,929	80	3,049
Oth	15	31	83	176	305
Total	82	1,161	3,054	291	4,588

Table 4: Confusion matrix.

The confusion matrix (Table 4) shows that the system distinguishes very well between the Kannada and Malayalam categories. It succeeds in identifying the true Kannada instances, but tends to assign instances of two other categories to it, as confirmed by the very clear difference between precision and recall for this category (Table 3). The errors for the Other-language category fall into the other three. It is difficult to go further in the analysis of this category without additional information on how it was constituted.

4.2 Factors Affecting the System Performance

As the organizers provided the gold-label for the test set, a series of analyzes were performed to assess almost all of the parameters and decisions made during the system development. As a reminder, the values of these paramters in the submitted system were a maximum n-gram length of 5, a frequency treshold of 2, a BM25 weighting, a L2 normalisation and a C equal to 9 with -wi. As above, both the WA-F1 and the Macro-F1 are provided in Table 5. It is interesting to note that the conclusions resulting from the analysis of the test set are generally identical to those obtained by the cross-validation approach. The main results are as follow:

- The maximal length of the character n-grams should at least be 4, but 5 is needed to get the best Macro-F1.
- Setting the minimum frequency threshold above 2 affects only the Macro-F1.
- Bestgen (2017) observed that the BM25 weighting was more effective than the sublinear TF-IDF. In the present study, the sublinear TF-IDF (Zampieri et al., 2015) and the log-entropy weighting schema (Jarvis et al., 2013) are as effective as BM25 for the WA-F1. On the other hand, for the Macro-F1, BM25 is more effective. It is also observed that a logarithmic weighting of the n-gram frequencies is desirable.
- L2 normalization clearly improves performance, especially on the Macro-F1.
- Using the -wi parameter improves the Macro-F1. This result was expected since this parameter was designed to improve LIBLINEAR processing of unbalanced data. On the other hand, the C parameter has only a limited impact, except when it is as small as 1.

Parameter	WA-F1	Macro-F1
N-gram length		
3	**-0.021**	**-0.049**
4	-0.005	-0.017
6	-0.001	-0.005
7	-0.001	-0.005
8	-0.003	-0.009
Freq. threshold		
3	-0.001	-0.004
5	-0.002	-0.010
10	**-0.003**	**-0.013**
Weighting		
Binary	-0.006	**-0.017**
Freq.	**-0.010**	**-0.017**
Logarithmic	-0.005	-0.012
TF-IDF	0.000	-0.003
Log-entropy	0.000	-0.004
Normalisation		
None	**-0.007**	**-0.030**
Range [0,1]	**-0.007**	**-0.030**
C without -wi		
1	**-0.038**	**-0.140**
9	-0.013	-0.038
50	-0.007	-0.017
200	-0.006	-0.017
1000	-0.005	-0.016
C with -wi		
1	**-0.014**	**-0.019**
5	-0.002	-0.005
8	-0.001	-0.002
10	0.000	-0.001
15	-0.001	-0.003

Table 5: Impact of the parameter values on the test set performance: difference from the submitted system. The most negative differences, corresponding to the worst value of a parameter, are in bold.

In the preceding analyzes, only one parameter was modified at a time in order to avoid a combinatorial explosion if a complete design had been evaluated. This last analysis presents the performance of a system that has not been fully optimized to compare it to the other three systems which participated in the shared task. This system employs n-grams from 1 to 5 characters, a frequency threshold of 10, a logarithmic weighting and no normalization. As the two LIBLINEAR parameters have little impact on its effectiveness, it is the version using the optimized C and wi parameters, which narrowly obtains the best scores, that is presented. Its WA-F1 was 0.915 (-0.014) and its Macro-F1 was 0.772 (-0.032). It would have been tied for 3rd, quite far from the system that came second (see Table 2). Above all, its Macro-F1 is much lower.

In these analyzes, the differences are clearly greater on the Macro-F1 than on the WA-F1. Moreover, the comparison of these two scores shows that, if one can have the impression that the automatic identification of the three Dravidian languages is on the way to being solved when using the WA-F1, it is very far from being the case if the Macro-F1 is privileged. Measuring performance in automatic classification on unbalanced data has already caused much debate and the present study was not designed to provide an answer. At the very least, it underlines how important it is that the measure used in a shared task is carefully considered and that the participants are informed before the start of the training phase.

5 Discussion and Conclusion

Given the difficulty of the DLI 2021 task, the level of performance achieved by the system is appreciable. Identifying the Other-language category was particularly difficult because it may be thought that it is not homogeneous but composed of different languages in varying proportions. It is not even certain that all the other languages present in the test set were also present in the learning set. The additional analyzes highlighted the positive impact of a series of decisions made during the development of the system, most notably a maximum length of n-grams greater than 3, a logarithmic weighting of the frequency, an L2 normalization and optimising LIBLINEAR parameters in cross validation.

The designed system completely neglects an important dimension of the task: code-switching. The main reason is that since a system participating in the *Closed* submission type was not allowed to use any data or linguistic resources other than those provided by the organizers (see the *Submission Types* section in `https://sites.google.com/view/vardial2021/evaluation-campaign`), trying to identify the English words might have required a lot of effort while the simple use of an English word lists would have made this task much simpler. Taking code-switching into account is certainly a development path.

A question that could be interesting to address in the future is to try to determine if certain parameters are generalizable to the previous VarDial shared tasks (see Jauhiainen et al. (2019) for an extensive survey). BM25 seems a good choice. One might think that logarithmic weighting and L2 normalization are too. Setting the n-gram length at 5 based on the present study is certainly much more questionable. A priori, the language to be identified should have a significant impact, but on the other hand, it's still about character n-grams with the same supervised classifier.

Acknowledgments

The author is a Research Associate of the Fonds de la Recherche Scientifique (FRS-FNRS).

References

Yves Bestgen. 2017. Improving the character ngram model for the DSL task with BM25 weighting and less frequently used feature sets. In *Proceedings of the Fourth Workshop on NLP for Similar Languages, Varieties and Dialects (VarDial)*, pages 115–123, Valencia, Spain.

Bharathi Raja Chakravarthi, Mihaela Găman, Radu Tudor Ionescu, Heidi Jauhiainen, Tommi Jauhiainen, Krister Lindén, Nikola Ljubešić, Niko Partanen, Ruba Priyadharshini, Christoph Purschke, Eswari Rajagopal, Yves Scherrer, and Marcos Zampieri. 2021. Findings of the VarDial Evaluation Campaign 2021. In *Proceedings of the Eighth Workshop on NLP for Similar Languages, Varieties and Dialects (VarDial)*.

Bharathi Raja Chakravarthi, Navya Jose, Shardul Suryawanshi, Elizabeth Sherly, and John Philip McCrae. 2020a. A sentiment analysis dataset for code-mixed Malayalam-English. In *Proceedings of the 1st Joint Workshop on Spoken Language Technologies for Under-resourced languages (SLTU) and Collaboration and Computing for Under-Resourced Languages (CCURL)*, pages 177–184, Marseille, France. European Language Resources association.

Bharathi Raja Chakravarthi, Vigneshwaran Muralidaran, Ruba Priyadharshini, and John Philip McCrae. 2020b. Corpus creation for sentiment analysis in code-mixed Tamil-English text. In *Proceedings of the 1st Joint Workshop on Spoken Language Technologies for Under-resourced languages (SLTU) and Collaboration and Computing for Under-Resourced Languages (CCURL)*, pages 202–210, Marseille, France. European Language Resources association.

Rong-En Fan, Kai-Wei Chang, Cho-Jui Hsieh, Xiang-Rui Wang, and Chih-Jen Lin. 2008. LIBLINEAR: A library for large linear classification. *Journal of Machine Learning Research*, 9:1871–1874.

Scott Jarvis, Yves Bestgen, and Steve Pepper. 2013. Maximizing classification accuracy in native language identification. In *Proceedings of The 8th Workshop on Innovative Use of NLP for Building Educational Applications (NAACL-HLT)*, pages 111–118.

Tommi Jauhiainen, Heidi Jauhiainen, Niko Partanen, and Krister Lindén. 2020. Uralic Language Identification (ULI) 2020 shared task dataset and the Wanca 2017 corpus. In *Proceedings of the Seventh Workshop on NLP for Similar Languages, Varieties and Dialects (VarDial)*, pages 688–698.

Tommi Jauhiainen, Marco Lui, Marcos Zampieri, Timothy Baldwin, and Krister Lindén. 2019. Automatic Language Identification in Texts: A Survey. *Journal of Artificial Intelligence Research*, 65:675–782.

Christopher D. Manning, Prabhakar Raghavan, and Hinrich Schütze. 2008. *An Introduction to Information Retrieval*. Cambridge University Press.

Juri Opitz and Sebastian Burst. 2021. Macro F1 and macro F1.

Stephen Robertson and Hugo Zaragoza. 2009. The probabilistic relevance framework: BM25 and beyond. *Foundations and Trends in Information Retrieval*, 3(4):333–389.

Marcos Zampieri, Binyam Gebrekidan Gebre, Hernani Costa, and Josef van Genabith. 2015. Comparing approaches to the identification of similar languages. In *Proceedings of the Joint Workshop on Language Technology for Closely Related Languages, Varieties and Dialects (LT4VarDial)*, pages 66–72, Hissar, Bulgaria.

Marcos Zampieri, Shervin Malmasi, Nikola Ljubešić, Preslav Nakov, Ahmed Ali, Jörg Tiedemann, Yves Scherrer, and Noëmi Aepli. 2017. Findings of the VarDial Evaluation Campaign 2017. In *Proceedings of the Fourth Workshop on NLP for Similar Languages, Varieties and Dialects (VarDial)*, Valencia, Spain.

Marcos Zampieri, Preslav Nakov, and Yves Scherrer. 2020. Natural language processing for similar languages, varieties, and dialects: A survey. *Natural Language Engineering*, 26(6):595–612.

Comparing the Performance of CNNs and Shallow Models for Language Identification

Andrea Ceolin
Università di Modena e Reggio Emilia
ceolin@unimore.it

Abstract

In this work we compare the performance of convolutional neural networks and shallow models on three out of the four language identification shared tasks proposed in the VarDial Evaluation Campaign 2021. In our experiments, convolutional neural networks and shallow models yielded comparable performance in the Romanian Dialect Identification (RDI) and the Dravidian Language Identification (DLI) shared tasks, after the training data was augmented, while an ensemble of support vector machines and Naïve Bayes models was the best performing model in the Uralic Language Identification (ULI) task. While the deep learning models did not achieve state-of-the-art performance at the tasks and tended to overfit the data, the ensemble method was one of two methods that beat the existing baseline for the first track of the ULI shared task. [1]

1 Introduction

In this paper, we present the submissions of Team Phlyers to the VarDial Evaluation Campaign 2021 (Chakravarthi et al., 2021). The campaign is part of a conference series, the Workshop on NLP for Similar Languages, Varieties and Dialects (VarDial), which has reached its eighth edition, five of which have included several shared tasks (Zampieri et al., 2017, 2018, 2019; Găman et al., 2020). The shared tasks typically involve the categorization of texts according to their language or their dialect. This task, known as language identification, is a classical NLP problem (House and Neuburg, 1977; Dunning, 1994; McNamee, 2005), because of its importance for information retrieval, machine translation, and more recently categorization of social media posts (Bergsma et al., 2012; Lui and Baldwin, 2014; Zubiaga et al., 2016).

[1]The code for the models employed in this work is found at https://github.com/AndreaCeolin/VarDial2021.

In the next sections, we briefly describe the three tasks that we participated in.

1.1 RDI

The VarDial 2019 edition (Zampieri et al., 2019) proposed the first shared task based on distinguishing standard Romanian from Moldavian newspaper articles. The task consisted in training a classifier on news articles in Romanian and Moldavian from the MOROCO corpus (Butnaru and Ionescu, 2019), and using it to classify other news articles yet to be added to the corpus. The best model achieved an F_1 score of 0.895 on the test set, using an ensemble method based on convolutional neural networks (CNN) and support vector machines (SVM) (Tudoreanu, 2019).

Last year's task asked participants to train a classifier on the news articles of the MOROCO corpus to distinguish standard Romanian from Moldavian tweets (Găman et al., 2020). The task was particularly interesting because the organizers provided a large validation dataset based on news articles (5923), and only a small validation dataset based on tweets (215). This made the validation stage challenging, because on the one hand a model trained on news articles which yields high accuracy on the news validation dataset could fail to generalize to a different domain, while on the other hand the size of the tweets validation dataset was so small that by training a model only on tweets, the risk of overfitting was considerable. The best result on the task was obtained by an ensemble of linear SVM classifiers (Çöltekin, 2020), which yielded an accuracy of F_1=0.788 on the test data. A similar accuracy (F_1=0.775) was reached by fine-tuned Romanian BERT models (Popa and Stefănescu, 2020). Attempts that relied on Naïve Bayes (NB) models yielded lower accuracies (Jauhiainen et al., 2020a; Ceolin and Zhang, 2020).

The shared task has been proposed again in this

Proceedings of the 8th VarDial Workshop on NLP for Similar Languages, Varieties and Dialects, pages 102–112
April 20, 2021 ©2021 Association for Computational Linguistics

year's VarDial edition, in which a new dataset of tweets in standard Romanian and Moldavian was made available to the participants.

1.2 ULI

The Uralic Language Identification task (ULI) differs from traditional tasks in the high number of language varieties that are present in the dataset (Jauhiainen et al., 2020b; Găman et al., 2020). In total, there are 178 languages that need to be distinguished, which include the 29 Uralic varieties which are the focus of the task, 3 extra Uralic languages (Finnish, Estonian, and Hungarian) and 146 other non-Uralic languages. Moreover, the classes are imbalanced: for the 29 Uralic varieties, the number of sentences vary from 19 to 214,225, while for the other languages the range is much higher (from 10K to 3 million).

The shared task is divided in three separate subtasks. The first subtask requires a model to distinguish among the 29 Uralic varieties giving equal importance to each of the classes, and is evaluated through a macro F_1 score. In the second subtask, classes are weighted according to their frequency, and thus a micro F_1 score is used. In the third subtask, the models are evaluated on all 178 languages.

The high number of classes, their overlap, and the imbalanced dataset all represent challenges for deep learning algorithms: in particular, they can lead to overfitting if the traning set is not balanced (Bernier-Colborne and Goutte, 2020). On the other hand, the same problem might affect shallow methods like SVMs, since they need to identify many distinct separation hyperplanes in a domain where many languages are virtually indistinguishable.

The shared task was presented for the first time during the VarDial Evaluation Campaign 2020 (Găman et al., 2020), and in that case the best performing system for all tracks was the HeLI method (Jauhiainen et al., 2016), which was the baseline presented by the organizers. Since the HeLI baselines were not improved, the task has been proposed again in this year's edition.

1.3 DLI

The Dravidian Language Identification task (DLI) requires participants to classify three South Dravidian languages (Tamil, Malayalam, and Kannada) using a dataset of 16,672 YouTube comments (Chakravarthi et al., 2020b,a; Hande et al., 2020). The comments are written in Roman script.

This task differs from the others in being focused on code-switching: all comments contain a mix of words from the target language and words from English, and in some cases native words can appear within an English grammatical structure. Classifiers must then be robust to this variability and be able to not be deceived by the English material. Another interesting feature of this task is the large class imbalance in the training set (with about 10K comments in Tamil, 4K in Malayalam, and only about 500 in Kannada) and the fact that both the training and the test datasets contain comments from other languages (under the label 'other-language', approximately 1K comments).

This is the first edition of this task.

2 Methods

Previous methods used for language identification typically involve SVMs (Goutte et al., 2014; Çöltekin and Rama, 2017; Medvedeva et al., 2017; Kreutz and Daelemans, 2018; Benites de Azevedo e Souza et al., 2018; Wu et al., 2019) and multinomial NB models applied to word and character ngrams (Barbaresi, 2016; Clematide and Makarov, 2017; Jauhiainen et al., 2016, 2020a). Deep learning methods based on CNNs and LSTMs have also been successfully applied to language identification tasks (Jaech et al., 2016; Butnaru and Ionescu, 2019; Hu et al., 2019; Tudoreanu, 2019), and the last two editions of VarDial also showed successful applications of BERT models (Bernier-Colborne et al., 2019; Popa and Stefănescu, 2020; Scherrer and Ljubešić, 2020; Zaharia et al., 2020).

For the current tasks, we employed NB and SVM models trained on character ngrams as baselines, and compared their performance with that of a CNN. For the CNN, we decided to use the character-based model for text classification that was developed by Zhang et al. (2015), and that was successfully adopted by Butnaru and Ionescu (2019) to distinguish between standard Romanian and Moldavian news texts. The architecture of the CNN is summarized in Table 1. All models were run using Google Colab, with 1 GPU.[2]

3 Results

This section summarizes our contributions to the three shared tasks, the evaluation of our models, and their performance on the test datasets.

[2]https://colab.research.google.com

	Type	In	Out	Kernel	MaxPool	Stride
1	Conv.	(*)	128	7	3	3
2	Conv.	128	128	7	3	3
3	Conv.	128	128	3	3	3
4	Linear	(*)	1000	-	-	-
5	Linear	1000	1000	-	-	-
6	Linear	1000	(*)	-	-	-

Table 1: CNN architecture. Filters applied over a single dimension. Loss function=CrossEntropy, Optimizer = Adam. DropOut is added to the two fully connected layers (0.5). ReLu threshold: 10^{-6}. Output is passed through Softmax. The dimensions marked with (*) are task specific.

3.1 RDI

A question that remains open after last year's edition is whether deep learning methods can achieve a good accuracy at distinguishing between standard Romanian and Moldavian tweets even with limited training data. The deep learning models that were used in last year's task (Popa and Stefănescu, 2020; Zaharia et al., 2020) all relied on pre-trained BERT models (Dumitrescu et al., 2020), which might not always be available when working on low-resource languages. Even though CNNs have been successfully applied to the task of distinguishing news texts between the two language varieties (Butnaru and Ionescu, 2019), in our contribution to last year's edition we have showed that the representations they learn fail to generalize to the tweets domain (Ceolin and Zhang, 2020). This year we readdressed this issue using the new dataset.

3.1.1 CNN

In last year's edition, a small dataset of 215 tweets was given to the participants to evaluate the model. Since this year's edition provides a larger amount of in-domain data (5237 tweets), we decided to use the model we trained last year and fine-tune it using the larger tweets validation dataset available for this year's task. We also decided to train a separate model on tweets-data only, to see if the use of out-of-domain news data leads to a better performance than a model trained only on tweets.

In order to augment the data, we experimented with some of the data augmentation techniques proposed by Wei and Zou (2019). The one which turned out to be the most successful was random swap, especially when it was used multiple times on the same sentence rather than just once (i.e., essentially shuffling the words in the sentence). See the Appendix for a more detailed summary of the data augmentation experiments.

After some trial runs, we decided to set a batch size of 128, and a learning rate of 0.001. We used 1/5 of the data to create a validation dataset, while the rest was used for training. The training data is augmented with 10 replications that involve shuffled sentences. On the basis of training and validation accuracies, we decided to interrupted training after 10 epochs on the original training data, and after 5 epochs on the augmented dataset.

3.1.2 Shallow models

We also trained a NB and a linear SVM model on TFIDF-transformed character ngrams in the [5-8] range, which was determined to be the optimal range for these languages in Ceolin and Zhang (2020). The models have not been fine-tuned, and have been evaluated using the same validation dataset selected to evaluate the CNN.

3.1.3 Evaluation

The tweets dataset was already balanced, with 2625 standard Romanian tweets and 2612 Moldavian tweets. As we see in Table 2, data augmentation improved the performance of the CNNs dramatically, to the point that it became comparable to that of shallow models.

Model	Macro F_1 score
NB	0.760
CNN (news+tweets) + data aug.	**0.756**
Linear SVM	0.756
CNN (tweets) + data aug.	0.749
CNN (news+tweets)	0.709
CNN (tweets)	0.700

Table 2: Final performance of the models on the evaluation of the RDI task.

For instance, if we take a look at the CNN (news+tweets) model, Figure 1 shows that after training for 10 epochs the performance on the validation set reaches a macro F_1 score of 0.709, while in Figure 2 we see that in the augmented dataset the accuracy is well above 0.7 after the first epoch, and converges to $\approx$0.76 after five epochs. The same is true for the model trained only on tweets, whose accuracy jumps from 0.7 to 0.75.

3.1.4 Results

We decided to submit two runs to the RDI shared task. Both contained the predictions of the CNN pre-trained on news articles and then fine-tuned on augmented tweets, but the second submission

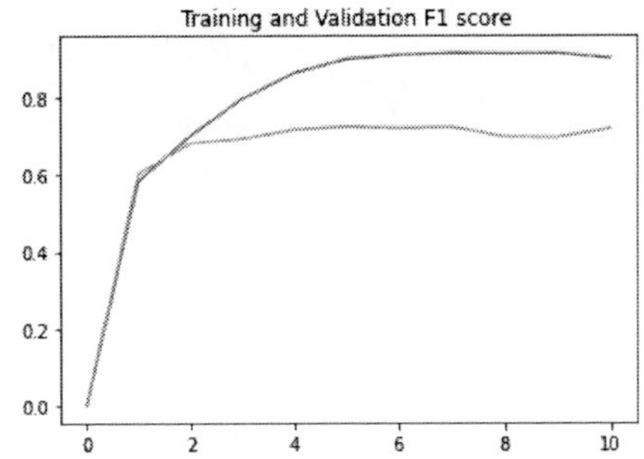

Figure 1: CNN news + tweets model. Comparing the training and validation performance measured by macro F_1 score through 10 epochs of training. Blue line: training; orange line: validation. The training dataset is not augmented.

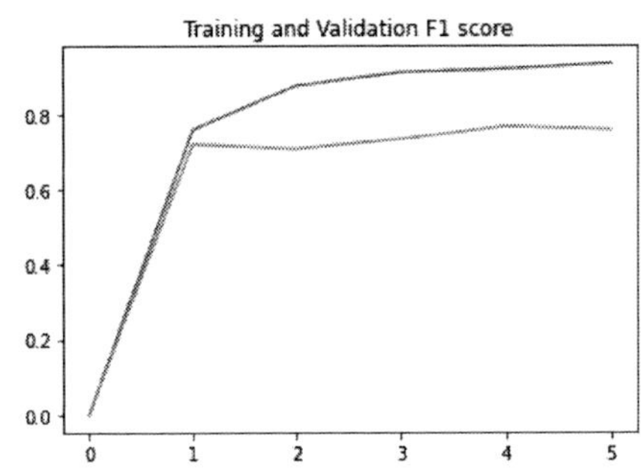

Figure 2: CNN news + tweets model. Comparing the training and validation performance measured by macro F_1 score through 5 epochs of training. Blue line: training; orange line: validation. Training set augmented.

resulted from a model were data augmentation had an increased weight (from x10 to x12).

Table 3 contains the results of the best runs of the three teams that took part in the task. The best accuracy (0.777) was reached by SUKI, who last year proposed a NB model trained on character ngrams (Jauhiainen et al., 2020a), while the second best accuracy (0.732) was reached by the UPB team (Zaharia et al., 2020), who last year addressed the task using a BERT model. The CNN we presented did not reach comparable performance, even though an inspection of precision and recall did not point to any obvious explanation: the network just ended up overfitting the training data. Our second run was not competitive, because increased data augmentation without changing the other parameters of the CNN led to even more overfitting.

Model	Macro F_1 score
SUKI	0.777
UPB	0.732
Phlyers	**0.653**

Table 3: Final performance of the teams' submissions to the RDI task.

Considering that the network was trained on the full tweets dataset rather than 80% of it before the submission, stopping the iterations after the first or the second epoch would have been a wiser choice, since we have seen that no considerable improvement of the valuation performance was made after the first few epochs, and therefore additional training might have led to overfitting.

3.2 ULI

As we previously mentioned, this task appeared to be the most challenging one, given the high amount of labels and the great class imbalance. In particular, the first subtask required the models to be able to accurately classify languages which were represented by a few dozen sentences.

The strategy we adopted to address these issues was to train two separate classifiers for two different classification problems. First, we want to be able to distinguish the 29 'target' Uralic languages from the 149 'non-target' languages. Once we have a model that can distinguish the two types of languages, we can train a second classifier to distinguish among the 29 target languages using features only extracted from such languages. In this way, the second model would be able to extract more features which are only needed to separate the 29 target languages, even though employing them in the first stage might produce some errors, in addition to more computational cost.

3.2.1 Distinguishing 'target' and 'non-target' languages

Defining a unique alphabet for the entire training dataset is unfeasible, since languages make use of different writing systems, and this fact makes it practically difficult to train a character-based CNN for the task. Therefore, we decided to focus on shallow models in this first stage. For this binary classification task, we trained a linear SVM and a NB method. In addition to the 646,043 sentences for the target languages, we used 5000 sentences for each of the non-target language, obtaining a total of 1,391,043 sentences for the 178 languages of the task. We then used 5-fold cross-validation to evaluate the classifier.

After some trial runs, we found that a linear SVM classifier trained on TF-IDF transformed character ngrams in the range [3,4], with the number of features limited to the 100,000 most frequent ones, converges to a 0.995 macro F_1 score. We will then use this classifier to single out the target languages in the test dataset.

Model	Ngrams	Macro F_1 score
Linear SVM	[3]	0.992
Linear SVM	[4]	0.994
Linear SVM	[5]	0.991
Linear SVM	[3,4]	**0.995**
NB	[3]	0.976
NB	[4]	0.986
NB	[5]	0.988
NB	[4,5]	0.985

Table 4: Evaluation of the models used to distinguish 'target' from 'non-target' languages.

3.2.2 Classifying 'target' languages

We first attempted to train a CNN for this subtask, but we could not develop a system that was able to deal with the large class imbalance and with the high number of different labels that need to be learned. We then retrained our shallow models for the task of distinguishing among the target languages. The best performing model was a NB model trained on TFIDF character ngrams, with ngrams in the range [3,5] and alpha=10^{-6} (cf. Table 5). Rare ngrams, those whose relative document frequency was less than $<10^{-4}$, were excluded. The model parameters were selected through 5-fold cross-validation.

Model	Ngrams	Macro F_1	Micro F_1
Linear SVM	[3]	0.748	0.964
Linear SVM	[4]	0.765	0.965
Linear SVM	[5]	0.772	0.962
NB	[3]	0.871	0.976
NB	[4]	0.909	0.983
NB	[5]	0.911	0.985
NB	[4,5]	0.907	0.985
NB	[3,5]	**0.915**	**0.986**

Table 5: Evaluation of the models used to distinguish among the 'target' languages.

3.2.3 Evaluation - Track 1 and 2

In order to evaluate our system, we decided to create a 80/20 training-test split. First, the SVM is trained on 80% of the dataset in order to determine whether the sentences in the test set are from target or non-target languages. Then, the NB model assigns a label to the sentences that are recognized as target sentences. The results are in Table 6.

Model	Macro F_1	Micro F_1
Linear SVM + NB	**0.905**	**0.988**

Table 6: Evaluation of the final model.

We see that the full model yields a macro F_1 score of 0.905. We noted that precision was higher than recall (0.958 versus 0.878), and in particular rare languages are associated to low recall scores. This means that the system does not make 'wrong' predictions often, but it can fail to identify the less common varieties.

The micro F_1 score for the system is about 0.99, as expected.

3.2.4 Evaluation - Track 3

The model we devised could not be used for a submission to Track 3, because the non-target languages are excluded in the first step. For this reason, we decided to retrain our models to directly predict the labels, and to use 5-fold cross-validation to evaluate them.

In this case, we need to increase the threshold for filtering rare ngrams to 10^{-3} for memory constraints, and to limit the analysis to NB systems, since the high number of labels makes working with SVMs more challenging. The best model we selected was a NB model with TFIDF transformed character 5-grams (F_1=0.949, see Table 7).

Model	Ngrams	Macro F1
NB	[3]	0.937
NB	[4]	0.946
NB	[5]	**0.949**

Table 7: Evaluation of the models developed for Track 3.

SVM+NB (1,2)	NB (3)	$Ensemble_1$	$Ensemble_2$
NA	NA	NA	NA
NA	$Target_b$	NA	$Target_b$
$Target_a$	NA	$Target_a$	NA
$Target_a$	$Target_b$	$\mathbf{Target_{a\text{-}b}}$	$\mathbf{Target_a}$

Table 8: Ensemble methods developed for the three subtasks. $Target_a$ refers to the prediction of a language on target made by the classifier developed for Track 1 and 2, while $Target_b$ refers to the prediction of a language on target made by the classifier developed for Track 3. Note how the predictions of the two ensemble models are essentially the same, respectively, of the two main models, but they differ in how they assign a label to a target language when there is disagreement between the two main classifiers.

3.2.5 Results

We submitted the two systems we described in the preceding sections (SVM+NB for Track 1 and 2, and NB for Track 3) for evaluation. In addition, we submitted the prediction of two ensemble models, that we summarize in Table 8. The models are derived from the two main models, but their predictions change when the two main models are in disagreement about which of two target languages is the correct label. The first ensemble ($Ensemble_1$) model uses all the predictions of the model developed for Track 1 and 2, but there is one case in which the prediction of the model developed for Track 3 are selected instead: when the first model predicts one of the five rare languages of the dataset, Ingrian (izh), Nganasan (nio), Kemi Sami (sjk), Ume Sami (sju), Votic (vot), and the second model predicts a different target language, then this second target language is selected instead. Our motivation is the following: if the model erroneously predicts a language which is not in the test set, precision for that language will go to zero, and the performance of the classifier will significantly drop. This strategy will make sure that the prediction is indeed accurate when dealing with rare languages. In this case, if the signal between the two classifiers is conflicting, it appears wiser to default to the prediction of the most common class.

The second ensemble ($Ensemble_2$) takes the predictions of the NB model developed for Track 3, but when the SVM+NB model predicts a different target language, then this more refined prediction is chosen instead, under the assumption that since the SVM+NB model has been developed specifically for distinguishing among target languages, its predictions should be more accurate.

The results for the three tasks are summarized in Table 9, Table 10 and Table 11.

As for Track 1 (Table 9), the first ensemble system was the best performing system among those we submitted, and the second best overall, although all teams provided systems with similar performances and architectures. It is noticeable how combining the predictions of the two different systems we devised for the task, with the aim of improving the classification of the rare languages, led to a significant improvement over the performance of the two systems taken separately.

Team	Model	Macro F_1
NRC	Probabilistic Classifier, ch.5grams	0.8138
Phlyers	**$\mathbf{Ensemble_1}$ (SVM+NB), ch. 3-5grams**	**0.8085**
Phlyers	$Ensemble_2$ (SVM+NB), ch. 3-5grams	0.8076
SUKI	HeLI	0.8004
Phlyers	NB ch. 5grams	0.7977
LAST	Logistic R., ch.1-3grams, BM25	0.7977
Phlyers	SVM (ch.3-4grams)+NB (ch.3-5grams)	0.7740

Table 9: Results for Track 1.

As for Track 2 (Table 10), $Ensemble_1$ and the SVM+NB model yielded the same performance (0.84), which was clearly below the baseline established by HeLI (Jauhiainen et al., 2020b), and below the performance of the systems submitted by the other teams. During the evaluation of our submissions, the organizers also provided us with the precision and recall scores, and it was clear that the failure was entirely due to the low precision of the systems. Since our evaluation set was balanced between target and non-target languages (with about 30% of the sentences belonging to the target set), the precision scores looked acceptable, but an error analysis clearly showed that the systems had the tendency of assigning a target label to a non-target language more often than the opposite, even though it was precisely this behavior that we were hoping to avoid with the SVM classifier.

Since our system still failed to filter out some non-target languages, precision was drastically reduced in the test phase, where non-target languages clearly outnumbered target languages (sentences belonging to target languages were about 2% of the whole sample, according to the SVM model).

Indeed, we also submitted the model we developed for Track 3, and the second ensemble, but both attempts yielded an even lower performance, which suggests that the SVM filter was partially successful at filtering out non-target languages, even though it was not sufficient to achieve state-of-the-art performance.

Team	Model	Micro F_1
NRC	Probabilistic Classifier using ch. 5grams	0.9668
SUKI	HeLI	0.9632
NRC	BERT Deep Neural Network	0.9530
LAST	Logistic R., ch.1-3grams, BM25	0.9496
Phlyers	**SVM(ch.3-4grams)+NB(ch.3-5grams)**	**0.8389**
Phlyers	NB ch. 5grams	0.5934
Phlyers	$Ensemble_2$ (SVM+NB), cf.3-5grams	0.5932

Table 10: Results for Track 2.

Finally, for Track 3 (Table 11) none of the systems submitted to the task were able to beat the strong baseline set by HeLI. Even though in this case the performance of our systems was close to that of the systems submitted by LAST and NRC, ours were not able to reach the performance of the other teams.

Team	Model	Macro F_1
SUKI	HeLI	0.9252
LAST	Logistic R., ch.1-3grams, BM25	0.9164
NRC	Probabilistic Classifier, ch.5grams	0.9079
NRC	BERT Deep Neural Network	0.9039
Phlyers	**$Ensemble_2$ (SVM+NB), ch.3-5grams**	**0.8847**
Phlyers	NB ch. 5grams	0.8831

Table 11: Results for Track 3.

3.3 DLI

As we said above, this task is focused on code-switching, and this means that many features that could be extracted are completely irrelevant to determine the original language of the text. The great class imbalance is another problem that needs to be addressed. Especially in the design of deep learning architectures, some strategy to prevent overfitting was required.

3.3.1 CNN

We addressed this task using the same CNN developed for the RDI task, with an important difference. Since in this case we have to deal with class imbalance, we decided to perform balanced sampling during the training phase.

First, 1/5 of the labeled data was randomly selected for evaluation purposes as a validation dataset, and the rest was used for training. Then, we sampled a total of 25,000 sentences uniformly across the four categories by selecting each of the four classes with p=0.25, and each sentence with p=$1/n_C$, with n_C being the number of sentences available for each class. This will necessarily imply that many sentences will be picked more than once, especially for the classes which are not well represented.

In order to avoid repeating the same sentences for the more uncommon classes, we decided to shuffle the order of the words in the sentences, essentially adopting the data augmentation strategy that was employed for the RDI task. This strategy had two purposes: dealing with class imbalance by augmenting the data of the classes which were not well represented, and addressing the problem of the influence of the English grammar, by exposing the network to sentences in which the order of the words was changed, with the aim of retrieving word sequences that were not in the training data, but were still possible in the language. We also trained a separate model where instead the order of the words was not shuffled, and therefore sentences in the training dataset were just repeated.

Since most of the comments are short, only the first 160 characters per comment were used as input to the network. After some parameter tuning, we set the learning rate to 0.001, and the batch size is 256. We also reduced the output of the second linear layer to 500. Training was interrupted after 10 epochs.

3.3.2 Shallow models

Following the strategy adopted for the RDI task, we trained a NB and a linear SVM model on TFIDF-transformed character ngrams in the [5-8] range. The models have not been fine-tuned, and have been evaluated using the same dataset used to evaluate the CNN.

3.3.3 Evaluation

Table 12 shows the micro F_1 score, which was the metric used to rank the submissions, for the models evaluated.

The patterns are similar to those we have obtained in the RDI task: shuffling words had the effect of improving the performance of the CNN. Figure 3 and Figure 4 show that in this case shuffling had only a marginal effect on the task, since in both cases training and validation performances were comparable.

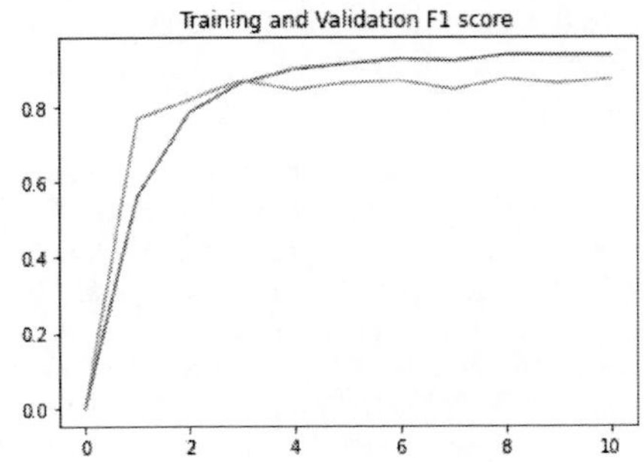

Figure 3: CNN model. Comparing the training and validation performance measured by micro F_1 score through 10 epochs of training. Blue line: training; orange line: validation. Sentences are not shuffled.

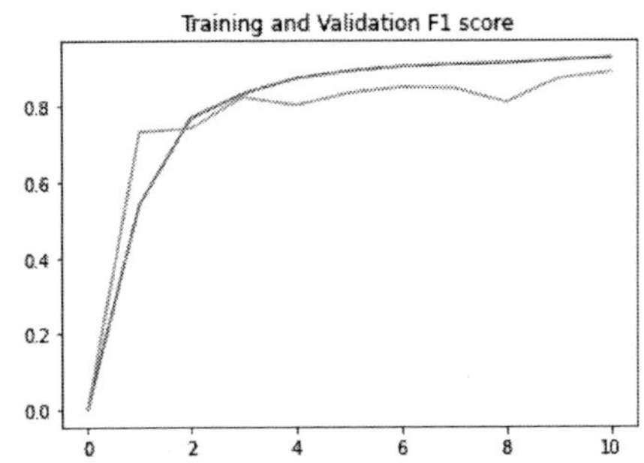

Figure 4: CNN model. Comparing the training and validation performance measured by micro F_1 score through 10 epochs of training. Blue line: training; orange line: validation. Sentences are shuffled.

We then submitted our best model for evaluation.

Model	Micro F_1 score
CNN (shuffle)	**0.880**
NB	0.878
CNN (no shuffle)	0.870
Linear SVM	0.848

Table 12: Final performance of the models on the evaluation of the DLI task.

3.3.4 Results

The results of the evaluation campaign are in Table 13. Our model performed as expected, with a micro F_1 score of 0.9. The performance was comparable to the submission of the other three teams, which however all yielded a better F_1 score.

The only systematic difference between our submission and the others was a low F_1 score for the 'other-languages' class (0.46), while all teams were able to achieve a score of at least 0.54. This suggests that our network was not able to obtain a representation of this class as robust as that obtained by the other classifiers.

Model	Micro F_1 score
LAST	0.93
Nayel	0.92
HWR	0.92
Phlyers	**0.90**

Table 13: Final performance of the teams' submissions to the DLI task.

4 Conclusion

The last editions of the VarDial evaluation campaign (Zampieri et al., 2019; Găman et al., 2020) have seen an increased use of deep learning techniques for language identification, which in several cases yielded the best performance at the tasks (Tudoreanu, 2019; Bernier-Colborne et al., 2019). In this work, we tried to compare the performance of CNNs and shallow models for three out of the four tasks at VarDial 2021. While for the ULI task developing a CNN turned out to be challenging, for both the RDI and the DLI task CNNs yielded performances which were in line with the baselines established by the more classic shallow models, even though the final results showed that they are prone to overfitting.

It is interesting to note that shuffling the words in the training data improved the accuracy of our CNN classifiers, in particular for the RDI task. The procedure essentially introduces noise in the data, because the order of the words in the sentences will be ungrammatical after they are shuffled, so why it improves the performance of the classifier is not clear. One possibility is that it introduces the network to word combinations that would be possible in the language (for instance, but switching a subject and an object, or by juxtaposing words separated by modifiers), increasing the diversification of the training data. Another possibility is that since shuffling words does not affect character sequences within words, but at word boundaries, shuffling has the effect of preventing the network from focusing on sequences with spaces in the middle, which could be less meaningful than sequences within words to learn the lexicon and the morphology associated to each language variety. In the current experiments, this strategy had the effect of reducing overfitting. This outcome will require more investigation in the future.

While data augmentation is popular in image

classification (Wang and Perez, 2017; Cubuk et al., 2019), it has so far had limited application in NLP (Coulombe, 2018; Kobayashi, 2018; Wei and Zou, 2019). Our experiments on the VarDial 2021 shared tasks suggest that data augmentation can play an important role in adapting neural models to the task of language identification.

Acknowledgments

Thanks to the co-founder of Team Phlyers, Hong Zhang.

References

Adrien Barbaresi. 2016. An Unsupervised Morphological Criterion for Discriminating Similar Languages. In *Proceedings of the Third Workshop on NLP for Similar Languages, Varieties and Dialects (VarDial3)*, pages 212–220, Osaka, Japan.

Shane Bergsma, Paul McNamee, Mossaab Bagdouri, Clayton Fink, and Theresa Wilson. 2012. Language identification for creating language-specific Twitter collections. In *Proceedings of the second workshop on language in social media*, pages 65–74.

Gabriel Bernier-Colborne and Cyril Goutte. 2020. Challenges in neural language identification: NRC at VarDial 2020. In *Proceedings of the 7th Workshop on NLP for Similar Languages, Varieties and Dialects*, pages 273–282.

Gabriel Bernier-Colborne, Cyril Goutte, and Serge Léger. 2019. Improving cuneiform language identification with BERT. In *Proceedings of the Sixth Workshop on NLP for Similar Languages, Varieties and Dialects*, pages 17–25.

Andrei M. Butnaru and Radu Tudor Ionescu. 2019. MOROCO: The Moldavian and Romanian Dialectal Corpus. In *Proceedings of ACL*, pages 688–698.

Andrea Ceolin and Hong Zhang. 2020. Discriminating between standard Romanian and Moldavian tweets using filtered character ngrams. In *Proceedings of the 7th Workshop on NLP for Similar Languages, Varieties and Dialects*, pages 265–272.

Bharathi Raja Chakravarthi, Mihaela Găman, Radu Tudor Ionescu, Heidi Jauhiainen, Tommi Jauhiainen, Krister Lindén, Nikola Ljubešić, Niko Partanen, Ruba Priyadharshini, Christoph Purschke, Eswari Rajagopal, Yves Scherrer, and Marcos Zampieri. 2021. Findings of the VarDial Evaluation Campaign 2021. In *Proceedings of the Eighth Workshop on NLP for Similar Languages, Varieties and Dialects (VarDial)*.

Bharathi Raja Chakravarthi, Navya Jose, Shardul Suryawanshi, Elizabeth Sherly, and John Philip McCrae. 2020a. A sentiment analysis dataset for code-mixed Malayalam-English. pages 177–184, Marseille, France. European Language Resources association.

Bharathi Raja Chakravarthi, Vigneshwaran Muralidaran, Ruba Priyadharshini, and John Philip McCrae. 2020b. Corpus creation for sentiment analysis in code-mixed Tamil-English text. In *Proceedings of the 1st Joint Workshop on Spoken Language Technologies for Under-resourced languages (SLTU) and Collaboration and Computing for Under-Resourced Languages (CCURL)*, pages 202–210, Marseille, France. European Language Resources association.

Simon Clematide and Peter Makarov. 2017. CLUZH at VarDial GDI 2017: Testing a variety of machine learning tools for the classification of swiss German dialects. In *Proceedings of the Fourth Workshop on NLP for Similar Languages, Varieties and Dialects (VarDial)*, pages 170–177, Valencia, Spain. Association for Computational Linguistics.

Çağrı Çöltekin. 2020. Dialect identification under domain shift: Experiments with discriminating Romanian and Moldavian. In *Proceedings of the 7th Workshop on NLP for Similar Languages, Varieties and Dialects*, pages 186–192.

Çağrı Çöltekin and Taraka Rama. 2017. Tübingen system in VarDial 2017 shared task: experiments with language identification and cross-lingual parsing. In *Proceedings of the Fourth Workshop on NLP for Similar Languages, Varieties and Dialects (VarDial)*, pages 146–155, Valencia, Spain.

Claude Coulombe. 2018. Text data augmentation made simple by leveraging NLP Cloud APIs. *arXiv preprint arXiv:1812.04718*.

Ekin D Cubuk, Barret Zoph, Dandelion Mane, Vijay Vasudevan, and Quoc V Le. 2019. Autoaugment: Learning augmentation strategies from data. In *Proceedings of the IEEE/CVF Conference on Computer Vision and Pattern Recognition*, pages 113–123.

Stefan Dumitrescu, Andrei-Marius Avram, and Sampo Pyysalo. 2020. The birth of Romanian BERT. In *Findings of the Association for Computational Linguistics: EMNLP 2020*, pages 4324–4328, Online. Association for Computational Linguistics.

Ted Dunning. 1994. *Statistical identification of language*. Computing Research Laboratory, New Mexico State University Las Cruces, NM, USA.

Cyril Goutte, Serge Léger, and Marine Carpuat. 2014. The NRC System for Discriminating Similar Languages. In *Proceedings of the First Workshop on Applying NLP Tools to Similar Languages, Varieties and Dialects (VarDial)*, pages 139–145, Dublin, Ireland.

Mihaela Găman, Dirk Hovy, Radu Tudor Ionescu, Heidi Jauhiainen, Tommi Jauhiainen, Krister Lindén, Nikola Ljubešić, Niko Partanen, Christoph

Purschke, Yves Scherrer, and Marcos Zampieri. 2020. A Report on the VarDial Evaluation Campaign 2020. In *Proceedings of the Seventh Workshop on NLP for Similar Languages, Varieties and Dialects (VarDial)*, pages 1–14.

Adeep Hande, Ruba Priyadharshini, and Bharathi Raja Chakravarthi. 2020. KanCMD: Kannada CodeMixed dataset for sentiment analysis and offensive language detection. In *Proceedings of the Third Workshop on Computational Modeling of People's Opinions, Personality, and Emotion's in Social Media*, pages 54–63, Barcelona, Spain (Online). Association for Computational Linguistics.

Arthur S House and Edward P Neuburg. 1977. Toward automatic identification of the language of an utterance. I. Preliminary methodological considerations. *The Journal of the Acoustical Society of America*, 62(3):708–713.

Hai Hu, Wen Li, He Zhou, Zuoyu Tian, Yiwen Zhang, and Liang Zou. 2019. Ensemble Methods to Distinguish Mainland and Taiwan Chinese. In *Proceedings of the Sixth Workshop on NLP for Similar Languages, Varieties and Dialects*, pages 165–171.

Aaron Jaech, George Mulcaire, Mari Ostendorf, and Noah A Smith. 2016. A neural model for language identification in code-switched tweets. In *Proceedings of The Second Workshop on Computational Approaches to Code Switching*, pages 60–64.

Tommi Jauhiainen, Heidi Jauhiainen, and Krister Lindén. 2020a. Experiments in language variety geolocation and dialect identification. In *Proceedings of the 7th Workshop on NLP for Similar Languages, Varieties and Dialects*, pages 220–231.

Tommi Jauhiainen, Heidi Jauhiainen, Niko Partanen, and Krister Lindén. 2020b. Uralic Language Identification (ULI) 2020 shared task dataset and the Wanca 2017 corpora. In *Proceedings of the 7th Workshop on NLP for Similar Languages, Varieties and Dialects*, pages 173–185.

Tommi Jauhiainen, Krister Lindén, and Heidi Jauhiainen. 2016. HeLI, a word-based backoff method for language identification. In *Proceedings of the Third Workshop on NLP for Similar Languages, Varieties and Dialects (VarDial 2016).*, pages 153–162.

Sosuke Kobayashi. 2018. Contextual augmentation: Data augmentation by words with paradigmatic relations. In *Proceedings of the 2018 Conference of the North American Chapter of the Association for Computational Linguistics: Human Language Technologies, Volume 2 (Short Papers)*, pages 452–457, New Orleans, Louisiana. Association for Computational Linguistics.

Tim Kreutz and Walter Daelemans. 2018. Exploring classifier combinations for language variety identification. In *Proceedings of the Fifth Workshop on NLP for Similar Languages, Varieties and Dialects (VarDial 2018)*, pages 191–198.

Marco Lui and Timothy Baldwin. 2014. Accurate language identification of Twitter messages. In *Proceedings of the 5th workshop on language analysis for social media (LASM)*, pages 17–25.

Paul McNamee. 2005. Language identification: a solved problem suitable for undergraduate instruction. *Journal of computing sciences in colleges*, 20(3):94–101.

Maria Medvedeva, Martin Kroon, and Barbara Plank. 2017. When sparse traditional models outperform dense neural networks: the curious case of discriminating between similar languages. In *Proceedings of the Fourth Workshop on NLP for Similar Languages, Varieties and Dialects (VarDial)*, pages 156–163, Valencia, Spain. Association for Computational Linguistics.

Cristian Popa and Vlad Stefănescu. 2020. Applying multilingual and monolingual transformer-based models for dialect identification. In *Proceedings of the 7th Workshop on NLP for Similar Languages, Varieties and Dialects*, pages 193–201.

Yves Scherrer and Nikola Ljubešić. 2020. HeLju@ VarDial 2020: Social media variety geolocation with BERT models. In *Proceedings of the 7th Workshop on NLP for Similar Languages, Varieties and Dialects*, pages 202–211.

Fernando Benites de Azevedo e Souza, Ralf Grubenmann, Pius von Däniken, Dirk Von Gruenigen, Jan Milan Deriu, and Mark Cieliebak. 2018. Twist bytes: German dialect identification with data mining optimization. In *27th International Conference on Computational Linguistics (COLING 2018), Santa Fe, August 20-26, 2018*, pages 218–227. VarDial.

Diana Tudoreanu. 2019. DTeam@ VarDial 2019: Ensemble based on skip-gram and triplet loss neural networks for Moldavian vs. Romanian cross-dialect topic identification. In *Proceedings of the Sixth Workshop on NLP for Similar Languages, Varieties and Dialects*, pages 202–208.

Jason Wang and Luis Perez. 2017. The effectiveness of data augmentation in image classification using deep learning. *arXiv preprint arXiv:1712.04621*.

Jason Wei and Kai Zou. 2019. EDA: Easy data augmentation techniques for boosting performance on text classification tasks. In *Proceedings of the 2019 Conference on Empirical Methods in Natural Language Processing and the 9th International Joint Conference on Natural Language Processing (EMNLP-IJCNLP)*, pages 6382–6388, Hong Kong, China. Association for Computational Linguistics.

Nianheng Wu, Eric DeMattos, Kwok Him So, Pin-zhen Chen, and Çağrı Çöltekin. 2019. Language discrimination and transfer learning for similar languages: experiments with feature combinations and adaptation. In *Proceedings of the Sixth Workshop on NLP for Similar Languages, Varieties and Dialects*, pages 54–63.

George-Eduard Zaharia, Andrei-Marius Avram, Dumitru-Clementin Cercel, and Traian Rebedea. 2020. Exploring the power of Romanian BERT for dialect identification. In *Proceedings of the 7th Workshop on NLP for Similar Languages, Varieties and Dialects*, pages 232–241.

Marcos Zampieri, Shervin Malmasi, Nikola Ljubešić, Preslav Nakov, Ahmed Ali, Jörg Tiedemann, Yves Scherrer, and Noëmi Aepli. 2017. Findings of the VarDial Evaluation Campaign 2017. In *Proceedings of the Fourth Workshop on NLP for Similar Languages, Varieties and Dialects (VarDial)*, pages 1–15, Valencia, Spain.

Marcos Zampieri, Shervin Malmasi, Preslav Nakov, Ahmed Ali, Suwon Shuon, James Glass, Yves Scherrer, Tanja Samardžić, Nikola Ljubešić, Jörg Tiedemann, Chris van der Lee, Stefan Grondelaers, Nelleke Oostdijk, Antal van den Bosch, Ritesh Kumar, Bornini Lahiri, and Mayank Jain. 2018. Language Identification and Morphosyntactic Tagging: The Second VarDial Evaluation Campaign. In *Proceedings of the Fifth Workshop on NLP for Similar Languages, Varieties and Dialects (VarDial)*, pages 1–17, Santa Fe, USA.

Marcos Zampieri, Shervin Malmasi, Yves Scherrer, Tanja Samardžić, Francis Tyers, Miikka Silfverberg, Natalia Klyueva, Tung-Le Pan, Chu-Ren Huang, Radu Tudor Ionescu, Andrei Butnaru, and Tommi Jauhiainen. 2019. A Report on the Third VarDial Evaluation Campaign. In *Proceedings of the Sixth Workshop on NLP for Similar Languages, Varieties and Dialects (VarDial)*. Association for Computational Linguistics.

Xiang Zhang, Junbo Zhao, and Yann LeCun. 2015. Character-level convolutional networks for text classification. In *Advances in neural information processing systems*, pages 649–657.

Arkaitz Zubiaga, Inaki San Vicente, Pablo Gamallo, José Ramom Pichel, Inaki Alegria, Nora Aranberri, Aitzol Ezeiza, and Víctor Fresno. 2016. TweetLID: a benchmark for tweet language identification. *Language Resources and Evaluation*, 50(4):729–766.

A Appendix - Data augmentation

Following Wei and Zou (2019), we ran some data augmentation experiments on the dataset of the RDI task. We experimented with Random Swap (swap the position of two words in the sentence), Random Delection (remove one word in the sentence), and Random Insertion (insert one extra word in the sentence). We did not experiment with Random Replacement, which involves the replacement of a word with a synonym. We also experimented with an additional technique, Shuffling, in which the words of the sentence are simply shuffled, and which is essentially a variation of Random Swap. We trained the network, on each augmented dataset, for 5 different times, and determined its test accuracy on the same hold-out dataset.

The results of the experiments on the model pretrained on news (the news+tweets model) are in Table 14. All techniques led to an improvement of the performance of the network, and the best improvement was obtained by shuffling the words of the sentences.

Technique	Training Epochs	Macro F_1
Shuffling	**5**	**0.756**
Random Swap	5	0.733
Random Deletion	5	0.733
Random Insertion	5	0.727
No augmentation	10	0.709

Table 14: Summary of our experiments on data augmentation in the RDI task, on the news+tweets model.

Dialect Identification through Adversarial Learning and Knowledge Distillation on Romanian BERT

George-Eduard Zaharia[1], Andrei-Marius Avram[1, 2], Dumitru-Clementin Cercel[1], Traian Rebedea[1]
University Politehnica of Bucharest, Faculty of Automatic Control and Computers[1]
Research Institute for Artificial Intelligence, Romanian Academy[2]
{george.zaharia0806, andrei_marius.avram}@stud.acs.upb.ro
{dumitru.cercel, traian.rebedea}@upb.ro

Abstract

Dialect identification is a task with applicability in a vast array of domains, ranging from automatic speech recognition to opinion mining. This work presents our architectures used for the VarDial 2021 Romanian Dialect Identification subtask. We introduced a series of solutions based on Romanian or multilingual Transformers, as well as adversarial training techniques. At the same time, we experimented with a knowledge distillation tool in order to check whether a smaller model can maintain the performance of our best approach. Our best solution managed to obtain a weighted F1-score of 0.7324, allowing us to obtain the 2nd place on the leaderboard.

1 Introduction

Dialect identification has attracted researchers from both the fields of speech and natural language processing, because of its wide appliance in different tasks such as automatic speech recognition (Biadsy, 2011), machine translation (Salloum et al., 2014), or opinion mining (Salamah and Elkhlifi, 2014). VarDial (Zampieri et al., 2020) is an yearly workshop that deals with boosting the research in this direction by creating computational resources for languages that are closely related with each other, varieties in language, and dialects. This year's edition (Chakravarthi et al., 2021) was composed of four subtasks: (1) Dravidian Language Identification (DLI), (2) Romanian Dialect Identification (RDI), (3) Social Media Variety Geolocation (SMG), and (4) Uralic Language Identification (ULI). We chose to participate in the second subtask of the workshop, the RDI subtask. This subtask was also proposed in the previous edition of the workshop (Gaman et al., 2020), but this time the participants are given an augmented version of the Moldavian and Romanian Dialectal Corpus (MOROCO) dataset (Butnaru and Ionescu, 2019) that contains texts from the news domain. Also, as in the previous edition, the test set comes from another domain, so cross-domain algorithms must be employed in order to maximize the results.

Romanian language resources are in an ongoing process of maturity, and the language is slowly starting to gain the datasets necessary to not be considered under-resourced anymore. Some of the recent publicly available Romanian corpora include the Large Romanian Sentiment DataSet (LaRoSeDa) (Tache et al., 2021), the Romanian Named Entity Corpus (RONEC) (Dumitrescu and Avram, 2020), and the Romanian version of the Cross-lingual Question Answering Dataset (xQuAD) (Artetxe et al., 2020). Moreover, with the rise of Transformer-based pretrained language models (Vaswani et al., 2017), some Romanian model versions have also been created (Dumitrescu et al., 2020; Masala et al., 2020). The speech resources are also starting to catch-up with the introduction of the Romanian Speech Corpus (RSC) (Georgescu et al., 2020) which was recently released for public usage, counting around 100 hours of speech, and with the introduction of a deep neural network architecture based on DeepSpeech2 (Amodei et al., 2016) for automatic speech recognition (Avram et al., 2020b).

In this work, we proposed a series of models based on Transformers, pre-trained on the Romanian language, and aimed to tackle the dialect identification task. By using different techniques, including adversarial training (Goodfellow et al., 2014b), knowledge distillation (Hinton et al., 2015), or Generative Adversarial Networks (GANs) (Goodfellow et al., 2014a), we managed to obtain good scores, allowing us to classify 2nd in the RDI subtask organized at VarDial 2021.

The current work is structured as follows. The next section presents the state of the art regarding the Romanian-Moldavian dialect identification

Proceedings of the 8th VarDial Workshop on NLP for Similar Languages, Varieties and Dialects, pages 113–119
April 20, 2021 ©2021 Association for Computational Linguistics

task. Section 3 outlines the methods created by us in order to tackle the previously mentioned challenge, while section 4 describes the results and displays the error analysis we conducted. Section 5 concludes the work and features some future improvements that can be made to further increase the performance.

2 Related Work

The third edition of the VarDial evaluation campaign (Zampieri et al., 2019) took place in 2019 and presented another challenging task for the Romanian language - Moldavian vs. Romanian Cross-dialect Topic identification. The task was composed of three smaller subtasks in which the participants had to (1) discriminate between the Moldavian (MD) and the Romanian (RO) dialects, (2) use Moldavian samples to classify Romanian samples by topic (MD $\rightarrow$ RO), and (3) use Romanian samples to classify Moldavian samples by topic (RO $\rightarrow$ MD). The highest macro F1-score on the first subtask was 89.50%, achieved by the `DTeam` team (Tudoreanu, 2019) with an ensemble model that combines a skip-gram convolutional neural network (CNN) (Kim, 2014) using the softmax loss and a CNN that was trained using a triplet loss. The highest scores for the cross-dialect subtasks 2 and 3 were obtained by the `tearsofjoy` team (Wu et al., 2019) that used a linear Support Vector Machine (SVM) classifier trained on a combination of character and word n-gram features. They obtained a 61.15% F1-score (macro) for the MD $\rightarrow$ RO subtasks and a 55.33% F1-score (macro) for the RO $\rightarrow$ MD subtask. Onose et al. (2019) adopted a non-Transformer approach and employed the usage of neural network models with Bidirectional Long Short-Term Memory cells (Hochreiter and Schmidhuber, 1997), Bidirectional Gated Recurrent units (Cho et al., 2014), as well as a Hierarchical Attention Network (Yang et al., 2016).

The fourth edition of VarDial (Gaman et al., 2020) occured in 2020 and came with the RDI task, a binary classification task where participants had to identify the dialect of a given text - either Romanian or Moldavian. To differentiate from the previous edition, the evaluation set was taken from another domain, namely Twitter messages. The highest F1-score (macro) of 78.75% was achieved by the `Tubingen` team (Çöltekin, 2020) by using an ensemble of SVMs trained on word and character n-grams. Also, this edition saw the appliance of the Romanian Bidirectional Encoder Representations from Transformers (BERT) by two teams (Popa and Ştefănescu, 2020; Zaharia et al., 2020a), with the best performing variant obtaining a 77.51% F1-score (macro).

3 Method

3.1 Transformer-based Models

Our architectures are based on multiple Transformer-based models, considering their performance on various natural language processing (NLP) tasks (Avram et al., 2020a; Dima et al., 2020; Ionescu et al., 2020; Paraschiv et al., 2020; Paraschiv and Cercel, 2019; Tanase et al., 2020b,a; Vlad et al., 2020; Zaharia et al., 2020b). For Romanian Dialect Identification, we employed the usage of a Transformer model extensively pre-trained on the Romanian language (Dumitrescu et al., 2020), as well as two multilingual models, namely XLM-RoBERTa (Conneau et al., 2019) and multilingual BERT (mBERT) (Pires et al., 2019). Their performance on the Romanian language is lower when compared to Romanian BERT, however, in an ensemble, their predictions can prove to increase the score of our approach.

3.2 Generative Adversarial Network Applied on Romanian BERT

Moreover, using a training technique similar to the ones employed by GANs proved to improve the performance of several NLP models (Croce et al., 2020). Similarly, we augment our Romanian BERT architecture with a generator, as well as a discriminator. The generator receives as input a 100-dimensional noise vector and produces an output vector as similar to real inputs as possible. Moreover, the discriminator acts as a classifier but, instead of only being forced to distinguish between the two classes of the RDI task (i.e., *RO* or *MD*), it also has the purpose to identify whether the input is fake or not and classify it accordingly, into a third class. The discriminator is penalized if it classifies a fake input as a true one or vice versa. After the training process, the generator components and the third output of the discriminator are disabled, therefore our architecture works as a classifier based on Romanian BERT features.

3.3 Knowledge Distillation Applied on Romanian BERT

We continued our experiments by applying a knowledge distillation technique, in order to check whether the high performance of Romanian BERT is maintained after it is distilled into a smaller model. For this approach, we used TextBrewer (Yang et al., 2020), a tool that receives as input a teacher model and trains a student model such that the latter is able to closely replicate the behavior of the former. We used Romanian BERT as the teacher, a Transformer-based model with 12 hidden layers, thus implying a large number of parameters. Moreover, the student model is also based on Transformers, however, it is not pre-trained on any corpus and it has only 3 hidden layers, instead of 12. This reduction greatly decreases the computational resources required for further fine-tuning or prediction.

3.4 Adversarial Training

Adversarial training has the purpose of enhancing the robustness of the model and, as a consequence, increase its performance in certain scenarios (Karimi et al., 2020). The system works by introducing adversarial perturbations at the level of the Transformer embeddings. The process turns into a minimization problem, with the purpose of determining the worst perturbations while minimizing the loss function.

The following formulas present the process of obtaining the adversarial perturbations, based on the gradient of the loss function g:

$$g = \nabla_x log\, p(y|x; \hat{\theta}) \quad (1)$$

$$r_{adv} = -\epsilon \frac{g}{||g||_2} \quad (2)$$

where $\hat{\theta}$ is a copy of the model's parameters, r_{adv} are the perturbations, and ϵ is the dimension of the perturbations.

After computing the perturbations, they are then added to the Transformer embeddings and an adversarial loss is obtained, given by Eq. 3:

$$-log\, p(y|x + r_{adv}; \theta) \quad (3)$$

The final loss represents the sum between the adversarial loss and the simple loss obtained by passing the unaltered input through the neural network.

3.5 Custom Selection Technique

The most important element that influenced the performance of our models is represented by the way we selected the training entries, as well as how we established the threshold for which an entry can be considered Romanian or Moldavian.

Firstly, the training dataset contains long entries, most of them surpassing the 512-token limit input by our Transformer models. At the same time, the validation entries are much shorter, with an average length of just 20 words.

Therefore, the first step we performed was to split the training entries into sentences and label each sentence with the label of the initial entry. However, the number of training entries was greatly increased, from 39,487 to 431,875. Considering this large number, we decided to filter the training entries, inasmuch as only the most relevant ones were kept for the final fine-tuning process. To do this, we initially trained our architecture, based on the Romanian BERT model, on the original validation entries. After four epochs, we tested the model on the split training entries and we selected only the ones that predicted Romanian or Moldavian with the confidence of over 95%. This way, we were able to select only the entries that are the closest in structure and context to the one from the validation dataset and, presumably, from the test one. We reduced the number of the split training entries to 158,363.

For determining the prediction threshold, we trained our architectures on the previously mentioned entries and, after the final epoch, we discovered a prediction threshold that maximized the performance. We performed the selection by trying different values such as, if the confidence of a prediction surpasses the threshold, then it is classified as Moldavian, for example, if not, it is classified as Romanian. The optimal value of the threshold was 0.21.

3.6 Machine Learning Approaches

We also experimented with various machine learning techniques, such as SVMs, Random Forest, Multinomial Naive Bayes, and Logistic Regression, alongside character n-gram features.

4 Experiments

4.1 Dataset Analysis and Preprocessing

The dataset is the one provided for the RDI subtask of the VarDial 2021 competition. There are three subsets, one for training, one for validation, and one for testing. The validation and testing datasets (5,237 and 5,282 entries, respectively) contain very short entries, with an average length of 20 words. At the same time, the training dataset (39,487 entries) contains much longer texts, many of them surpassing 512 words. The class distribution is relatively balanced, with 21,366 Romanian entries and 18,121 Moldavian entries in the training dataset plus 2,625 and 2,612 entries, respectively, in the validation one.

In terms of preprocessing, we standardized the punctuation, by removing repeated characters such as question marks. Moreover, we cleaned the entries that contained an unnecessary number of whitespaces.

4.2 Implementation Details

For running the Transformer-based models we used Adam with weight decay optimizer (AdamW) (Kingma and Ba, 2014) and an epsilon value of *1e-8*. We fine-tuned them for four epochs with a learning rate of *2e-5*. Moreover, for the GAN approach, we allowed the generator to back-propagate its loss every 200 steps, such that the discriminator, which also performs as the classifier, had a small advantage.

4.3 Results

Table 1 presents all the results obtained with neural network approaches. The best results are obtained by the ensemble used by taking the predictions from the six deep learning models used in our experiments. With a weighted F1-score of 0.7324, the ensemble slightly surpasses the Romanian BERT model trained under adversarial circumstances, which scored a weighted F1 of 0.7318. The small performance improvement is noticeable on the validation dataset, as well, the ensemble scoring a 0.8564 weighted F1.

The adversarial training technique helps the Romanian BERT model improve its performance, considering the higher weighted F1-score on the validation dataset, 0.8559, obtained by the adversarial model when compared to the standard counterpart (0.8492). In contrast, the GAN training approach does not help the model achieve improved performance. The weighted F1-score is slightly higher than the standard Romanian BERT. However, when compared to the adversarial training technique, GAN+Romanian BERT lacks behind in terms of performance.

The distilled model obtained by using TextBrewer with Romanian BERT comes last in terms of performance in the group of the Romanian BERT-based models. The weighted F1-scores of 0.7891 and 0.6744 obtained on the validation and test datasets are behind all the scores obtained by using variations of the Romanian BERT. The lack of performance can be attributed to the lower number of parameters of the distilled model, which it is not able to grasp the distinctive features of Romanian and Moldavian entries as well as the full model.

The last models in terms of performance are Multilingual BERT and XLM-RoBERTa. Even though the pre-training corpus of XLM-RoBERTa is bigger, the model is surpassed by mBERT. One reason for this can be represented by the inclusion of more Romanian entries in the mBERT pre-training corpus.

Table 2 contains the results obtained by using various machine learning techniques alongside character n-gram features. The scores are much lower when compared to the ones achieved by the neural network approaches. The best performing model is the SVM trained with the parameter C equal to 3. The model achieves a weighted F1-score of 0.6298, 0.1324 lower than the worst score obtained by the neural network approaches.

4.4 Error Analysis

Most misclassifications come from the inability of the models to identify dialect-specific features in the input entries. Taking as an example the validation dataset, many entries that are classified as Romanian or Moldavian have no surface differences in terms of structure or the used words (i.e., "*Ultimele știri despre coronavirus NE*" is labeled with the Romanian dialect, while "*Cum te protejezi împotriva coronavirusului NE*" is Moldavian). At the same time, the entries that are classified with high confidence as either Romanian or Moldavian are the ones with unmasked named entities, that are also present in the training dataset (i.e., "*Arafat*", "*Ceban*", "*Igor*") or dialect-specific words (i.e., "*raional*").

Some entires are obstructed by the masked named entities (i.e., "*Este criză în NE și NE NE*", "*FOTO-VIDEO. Ministrul NE NE NE și NE NE NE la NE NE Nu este vorba*") and therefore our models cannot properly identify features specific to one dialect or the other.

Table 1: Deep learning results.

Model	Validation			Test		
	macro-F1	weighted-F1	micro-F1	macro-F1	weighted-F1	micro-F1
Romanian BERT	0.8492	0.8492	0.8495	-	-	-
Romanian BERT + Adversarial Training	0.8558	0.8559	0.8564	0.7319	0.7318	0.7319
Multilingual BERT	0.8097	0.8097	0.8098	-	-	-
XLM-RoBERTa	0.7619	0.7619	0.7622	-	-	-
Romanian BERT + GAN	0.8516	0.8516	0.8523	-	-	-
Romanian BERT + TextBrewer	0.7891	0.7891	0.7893	0.6743	0.6744	0.6749
Ensemble	**0.8564**	**0.8564**	**0.8566**	**0.7324**	**0.7324**	**0.7324**

Table 2: Machine learning results on the validation dataset.

Model	Validation		
	macro-F1	weighted-F1	micro-F1
SVM	**0.6297**	**0.6298**	**0.6324**
Random Forest	0.5216	0.5218	0.5379
Multinomial Naive Bayes	0.5726	0.5728	0.5921
Logistic Regression	0.6250	0.6251	0.6270

Moreover, the performance difference between the validation and test sets (i.e., 0.8564 vs. 0.7324) can be attributed to the selection technique we used for filtering the training entries. The new inputs are chosen such that they are similar to the validation entries, not the test ones.

5 Conclusions and Future Work

This work presents our approaches for the Romanian Dialect Identification subtask organized by VarDial 2021. We proposed a series of systems based on state-of-the-art, Transformer-based models, which imply the usage of adversarial techniques for improving the robustness. At the same time, we also experimented with TextBrewer, a knowledge distillation tool that allows us to compress a teacher model into a student model such that the performance can be maintained while reducing the size. Moreover, by using an ensemble of all the models we experimented with, we managed to improve the overall performance.

For future work, we intend to experiment with different variants of adversarial training for increasing the scores obtained by our models.

References

Dario Amodei, Sundaram Ananthanarayanan, Rishita Anubhai, Jingliang Bai, Eric Battenberg, Carl Case, Jared Casper, Bryan Catanzaro, Qiang Cheng, Guoliang Chen, et al. 2016. Deep speech 2: End-to-end speech recognition in english and mandarin. In *International conference on machine learning*, pages 173–182. PMLR.

Mikel Artetxe, Sebastian Ruder, and Dani Yogatama. 2020. On the cross-lingual transferability of monolingual representations. In *Proceedings of the 58th Annual Meeting of the Association for Computational Linguistics*, pages 4623–4637.

Andrei-Marius Avram, Dumitru-Clementin Cercel, and Costin-Gabriel Chiru. 2020a. Upb at semeval-2020 task 6: Pretrained language models for definitionextraction. *arXiv preprint arXiv:2009.05603*.

Andrei-Marius Avram, PĂIȘ Vasile, and Dan Tufis. 2020b. Towards a romanian end-to-end automatic speech recognition based on deepspeech2. In *Proc. Rom. Acad. Ser. A*, volume 21, pages 395–402.

Fadi Biadsy. 2011. *Automatic dialect and accent recognition and its application to speech recognition*. Ph.D. thesis, Columbia University.

Andrei Butnaru and Radu Tudor Ionescu. 2019. Moroco: The moldavian and romanian dialectal corpus. In *Proceedings of the 57th Annual Meeting of the Association for Computational Linguistics*, pages 688–698.

Bharathi Raja Chakravarthi, Mihaela Găman, Radu Tudor Ionescu, Heidi Jauhiainen, Tommi Jauhiainen, Krister Lindén, Nikola Ljubešić, Niko Partanen, Ruba Priyadharshini, Christoph Purschke, Eswari Rajagopal, Yves Scherrer, and Marcos Zampieri. 2021. Findings of the VarDial Evaluation Campaign 2021. In *Proceedings of the Eighth Workshop on NLP for Similar Languages, Varieties and Dialects (VarDial)*.

Kyunghyun Cho, Bart van Merriënboer, Caglar Gulcehre, Dzmitry Bahdanau, Fethi Bougares, Holger

Schwenk, and Yoshua Bengio. 2014. Learning phrase representations using rnn encoder–decoder for statistical machine translation. In *Proceedings of the 2014 Conference on Empirical Methods in Natural Language Processing (EMNLP)*, pages 1724–1734.

Çağrı Çöltekin. 2020. Dialect identification under domain shift: Experiments with discriminating romanian and moldavian. In *Proceedings of the 7th Workshop on NLP for Similar Languages, Varieties and Dialects*, pages 186–192.

Alexis Conneau, Kartikay Khandelwal, Naman Goyal, Vishrav Chaudhary, Guillaume Wenzek, Francisco Guzmán, Edouard Grave, Myle Ott, Luke Zettlemoyer, and Veselin Stoyanov. 2019. Unsupervised cross-lingual representation learning at scale. *arXiv preprint arXiv:1911.02116*.

Danilo Croce, Giuseppe Castellucci, and Roberto Basili. 2020. Gan-bert: Generative adversarial learning for robust text classification with a bunch of labeled examples. In *Proceedings of the 58th Annual Meeting of the Association for Computational Linguistics*, pages 2114–2119.

George-Andrei Dima, Andrei-Marius Avram, and Dumitru-Clementin Cercel. 2020. Approaching smm4h 2020 with ensembles of bert flavours. In *Proceedings of the Fifth Social Media Mining for Health Applications Workshop & Shared Task*, pages 153–157.

Stefan Dumitrescu, Andrei-Marius Avram, and Sampo Pyysalo. 2020. The birth of romanian bert. In *Proceedings of the 2020 Conference on Empirical Methods in Natural Language Processing: Findings*, pages 4324–4328.

Stefan Daniel Dumitrescu and Andrei-Marius Avram. 2020. Introducing ronec-the romanian named entity corpus. In *Proceedings of The 12th Language Resources and Evaluation Conference*, pages 4436–4443.

Mihaela Gaman, Dirk Hovy, Radu Tudor Ionescu, Heidi Jauhiainen, Tommi Jauhiainen, Krister Lindén, Nikola Ljubešić, Niko Partanen, Christoph Purschke, Yves Scherrer, et al. 2020. A report on the vardial evaluation campaign 2020. In *Proceedings of the 7th Workshop on NLP for Similar Languages, Varieties and Dialects*, pages 1–14.

Alexandru-Lucian Georgescu, Horia Cucu, Andi Buzo, and Corneliu Burileanu. 2020. Rsc: A romanian read speech corpus for automatic speech recognition. In *Proceedings of The 12th Language Resources and Evaluation Conference*, pages 6606–6612.

Ian J Goodfellow, Jean Pouget-Abadie, Mehdi Mirza, Bing Xu, David Warde-Farley, Sherjil Ozair, Aaron Courville, and Yoshua Bengio. 2014a. Generative adversarial networks. *arXiv preprint arXiv:1406.2661*.

Ian J Goodfellow, Jonathon Shlens, and Christian Szegedy. 2014b. Explaining and harnessing adversarial examples. *arXiv preprint arXiv:1412.6572*.

Geoffrey Hinton, Oriol Vinyals, and Jeff Dean. 2015. Distilling the knowledge in a neural network. *arXiv preprint arXiv:1503.02531*.

Sepp Hochreiter and Jürgen Schmidhuber. 1997. Long short-term memory. *Neural computation*, 9(8):1735–1780.

Marius Ionescu, Andrei-Marius Avram, George-Andrei Dima, Dumitru-Clementin Cercel, and Mihai Dascalu. 2020. Upb at fincausal-2020, tasks 1 & 2: Causality analysis in financial documents using pretrained language models. In *Proceedings of the 1st Joint Workshop on Financial Narrative Processing and MultiLing Financial Summarisation*, pages 55–59.

Akbar Karimi, Leonardo Rossi, Andrea Prati, and Katharina Full. 2020. Adversarial training for aspect-based sentiment analysis with bert. *arXiv preprint arXiv:2001.11316*.

Yoon Kim. 2014. Convolutional neural networks for sentence classification. *arXiv preprint arXiv:1408.5882*.

Diederik P Kingma and Jimmy Ba. 2014. Adam: A method for stochastic optimization. *arXiv preprint arXiv:1412.6980*.

Mihai Masala, Stefan Ruseti, and Mihai Dascalu. 2020. Robert–a romanian bert model. In *Proceedings of the 28th International Conference on Computational Linguistics*, pages 6626–6637.

Cristian Onose, Dumitru-Clementin Cercel, and Stefan Trausan-Matu. 2019. Sc-upb at the vardial 2019 evaluation campaign: Moldavian vs. romanian cross-dialect topic identification. In *Proceedings of the Sixth Workshop on NLP for Similar Languages, Varieties and Dialects*, pages 172–177.

Andrei Paraschiv and Dumitru-Clementin Cercel. 2019. Upb at germeval-2019 task 2: Bert-based offensive language classification of german tweets. In *KONVENS*.

Andrei Paraschiv, Dumitru-Clementin Cercel, and Mihai Dascalu. 2020. Upb at semeval-2020 task 11: Propaganda detection with domain-specific trained bert. *arXiv preprint arXiv:2009.05289*.

Telmo Pires, Eva Schlinger, and Dan Garrette. 2019. How multilingual is multilingual bert? In *Proceedings of the 57th Annual Meeting of the Association for Computational Linguistics*, pages 4996–5001.

Cristian Popa and Vlad Ştefănescu. 2020. Applying multilingual and monolingual transformer-based models for dialect identification. In *Proceedings of the 7th Workshop on NLP for Similar Languages, Varieties and Dialects*, pages 193–201.

Jana Ben Salamah and Aymen Elkhlifi. 2014. Microblogging opinion mining approach for kuwaiti dialect. In *The International Conference on Computing Technology and Information Management (ICCTIM)*, page 388. Society of Digital Information and Wireless Communication.

Wael Salloum, Heba Elfardy, Linda Alamir-Salloum, Nizar Habash, and Mona Diab. 2014. Sentence level dialect identification for machine translation system selection. In *Proceedings of the 52nd Annual Meeting of the Association for Computational Linguistics (Volume 2: Short Papers)*, pages 772–778.

Anca Maria Tache, Mihaela Gaman, and Radu Tudor Ionescu. 2021. Clustering word embeddings with self-organizing maps. application on laroseda–a large romanian sentiment data set. *arXiv preprint arXiv:2101.04197*.

Mircea-Adrian Tanase, Dumitru-Clementin Cercel, and Costing-Gabriel Chiru. 2020a. Upb at semeval-2020 task 12: Multilingual offensive language detection on social media by fine-tuning a variety of bert-based models. *arXiv preprint arXiv:2010.13609*.

Mircea-Adrian Tanase, George-Eduard Zaharia, Dumitru-Clementin Cercel, and Mihai Dascalu. 2020b. Detecting aggressiveness in mexican spanish social media content by fine-tuning transformer-based models. In *Proceedings of the Iberian Languages Evaluation Forum (IberLEF 2020) co-located with 36th Conference of the Spanish Society for Natural Language Processing (SEPLN) 2020*, pages 236–245.

Diana Tudoreanu. 2019. Dteam@ vardial 2019: Ensemble based on skip-gram and triplet loss neural networks for moldavian vs. romanian cross-dialect topic identification. In *Proceedings of the Sixth Workshop on NLP for Similar Languages, Varieties and Dialects*, pages 202–208.

Ashish Vaswani, Noam Shazeer, Niki Parmar, Jakob Uszkoreit, Llion Jones, Aidan N Gomez, Łukasz Kaiser, and Illia Polosukhin. 2017. Attention is all you need. In *Proceedings of the 31st International Conference on Neural Information Processing Systems*, pages 6000–6010.

George-Alexandru Vlad, George-Eduard Zaharia, Dumitru-Clementin Cercel, Costin-Gabriel Chiru, and Stefan Trausan-Matu. 2020. Upb at semeval-2020 task 8: Joint textual and visual modeling in a multi-task learning architecture for memotion analysis. *arXiv preprint arXiv:2009.02779*.

Nianheng Wu, Eric DeMattos, Kwok Him So, Pin-zhen Chen, and Çağrı Çöltekin. 2019. Language discrimination and transfer learning for similar languages: experiments with feature combinations and adaptation. In *Proceedings of the Sixth Workshop on NLP for Similar Languages, Varieties and Dialects*, pages 54–63.

Zichao Yang, Diyi Yang, Chris Dyer, Xiaodong He, Alex Smola, and Eduard Hovy. 2016. Hierarchical attention networks for document classification. In *Proceedings of the 2016 conference of the North American chapter of the association for computational linguistics: human language technologies*, pages 1480–1489.

Ziqing Yang, Yiming Cui, Zhipeng Chen, Wanxiang Che, Ting Liu, Shijin Wang, and Guoping Hu. 2020. Textbrewer: An open-source knowledge distillation toolkit for natural language processing. *arXiv preprint arXiv:2002.12620*.

George-Eduard Zaharia, Andrei-Marius Avram, Dumitru-Clementin Cercel, and Traian Rebedea. 2020a. Exploring the power of romanian bert for dialect identification. In *Proceedings of the 7th Workshop on NLP for Similar Languages, Varieties and Dialects*, pages 232–241.

George-Eduard Zaharia, Dumitru-Clementin Cercel, and Mihai Dascalu. 2020b. Cross-lingual transfer learning for complex word identification. In *2020 IEEE 32nd International Conference on Tools with Artificial Intelligence (ICTAI)*, pages 384–390. IEEE.

Marcos Zampieri, Shervin Malmasi, Yves Scherrer, Tanja Samardzic, Francis Tyers, Miikka Silfverberg, Natalia Klyueva, Tung-Le Pan, Chu-Ren Huang, Radu Tudor Ionescu, et al. 2019. A report on the third vardial evaluation campaign. In *Proceedings of the Sixth Workshop on NLP for Similar Languages, Varieties and Dialects*, pages 1–16.

Marcos Zampieri, Preslav Nakov, and Yves Scherrer. 2020. Natural language processing for similar languages, varieties, and dialects: A survey. *Natural Language Engineering*, 26(6):595–612.

Comparing Approaches to Dravidian Language Identification

Tommi Jauhiainen[1,3], Tharindu Ranasinghe[2], Marcos Zampieri[3]
[1]University of Helsinki, Finland
[2]University of Wolverhampton
[3]Rochester Institute of Technology, USA
tommi.jauhiainen@helsinki.fi

Abstract

This paper describes the submissions by team HWR to the Dravidian Language Identification (DLI) shared task organized at VarDial 2021 workshop. The DLI training set includes 16,674 YouTube comments written in Roman script containing code-mixed text with English and one of the three South Dravidian languages: Kannada, Malayalam, and Tamil. We submitted results generated using two models, a Naive Bayes classifier with adaptive language models, which has shown to obtain competitive performance in many language and dialect identification tasks, and a transformer-based model which is widely regarded as the state-of-the-art in a number of NLP tasks. Our first submission was sent in the closed submission track using only the training set provided by the shared task organisers, whereas the second submission is considered to be open as it used a pretrained model trained with external data. Our team attained shared second position in the shared task with the submission based on Naive Bayes. Our results reinforce the idea that deep learning methods are not as competitive in language identification related tasks as they are in many other text classification tasks.

1 Introduction

Discriminating between similar languages (e.g. Bulgarian and Macedonian or Croatian and Serbian), language varieties (e.g. Brazilian and European Portuguese), and dialects is one of the main challenges in automatic language identification (LI) in texts. This issue has been addressed in a couple recent surveys (Jauhiainen et al., 2019c; Zampieri et al., 2020) and evaluation papers (Goutte et al., 2016). Furthermore, it has been the topic of a number of competitions such as TweetLID (Zubiaga et al., 2016) and many shared tasks organized in past VarDial workshops (Zampieri et al., 2018, 2019; Găman et al., 2020).

In this paper, we revisit the challenge of discriminating between similar languages on a challenging code-mixed data set containing three South Dravidian Languages: Kannada, Malayalam, and Tamil. In addition, there were code-mixed comments on other languages as well. The data set contains 22,164 YouTube comments divided into 16,674 instances for training and 4,590 instances for testing, each containing a mix of languages. The data set was released by the organizers of the Dravidian Language Identification (DLI) shared task part of the VarDial Evaluation Campaign 2020 (Chakravarthi et al., 2021).[1] The goal of the task is to train computational models able to identify the language of each comment in a test set presented in Section 3.

The DLI debuted as the first competition on similar language identification using code-mixed data associated with the VarDial workshops. Very similar multilingual language identification shared tasks were organized as part of Forum for Information Retrieval Evaluation (FIRE) meetings in 2013 and 2014 (Roy et al., 2013; Choudhury et al., 2014).[2] A similar competition to the DLI are also the shared tasks on Language Identification in Code-Switched Data (Solorio et al., 2014; Molina et al., 2016). These shared tasks addressed intra-sentential language identification with word level labeling whereas the DLI shared task is language identification shared task with predictions at the document level. We take this opportunity to evaluate the performance of two models for this task, a Naive Bayes classifier using adaptive language models and a transformers-based system described in detail in Section 4.

[1]https://sites.google.com/view/vardial2021/evaluation-campaign

[2]http://fire.irsi.res.in/fire/2021/home

Proceedings of the 8th VarDial Workshop on NLP for Similar Languages, Varieties and Dialects, pages 120–127
April 20, 2021

2 Related Work

The task of automatic language identification of texts has been under continuous research since 1960s as is witnessed, for example, by the works of Mustonen (1965), House and Neuburg (1977), Henrich (1989), Grefenstette (1995), and Martins and Silva (2005). The problem of discriminating between similar languages, language varieties, and dialects is a particularly challenging one and it has also been addressed by a number of studies such as Tiedemann and Ljubešić (2012); Tan et al. (2014); Malmasi and Zampieri (2017b,a), and the aforementioned shared tasks at the VarDial workshop. In addition to addressing the issue of discriminating between similar languages, Jauhiainen et al. (2019c) provide an extensive overview of the history and methods used in language identification of texts in general.

2.1 Language Identification of South Dravidian Languages

Even though the DLI 2021 shared task was the first time a shared task solely focused on discriminating between Dravidian languages, Dravidian languages have been part of language repertoire of LI research before. Most of the research so far has focused on texts written with non-Roman script. Notable exception to the trend is the first subtask of the Transliterated Search shared which was organized as part of FIRE 2014 (Choudhury et al., 2014), where the goal was to label individual transliterated words in code-mixed search queries. The training set of the subtask included code-mixed sentences in English together with one of the Indian languages: Bangla, Gujarati, Hindi, or Malayalam. In addition, the test set included code-mixed sentences with Kannada and Tamil as unseen languages. Choudhury et al. (2014) list three teams which submitted results for the Dravidian languages, but to the best of our knowledge there are no system description papers available for these submissions.

Using Multivariate Analysis (MVA) and Principal Component Analysis (PCA), Vinosh Babu and Baskaran (2005) attained a 100% performance in language identification between six Tamil dialects (Iscii, Shree-Tam, Tab, Tam, Tscii, and Vikatan). The exact test sizes they used are not known, but they considered 500 bytes "too small", which indicates that the texts they processed were generally much longer than those part of the DLI shared task test set.

Murthy and Kumar (2006) focused on smaller text samples in pair wise language identification of several Indian languages, including those of Tamil, Malayalam, and Kannada with Multiple Linear Regression (MLR). They used the number of aksharas (a sort of syllables generally used in Indian scripts) as the measure of the length of text and obtained F-scores of over 0.99 with texts of only 10 aksharas in length when discriminating between two of the South Dravidian languages. In their research, they show that features based on aksharas (*e.g.* akshara *n*-grams) work better than features based on bytes.

Goswami et al. (2020) experiment with supervised and unsupervised methods in dialect identification using, among others, a Dravidian data set containing Tamil, Telugu, Malayalam, and Kannada.

The three South Dravidian languages were a part of larger repertoire of the language identifiers presented by, for example, Majliš (2011) and Kocmi and Bojar (2017). Hanumathappa and Reddy (2012) conducted identification experiments between Kannada and Telugu, a Central Dravidian language.

3 Shared Task Setup and Data

The evaluation measure in the DLI shared task was the macro F_1 score, which gives equal value for each language independent of their actual distribution in the test set.

The data set provided by the DLI organizers contains a total of 22,164 YouTube comments written in a mix of English and one of the aforementioned South Dravidian languages (Chakravarthi et al., 2020a,b; Hande et al., 2020). In addition to the target languages, the data included comments in other languages as well. It was divided into 16,674 instances for training and 4,590 instances for testing. The number of instances for each language is show in Figure 1.

Set	**kan**	**mal**	**tam**	**other**	**Total**
Training	493	4,204	10,969	1,008	16,674
Test					4,590
Total					22,164

Table 1: Number of instances in the DLI dataset for Kannada (kan), Malayalam (mal), and Tamil (tam).

In order to evaluate and compare our methods using the training data, we divided the training data into training and development portions. For training, we used the first 90% of comments for each language and the rest was set aside for development. This way, we retained the original distribution of different labels as the provided training data seemed not to be in a random order. For example, the last 10% of the training comments did not include comments in Malayalam at all.

For the open track, we considered using corpora collected for the use of the SUKI-project (Jauhiainen et al., 2015a), but quickly found that for example the SUKI data for Tamil consisted of texts written completely using the Devanagari script. As the YouTube comments used in the shared task were mostly written in Latin alphabet, we did not pursue using external corpora further.

4 Methods and Experiments with the development data

In our development environment, we experimented with several different methods: simple scoring, sum of relative frequencies, the product of relative frequencies (Naive Bayes, NB), NB with language model adaptation, HeLI, language set identification, and transformers.

4.1 Simple scoring, sum of relative frequencies, and Naive Bayes

None of the three methods are equipped with any special ways of handling multilingual texts and simply act in a similar fashion as each line would actually be monolingual. The possible multilinguality of the input texts is handled by the language models derived from the training material actually representing a mixture of languages.

The implementation of these methods was the same, which was used by Jauhiainen et al. (2019a) in the Discriminating between Mainland and Taiwan variation of Mandarin Chinese (DMT) shared task. We have now published this software titled "Tunnista" in GitHub with an MIT license.[3] The software is used to automatically evaluate the performance of the methods using different ranges of character n-grams and penalty modifiers.

In the evaluations of all three methods, we removed all non-alphabetical characters from the training and the test material and also lowercased all the remaining characters.

Simple scoring was evaluated with all possible character n-gram ranges from 1 to 10 and from 6 to 11. The best micro-F_1 score of 0.9225 was attained using character n-grams from 7 to 8 and the best macro-F_1 of **0.7321** with character n-grams from 7 to 10. The sum of relative frequencies was evaluated with all possible character n-gram ranges from 1 to 11. The best micro-F_1 score of 0.8048 was attained using character n-grams from 3 to 9 and the best macro-F_1 of **0.6897** with character n-grams from 7 to 9. It is noticeable how much closer the macro F_1 scores are to each other when compared with the micro F_1 scores.

The NB classifier was evaluated with several combinations of character n-grams and penalty modifiers ranging from n-gram length of 1 to 11 and penalty modifiers between 1.2 and 2.5. The classifier obtained its best micro F_1 score of 0.9339 using character n-grams from 1 or 2 to 6 with penalty modifiers ranging from 2.37 to 2.42. The best macro F_1 score, **0.8609** was attained using character n-grams from 2 to 6 with penalty modifiers ranging from 2.14 to 2.16. The NB classifier was clearly the best of the three methods provided by the "Tunnista" program.

4.2 Product of Relative Frequencies with Adaptive Language Models

As the macro F_1 score was used as the evaluation measure of the shared task, we used the best parameters (character n-grams from 2 to 6, with penalty modifier of 2.15) from the previous experiments as the basis for our experiments with the adaptive version of the naive Bayes classifier.

The adaptation method uses several parameters which have to be optimized using the training and the development material. The first parameter is the number of splits the whole material to be identified is divided in. The actual division into splits happens after each time the test set is preliminarily identified and ordered so that the mystery texts with the highest difference between the log probabilities of the most probable and the second most probable language are on the top of the list. When incorporating new information from the text to be identified, the highest split is processed first. After its information has been added to the language models, all the remaining mystery texts are again preliminarily identified and divided into same sized splits. Again the information from the best split is incorporated into language models and so on, until all the splits have been processed.

We evaluated different split sizes between zero and the so called full split, which means the number

[3]https://github.com/tosaja/Tunnista

of splits was equal to the number of mystery texts in the test set. Table 2 shows the development of the F_1 score relative to the number of splits k.

k	**macro F_1-score**
1	0.8609
2	0.8595
4	0.8623
10	0.8648
20, 40, 100, 200, 400, 800, max	**0.8663**

Table 2: The macro F1-scores obtained by the NB identifier using adaptation with different values of k when evaluated on the development partition of the DLI training set.

We also use the log probability difference between the best and second best scores as a confidence score. In case confidence threshold, CT, is used, no information from mystery lines with confidence score equal or below CT is incorporated into the language models. We evaluated several CT values with k of 20, but the best results were obtained without using the confidence threshold at all.

4.3 HeLI 2.0 method

The third series of experiments was conducted using a language identifier based on the HeLI method (Jauhiainen et al., 2016). The actual implementation used was that of the HeLI 2.0 method (Jauhiainen et al., 2019b) with adaptive language models from the GDI 2019 shared task (Jauhiainen et al., 2019a).[4] We used the $createmodels.java$[5] program to generate language models of words and character n-grams of up to 12 characters in length, both lowercased and with the original casing. All non-alphabetical characters were also removed.

Table 3 lists some combinations of parameters and the results they achieved for the development data in our experiments. Column heading lnr refers to the length range of lowercased character n-grams, onr to those with original casing, lw and ow tell whether lowercased or origical words were used (y) or not (n). Column heading pm refers to the used penalty modifier.

From these experiments, it was clear that the naive Bayes based language identifier fared better than the one implementing the HeLI method. We also experimented with HeLI 2.0 using language model adaptation scheme identical to what we described in Section 4.2. These experiments failed to increase the macro F_1 score at all.

lnr	*onr*	*lw*	*ow*	*pm*	**macro F1-score**
1-11	1-11	y	y	1.17	0.8334
1-11	1-11	y	n	1.14	0.8305
1-11	-	y	y	1.18	0.8308
-	1-11	y	y	1.17	0.8334
1-10	1-10	y	y	1.17	0.8334
1-9	1-9	y	y	1.17	0.8334
1-8	1-8	y	y	1.17	0.8334
1-7	1-7	y	y	1.10	0.8338
1-6	1-6	y	y	1.11	**0.8403**
1-5	1-5	y	y	1.09	0.8369
2-6	2-6	y	y	1.11	**0.8403**
3-6	3-6	y	y	1.10	0.8396
2-6	2-6	y	n	1.10	0.8319
2-6	2-6	n	y	1.11	**0.8403**

Table 3: The macro F1-scores obtained by HeLI-based identifier when evaluated on the development partition of the DLI training set. See Section 4.3 for the explanations of the column headings. The best results are in bold.

4.4 Language Set Identification

As the mystery lines in the DLI data set were actually multilingual, we wanted to experiment with a system capable of detecting several languages in one text. We set out to incorporate the language set identification method deviced by Jauhiainen et al. (2015b) into the naive Bayes identifier with adaptive language models. A server version of the language set identifier using the HeLI method is currently available at GitHub.[6] It has been successfully used as part of corpus collection and creation pipeline resulting to the Wanca corpora, which has been used in the Uralic Language Identification (ULI) shared task (Jauhiainen et al., 2020a,b). We managed to combine the method to the naive Bayes classifier and run some initial experiments, in which using the language set identification did not improve the results. Unfortunately, we did not have time to finalize our experiments as we were left contemplating about the nature of the multilinguality inherent in the DLI data set and were not encouraged by our initial results.

4.5 Transformers

The system for our second submission (described in Section 5.2) was based on pretrained transformer

[4]The publication of the HeLI 2.0 implementation is still currently in our queue.

[5]https://github.com/tosaja/HeLI

[6]https://github.com/tosaja/TunnistinPalveluMulti

models: multilingual BERT (Devlin et al., 2019) and XLM-RoBERTa (XLM-R) (Conneau et al., 2019). The system used pretrained language models available from the Hugging Face Team [7]. Transformer are effective than RNN based deep learning architectures (Hettiarachchi and Ranasinghe, 2019) in text classification tasks (Ranasinghe et al., 2019; Ranasinghe and Hettiarachchi, 2020; Pitenis et al., 2020).

It was also evaluated using the same development set which was used in the previously described experiments. It the initial experiments it achieved a macro F_1 score of 0.785, which was considerably lower than the 0.861 gained by the simple naive Bayes model even though it used pretrained models as opposed to the naive Bayes which was using only the data provided for the DLI task. We considered generating additional training material from the SUKI data and other available Dravidian corpora written with the native script using automatic transliteration.[8] However, we were doubtful about the performance of such libraries since the texts they were trained with were not natural romanized writing as opposed to the YouTube comments part of the DLI shared task and did not pursue this further.

5 Submissions and Results

In this Section, we summarize the systems we used in our submission and provide the results obtained on the test set.

5.1 System 1: Bayesian Classifier

The results of our first submission were produced using the adaptive version of the naive Bayes classifier with the best parameters attained in the experiments detailed in Sections 4.1 and 4.2.

The system is based on a naive Bayes classifier using the relative frequencies of character n-grams as probabilities (Jauhiainen et al., 2019a). Non-alphabetic characters were removed and the rest were lowercased. The lengths of the character n-grams used were from two to six. Instead of multiplying the relative frequencies we summed up their negative logarithms. As a smoothing value we used the negative logarithm of an n-gram appearing only once multiplied by a penalty modifier. In this case, the penalty modifier was 2.15.

In addition, we used identical language model adaptation technique as was used with the HeLI method in GDI 2018 (Jauhiainen et al., 2018). We used one epoch of language model adaptation to the test data. The n-gram models used, the penalty modifier, the confidence value, and the number of splits in adaptation were optimized using 10% of the training data as the development data.

5.2 System 2: Transformers

These results were produced by using a pretrained transformer model which has been used in a number of NLP tasks like text classification (Pitenis et al., 2020), span classification (Ranasinghe and Zampieri, 2021), word similarity (Hettiarachchi and Ranasinghe, 2020a), question answering (Yang et al., 2019) etc. We pass the sentence through the transformer model and add a softmax layer on top of the [CLS] token as a normal classification architecture with transformers (Ranasinghe and Hettiarachchi, 2020). We fine-tune all the parameters from transformer model as well as the softmax layer jointly by maximising the log-probability of the correct label. This architecture has been used widely in many text classification tasks (Ranasinghe et al., 2019; Ranasinghe and Zampieri, 2020) that includes Malayalam code-mix texts too (Ranasinghe et al., 2020). We did not perform any preprocessing to this architecture. Considering the pretrained transformer models that supports Kannada, Malayalam and Tamil we used multilingual bert (Devlin et al., 2019) and XLM-R large (Conneau et al., 2019) models.

We divided the dataset into a training set and a validation set using 0.8:0.2 split on the data set. We predominantly fine tuned the learning rate and number of epochs of the classification model manually to obtain the best results for the validation set. We obtained $1e^{-}5$ as the best value for learning rate and 3 as the best value for number of epochs. We first fine-tune multiple transformer models with different random seeds. For each input, we output the best predictions made by the transformer along with the probability and sum up the probability of the predictions from each model together. The output of the ensemble model is the prediction with the highest probability. This voted ensemble method has improved results in many tasks (Hettiarachchi and Ranasinghe, 2020b) for transformers.

[7] https://huggingface.co/transformers/pretrained_models.html

[8] Indic transliteration tools provide such functionalities - https://pypi.org/project/indic-transliteration/

5.3 Results on the Test Set

Table 4 shows the results of the shared task. Our first run was clearly better than the second and not far behind the results of the LAST-team.

Rank	Team	Run	Macro F_1
1	LAST	1	0.93
	LAST	2	0.92
	LAST	3	0.92
2	**HWR**	**1**	**0.92**
2	NYAEL	1	0.92
	NAYEL	2	0.91
4	Phlyers	1	0.89
	Phlyers	2	0.89
	HWR	**2**	**0.89**
	NAYEL	3	0.84

Table 4: The results of each team participating on the DLI shared task in terms of Macro F1. Our results are displayed in bold.

6 Discussion

We did not experiment with the NB identifier using non-alphabetic characters nor with the original casing of the alphabetic characters. In light of the results for the HeLI method in Table 3, it might be a promising direction. It seems that at least for the HeLI method, the original character n-grams were more important than lowercased as can be seen from the third and fourth rows of the table. The same NB method was used also in the winning submission of the Romanian Dialect Identification (RDI 2021) shared task organized as part of the same campaign as DLI (Chakravarthi et al., 2021). In RDI, the use of non-alphabetic characters and original casing proved out to be quite important (Jauhiainen et al., 2021) and might have very well cost us the small difference between the second and the first positions in the DLI shared task.

Even though the difference in performance between the NB model and the transformers was only 3 percentage points in the test set, the fact that the transformers did not outperform the simple naive Bayes classifier deserves special attention. One of the reasons to the inferior performance of the pretrained models is probably that the comments contained code-mixed sentences kind of which the pretrained language models like BERT and XLM-R had not seen before.

7 Conclusion

We present the submissions by team HWR to the Dravidian Language Identification (DLI) shared task at VarDial 2021. The DLI shared task featured a challenging dataset including YouTube comments written in Roman script containing code-mixed text with English and one of the three South Dravidian languages: Kannada, Malayalam, and Tamil. Our two systems, obtained competitive performance with the NB system achieving 2nd position in the competition.

Our results are in line with the general trend of deep learning methods not being overtly competitive in language identification tasks as discussed in Medvedeva et al. (2017).

Acknowledgments

We would like to thank the DLI organizers for making this interesting dataset available.

This research has been partly funded by The Finnish Research Impact Foundation in cooperation with Lingsoft.

References

Bharathi Raja Chakravarthi, Mihaela Găman, Radu Tudor Ionescu, Heidi Jauhiainen, Tommi Jauhiainen, Krister Lindén, Nikola Ljubešić, Niko Partanen, Ruba Priyadharshini, Christoph Purschke, Eswari Rajagopal, Yves Scherrer, and Marcos Zampieri. 2021. Findings of the VarDial Evaluation Campaign 2021. In *Proceedings of the Eighth Workshop on NLP for Similar Languages, Varieties and Dialects (VarDial)*.

Bharathi Raja Chakravarthi, Navya Jose, Shardul Suryawanshi, Elizabeth Sherly, and John Philip McCrae. 2020a. A sentiment analysis dataset for code-mixed Malayalam-English. In *Proceedings of SLTU/CCURL*.

Bharathi Raja Chakravarthi, Vigneshwaran Muralidaran, Ruba Priyadharshini, and John Philip McCrae. 2020b. Corpus creation for sentiment analysis in code-mixed Tamil-English text. In *Proceedings of SLTU/CCURL*.

Monojit Choudhury, Gokul Chittaranjan, Parth Gupta, and Amitava Das. 2014. Overview of FIRE 2014 Track on Transliterated Search. In *Proceedings of FIRE*.

Alexis Conneau, Kartikay Khandelwal, Naman Goyal, Vishrav Chaudhary, Guillaume Wenzek, Francisco Guzmán, Edouard Grave, Myle Ott, Luke Zettlemoyer, and Veselin Stoyanov. 2019. Unsupervised cross-lingual representation learning at scale. In *Proceedings of ACL*.

Jacob Devlin, Ming-Wei Chang, Kenton Lee, and Kristina Toutanova. 2019. Bert: Pre-training of deep bidirectional transformers for language understanding. In *Proceedings of NAACL*.

Koustava Goswami, Rajdeep Sarkar, Bharathi Raja Chakravarthi, Theodorus Fransen, and John Philip McCrae. 2020. Unsupervised deep language and dialect identification for short texts. In *Proceedings of COLING*.

Cyril Goutte, Serge Léger, Shervin Malmasi, and Marcos Zampieri. 2016. Discriminating Similar Languages: Evaluations and Explorations. In *Proceedings of LREC*.

Gregory Grefenstette. 1995. Comparing Two Language Identification Schemes. In *Proceedings of JADT*.

Mihaela Găman, Dirk Hovy, Radu Tudor Ionescu, Heidi Jauhiainen, Tommi Jauhiainen, Krister Lindén, Nikola Ljubešić, Niko Partanen, Christoph Purschke, Yves Scherrer, and Marcos Zampieri. 2020. A Report on the VarDial Evaluation Campaign 2020. In *Proceedings of VarDial*.

Adeep Hande, Ruba Priyadharshini, and Bharathi Raja Chakravarthi. 2020. KanCMD: Kannada CodeMixed dataset for sentiment analysis and offensive language detection. In *Proceedings of PEOPLES*.

M. Hanumathappa and Mallamma V. Reddy. 2012. Natural Language Identification and Translation Tool for Natural Language Processing. *International Journal of Science and Applied Information Technology*, 1(4).

Peter Henrich. 1989. Language Identification for the Automatic Grapheme-to-phoneme Conversion of Foreign Words in a German Text-to-speech System. In *Proceedings of EUROSPEECH*.

Hansi Hettiarachchi and Tharindu Ranasinghe. 2019. Emoji powered capsule network to detect type and target of offensive posts in social media. In *Proceedings of RANLP*.

Hansi Hettiarachchi and Tharindu Ranasinghe. 2020a. BRUMS at SemEval-2020 task 3: Contextualised embeddings for predicting the (graded) effect of context in word similarity. In *Proceedings of SemEval*.

Hansi Hettiarachchi and Tharindu Ranasinghe. 2020b. InfoMiner at WNUT-2020 task 2: Transformer-based covid-19 informative tweet extraction. In *Proceedings of W-NUT*.

Arthur S. House and Edward P. Neuburg. 1977. Toward Automatic Identification of the Language of an Utterance. I. Preliminary Methodological Considerations. *The Journal of the Acoustical Society of America*, 62(3):708–713.

Heidi Jauhiainen, Tommi Jauhiainen, and Krister Lindén. 2015a. The Finno-Ugric Languages and The Internet Project. In *Proceedings of IWCLUL*.

Heidi Jauhiainen, Tommi Jauhiainen, and Krister Lindén. 2020a. Building web corpora for minority languages. In *Proceedings of WAC*.

Tommi Jauhiainen, Heidi Jauhiainen, and Lindén. 2021. Naive Bayes-based Experiments in Romanian Dialect Identification. In *Proceedings of VarDial*.

Tommi Jauhiainen, Heidi Jauhiainen, and Krister Lindén. 2018. HeLI-based experiments in Swiss German dialect identification. In *Proceedings of VarDial*.

Tommi Jauhiainen, Heidi Jauhiainen, and Krister Lindén. 2019a. Discriminating between Mandarin Chinese and Swiss-German varieties using adaptive language models. In *Proceedings of VarDial*.

Tommi Jauhiainen, Heidi Jauhiainen, Niko Partanen, and Krister Lindén. 2020b. Uralic Language Identification (ULI) 2020 shared task dataset and the Wanca 2017 corpora. In *Proceedings of VarDial*.

Tommi Jauhiainen, Krister Lindén, and Heidi Jauhiainen. 2015b. Language Set Identification in Noisy Synthetic Multilingual Documents. In *Proceedings of CICLing*.

Tommi Jauhiainen, Krister Lindén, and Heidi Jauhiainen. 2016. HeLI, a Word-Based Backoff Method for Language Identification. In *Proceedings of VarDial*.

Tommi Jauhiainen, Krister Lindén, and Heidi Jauhiainen. 2019b. Language model adaptation for language and dialect identification of text. *Natural Language Engineering*, 25(5):561–583.

Tommi Jauhiainen, Marco Lui, Marcos Zampieri, Timothy Baldwin, and Krister Lindén. 2019c. Automatic Language Identification in Texts: A Survey. *Journal of Artificial Intelligence Research*, 65:675–782.

Tom Kocmi and Ondřej Bojar. 2017. LanideNN: Multilingual Language Identification on Character Window. In *Proceedings of EACL*.

Martin Majliš. 2011. Large Multilingual Corpus. Master's thesis, Charles University in Prague, Prague.

Shervin Malmasi and Marcos Zampieri. 2017a. Arabic Dialect Identification Using iVectors and ASR Transcripts. In *Proceedings of VarDial*.

Shervin Malmasi and Marcos Zampieri. 2017b. German Dialect Identification in Interview Transcriptions. In *Proceedings of VarDial*.

Bruno Martins and Mário J. Silva. 2005. Language Identification in Web Pages. In *Proceedings of SAC*.

Maria Medvedeva, Martin Kroon, and Barbara Plank. 2017. When sparse traditional models outperform dense neural networks: the curious case of discriminating between similar languages. In *Proceedings of VarDial*.

Giovanni Molina, Fahad AlGhamdi, Mahmoud Ghoneim, Abdelati Hawwari, Nicolas Rey-Villamizar, Mona Diab, and Thamar Solorio. 2016. Overview for the second shared task on language identification in code-switched data. In *Proceedings of CodeSwitch*.

Kavi Narayana Murthy and G. Bharadwaja Kumar. 2006. Language Identification from Small Text Samples. *Journal of Quantitative Linguistics*, 13(1):57–80.

Seppo Mustonen. 1965. Multiple Discriminant Analysis in Linguistic Problems. *Statistical Methods in Linguistics*, 4:37–44.

Zeses Pitenis, Marcos Zampieri, and Tharindu Ranasinghe. 2020. Offensive Language Identification in Greek. In *Proceedings of LREC*.

Tharindu Ranasinghe, Sarthak Gupte, Marcos Zampieri, and Ifeoma Nwogu. 2020. WLV-RIT at HASOC-Dravidian-CodeMix-FIRE2020: Offensive Language Identification in Code-switched YouTube Comments. In *Proceedings of FIRE*.

Tharindu Ranasinghe and Hansi Hettiarachchi. 2020. BRUMS at SemEval-2020 task 12: Transformer based multilingual offensive language identification in social media. In *Proceedings of SemEval*.

Tharindu Ranasinghe and Marcos Zampieri. 2020. Multilingual offensive language identification with cross-lingual embeddings. In *Proceedings of EMNLP*.

Tharindu Ranasinghe and Marcos Zampieri. 2021. MUDES: Multilingual Detection of Offensive Spans. In *arXiv preprint arXiv:2102.09665*.

Tharindu Ranasinghe, Marcos Zampieri, and Hansi Hettiarachchi. 2019. BRUMS at HASOC 2019: Deep Learning Models for Multilingual Hate Speech and Offensive Language Identification. In *Proceedings of FIRE*.

Rishiraj Saha Roy, Monojit Choudhury, Prasenjit Majumder, and Komal Agarwal. 2013. Overview of the FIRE 2013 Track on Transliterated Search. In *Proceedings of FIRE*.

Thamar Solorio, Elizabeth Blair, Suraj Maharjan, Steven Bethard, Mona Diab, Mahmoud Ghoneim, Abdelati Hawwari, Fahad AlGhamdi, Julia Hirschberg, Alison Chang, et al. 2014. Overview for the first shared task on language identification in code-switched data. In *Proceedings of CodeSwitch*.

Liling Tan, Marcos Zampieri, Nikola Ljubešic, and Jörg Tiedemann. 2014. Merging Comparable Data Sources for the Discrimination of Similar Languages: The DSL Corpus Collection. In *Proceedings of BUCC*.

Jörg Tiedemann and Nikola Ljubešić. 2012. Efficient Discrimination between Closely Related Languages. In *Proceedings of COLING*.

J. Vinosh Babu and S. Baskaran. 2005. Automatic Language Identification Using Multivariate Analysis. In *Proceedings of CICLing*.

Wei Yang, Yuqing Xie, Aileen Lin, Xingyu Li, Luchen Tan, Kun Xiong, Ming Li, and Jimmy Lin. 2019. End-to-end open-domain question answering with BERTserini. In *Proceedings of NAACL*.

Marcos Zampieri, Shervin Malmasi, Preslav Nakov, Ahmed Ali, Suwon Shon, James Glass, Yves Scherrer, Tanja Samardžić, Nikola Ljubešić, Jörg Tiedemann, Chris van der Lee, Stefan Grondelaers, Nelleke Oostdijk, Dirk Speelman, Antal van den Bosch, Ritesh Kumar, Bornini Lahiri, and Mayank Jain. 2018. Language Identification and Morphosyntactic Tagging: The Second VarDial Evaluation Campaign. In *Proceedings of VarDial*.

Marcos Zampieri, Shervin Malmasi, Yves Scherrer, Tanja Samardžić, Francis Tyers, Miikka Silfverberg, Natalia Klyueva, Tung-Le Pan, Chu-Ren Huang, Radu Tudor Ionescu, Andrei Butnaru, and Tommi Jauhiainen. 2019. A Report on the Third VarDial Evaluation Campaign. In *Proceedings of VarDial*.

Marcos Zampieri, Preslav Nakov, and Yves Scherrer. 2020. Natural Language Processing for Similar Languages, Varieties, and Dialects: A Survey. *Natural Language Engineering*, 26:595–612.

Arkaitz Zubiaga, Inaki San Vicente, Pablo Gamallo, José Ramom Pichel, Inaki Alegria, Nora Aranberri, Aitzol Ezeiza, and Víctor Fresno. 2016. Tweetlid: a benchmark for tweet language identification. *Language Resources and Evaluation*, 50(4):729–766.

N-gram and Neural Models for Uralic Language Identification: NRC at VarDial 2021

Gabriel Bernier-Colborne, Serge Léger, Cyril Goutte
National Research Council Canada
{Gabriel.Bernier-Colborne, Serge.Leger, Cyril.Goutte}@nrc-cnrc.gc.ca

Abstract

We describe the systems developed by the National Research Council Canada for the Uralic language identification shared task at the 2021 VarDial evaluation campaign. We evaluated two different approaches to this task: a probabilistic classifier exploiting only character 5-grams as features, and a character-based neural network pre-trained through self-supervision, then fine-tuned on the language identification task. The former method turned out to perform better, which casts doubt on the usefulness of deep learning methods for language identification, where they have yet to convincingly and consistently outperform simpler and less costly classification algorithms exploiting n-gram features.

1 Introduction

The goal of the Uralic language identification (ULI) shared task at VarDial 2021 (Chakravarthi et al., 2021) was to identify and discriminate 29 Uralic language varieties, among a total of 178 language varieties from various families, given a short text (typically a sentence). This was a re-run of the ULI task at VarDial 2020 (Găman et al., 2020).

We experimented with two different approaches to the ULI task. The first is a probabilistic classifier that exploits only character 5-grams as features. The second is a deep learning approach based on character embeddings and a transformer network (Vaswani et al., 2017), which is first pre-trained through self-supervision, then fine-tuned on the ULI task, in a similar fashion to BERT (Devlin et al., 2019).

This second approach is essentially an improved version of the one developed by the NRC team for the first run of the ULI task (Bernier-Colborne and Goutte, 2020). By improving the sampling functions used to sample training and evaluation data, and making a few other small changes to the model, we were able to achieve much better results. However, our best results were achieved using the simpler approach, based on character 5-grams.

In this paper, we explain these two approaches to language identification and compare the results obtained on the ULI task.

2 Data and Task Definition

The ULI data and task are described by Jauhiainen et al. (2020). The goal of the task is to identify the language of a short text, typically a single sentence. If more than one language is used (e.g. code switching), the main language must be identified.

This was a closed task, so the only data that could be used was the training set provided. The data contain both relevant and non-relevant languages. The 29 relevant languages are part of the Uralic group of languages, spoken mainly in northern Eurasia. Some are very under-resourced, and some are already extinct. Besides these, there are 149 non-relevant languages, belonging to various language families. These include the three largest Uralic languages, i.e. Estonian, Finnish, and Hungarian. In total, the data covers 178 language varieties, which is the highest number covered so far in a language identification shared task.

The training set contains 646,043 examples for the relevant languages and 63,772,445 examples for the non-relevant ones. So there is about 100 times more data for the non-relevant languages, and there are 5 times more non-relevant languages than relevant ones, therefore the number of examples is about 20 times greater for non-relevant languages, on average. Both parts of the training set are highly unbalanced. The class frequencies of relevant languages range from 19 to 214,225, and those of non-relevant ones range from 10,000 to 3,000,000.

The task was divided into three tracks, the difference being the way in which the evaluation metric

Proceedings of the 8th VarDial Workshop on NLP for Similar Languages, Varieties and Dialects, pages 128–134
April 20, 2021 ©2021 Association for Computational Linguistics

is computed. For tracks 1 and 2, the evaluation metrics are the macro-averaged F1 and micro-averaged F1 respectively, and it only considers examples where either the predicted label or the true label is a relevant language. For track 3, the metric is macro-averaged F1, computed over all examples.

Some of the challenges of this task were highlighted by Bernier-Colborne and Goutte (2020) and Jauhiainen et al. (2020). These include: the presence of low-resource and closely-related language varieties; the large size of the training set; the large and complex class imbalances in the training set; and the absence of an official development set, which, while a valid design choice for this competition, added a degree of complexity.

3 Models

We evaluated two approaches to this task, which we describe in this section.

3.1 Probcat

The first approach employs a probabilistic classifier (Gaussier et al., 2002), that we call Probcat, which we trained using character 5-grams as features. The classifier is similar to multinomial Naive Bayes except that it does not assume that all n-grams in a given text are generated from a single class. It has been used in the past to obtain state-of-the-art results on language identification tasks (Goutte and Léger, 2016) . For more details on this classification algorithm, refer to Goutte et al. (2014, Sec. 2.2).

For reference, running inference on the official test, which contains over 1.5 million examples, takes about four and a half hours using four Intel Xeon CPUs @ 2.6 GHz, and could be reduced by using more CPUs. Training takes about five and a half hours. Memory requirement is below 32 GB.

3.2 Transformer

The second approach is a deep learning approach, which the NRC team has previously applied, with very different levels of success, to Cuneiform language identification (Bernier-Colborne et al., 2019) and Uralic language identification (Bernier-Colborne and Goutte, 2020). In the former case, it produced a winning submission, whereas in the latter, it was well under the baseline, because of a flaw in the methods used to sample training and evaluation data.

The model is a deep neural network which takes sequences of characters as input. Characters are embedded and fed through a stack of bidirectional transformers (Vaswani et al., 2017), which encodes the sequence. The output of this encoder is a sequence of hidden state vectors (one per input character), which is then fed to various output heads (or modules) during training.

The model is trained in two stages: self-supervised pre-training on a masked language modeling (MLM) task (Devlin et al., 2019), followed by supervised fine-tuning on the target task, i.e. language identification. For MLM, the objective is to predict one or more randomly chosen characters in the input sequence, which are replaced with a special masking symbol before the embedding stage. This produces a model that can predict characters in context for any of the languages used for training, and must therefore have learned some of the specific surface regularities of each. The output head for this task is a softmax over the vocabulary (or alphabet), which takes as input the encoding (i.e. final hidden state) of a masked character, and the loss is cross-entropy.

After pre-training, we fine-tune for language identification by keeping the pre-trained encoder, discarding the MLM head, and replacing it with a head containing: an average pooling layer, that averages the final hidden states of the encoder to produce a fixed-length encoding of the sentence (Reimers and Gurevych, 2019); followed by a relu activation; and finally a softmax over the 178 languages. Again, the loss is cross-entropy.

The vocabulary (or alphabet) contains every character that appears more than once in the training portion of the train/dev/test split we created (see Section 4.1). Characters that are not in this vocab are replaced with a special symbol reserved for unknown characters, before the encoding stage.

The hyperparameter settings we used largely follow the recommendations of Devlin et al. (2019), except that we use fewer layers than their base architecture (to reduce training time and memory requirements):

- Nb transformer layers: 8
- Nb attention heads: 12
- Hidden layer size: 768
- Feed forward/filter size: 3072
- Hidden activation: gelu

- Dropout probability: 0.1
- Optimizer: Adam
- Learning rate (pre-training): 1e-4
- Nb steps (pre-training): 1M
- Warmup steps (pre-training): 10K
- Batch size (pre-training): 64
- Maximum input length (pre-training): 128
- Learning rate (fine-tuning): 1e-5
- Batch size (fine-tuning): 32
- Maximum input length (fine-tuning): 256

During pre-training, examples were sampled from our training set using the frequency-based sampling function described by Bernier-Colborne and Goutte (2020). We refer the reader to this paper for the full equations. In essence, we compute the relative frequencies of relevant and non-relevant languages separately, damp each of the two resulting distributions using exponent α, multiply the distribution of relevant languages by coefficient γ, then combine the two distributions and re-normalize. We arbitrarily set $\alpha = 1$ and $\gamma = 1$, which means that relevant and non-relevant examples are sampled in approximately equal proportion, so the relevant languages will end up being sampled about 5 times more frequently than non-relevant ones, on average, as there are about 5 times fewer relevant languages.

During fine-tuning, we experimented with various functions to sample the labeled training examples from the training set, including this frequency-based function. The other functions we experimented with were:

- Class-wise uniform sampling
- Accuracy-based sampling using a dynamic estimate of class-wise accuracy. We tested two different functions to estimate this, both based on the same score, which is the class-wise, one-vs-rest binary accuracy on the dev set. If we call the set of class-wise scores m, then the two functions we tested to compute sampling probabilities can be formulated as follows:

$$p_{\text{inv}}(m_i) = \frac{1 - m_i}{\sum_j (1 - m_j)}$$

$$p_{\text{rank}}(m_i) = \frac{\text{rank}(m_i, m)}{\sum_j \text{rank}(m_j, m)}$$

where $\text{rank}(m_i, m)$ returns the rank of m_i.

During fine-tuning, the maximum input length was increased to 256; the extra position embeddings are still randomly initialized at this point, and are learned during fine-tuning. To reduce useless computation, rather than padding or truncating all sequences in a given batch to the maximum length of 256, we pad or truncate them to the length of the longest sequence in the batch. This change reduced computation time significantly with respect to our previous implementation, as the vast majority (over 99%) of examples in the ULI training data are shorter than 256 characters.

Our code, which exploits the Transformers library by HuggingFace (Wolf et al., 2020), is available is at `https://www.github.com/gbcolborne/vardial2021`.

All experiments were conducted on a single GPU with 12 GB of memory. Inference on the official test set takes about 70 minutes using a v100. Pre-training took about 10 days, and we fine-tuned for about 3 days.

4 Experiments

To evaluate and optimize our two approaches, we first had to create a development set, as none was provided for this shared task, as mentioned in Section 2.

4.1 Making a Development Set

To sample our development sets, we used the frequency-based sampling function described in Section 3.2, with $\alpha = 1$ and $\gamma = 1$, to sample a 'dev' set containing 20,000 examples and a 'dev-test' set containing 100,000 examples. The idea was to use the dev set to tune the hyperparameters of the models, then use the dev-test set to get an unbiased estimate of the accuracy of the fully tuned models. However, due to time constraints, in the case of the transformer model, we ended up adding the dev-test set to the training set, and using the dev set for model selection. We will come back to this in the following section.

4.2 Model Selection

To optimize Probcat, we compared 4 different n-gram lengths, from 2 to 5. The models were trained on our training set and evaluated on both our development sets. Results showed that 5-grams produced the best results, as shown in Table 1. Note that after the official evaluation, we tried combining various n-gram lengths, but did not observe any improvements on our development sets.

n	Track 1		Track 2		Track 3	
	Dev	Test	Dev	Test	Dev	Test
2	0.760	0.763	0.769	0.774	0.766	0.743
3	0.917	0.844	0.941	0.936	0.912	0.890
4	0.960	0.916	0.973	0.970	0.939	0.929
5	**0.963**	**0.936**	**0.978**	**0.976**	**0.951**	**0.943**

Table 1: F-scores of Probcat on dev and dev-test sets, with respect to n-gram length (n).

We made a single submission using this approach, using only 5-grams as features. The entire training set was used to train the classifier for this submission.

As for the transformer model, we conducted various experiments involving: optimizing the architecture (e.g. replacing the tanh activation in the pooling layer with a relu activation); developing better sampling functions for training; and tuning a few hyperparameters, such as the learning rate and batch size. We will not present the full results of these experiments here, because of their ad hoc nature.

We ended up making a first set of two submissions, and a final set of four submissions. As the results of the latter were better, we will not go into the model selection tests that led to the first set of submissions.

For our final model selection experiment, we decided to add the dev-test set to the training set (for lack of time to re-train models on the entire training set), and rely on the dev set evaluation to select models. Note that, because of this reason, the results of these tests are not directly comparable to the dev scores of Probcat.

We focused on the sampling function used to fine-tune the model, and compared the functions described in Section 3.2:

- Frequency-based sampling, with a few different values of α and γ, i.e. ($\alpha = 1, \gamma = 1$), ($\alpha = 0.75, \gamma = 1$), and ($\alpha = 0.75, \gamma = 0.5$).
- Uniform sampling.
- Accuracy-based sampling, using either p_{inv} or p_{rank} to convert class-wise dev-scores to sampling probabilities.

We compared a couple different learning rates (i.e. 3e-6 and 1e-5). Models were fine-tuned for a maximum of 820K steps, and validated every 20K steps, with early stopping on the dev set, using either the track 1 or track 3 score as stopping criterion.

Sampling	Track 1	Track 2	Track 3
Frequency	**0.977**	**0.989**	**0.978**
Uniform	0.973	0.986	0.969
Acc. (p_{inv})	0.974	0.988	0.977
Acc. (p_{rank})	0.975	0.987	0.974

Table 2: Best F-scores of transformer model on dev set, with respect to sampling function.

The results, summarized in Table 2, suggested frequency-based sampling worked best, but all sampling functions achieved high scores, with accuracy-based sampling working slightly better than uniform sampling. The optimal learning rate was 1e-5.

We submitted four runs, two of which were tuned (in terms of the sampling function and early stopping) to track 1, and two of which were tuned to track 3:

- Track 1, run 1: frequency-based sampling (with $\alpha = 0.75, \gamma = 0.5$), early stopped for track 1.
- Track 1, run 2: accuracy-based sampling (with p_{rank}), early stopped for track 1.
- Track 3, run 1: frequency-based sampling (with $\alpha = 0.75, \gamma = 0.5$), early stopped for track 3.
- Track 3, run 2: accuracy-based sampling (with p_{inv}), early stopped for track 3.

5 Official Results

The scores of our best runs on the official test set are shown in Table 3. The baseline scores were computed using the HeLI method (Jauhiainen et al., 2017). Probcat was the only system to beat the baseline on track 2, and one of two systems that beat the baseline on track 1 (along with an ensemble of SVM and naive Bayes models exploiting 3-, 4-, and 5-grams, which scored 0.809 on track 1, but only 0.593 on track 2 according to the leaderboard[1]

[1] `http://urn.fi/urn:nbn:fi:lb-2020102201`

at the time of writing). The baseline on track 3 has yet to be beaten.

Our results using the transformer model are competitive on tracks 2 and 3, but less so on track 1, which focuses on the macro-averaged F-score on relevant languages.

System	Track 1	Track 2	Track 3
Baseline	0.800	0.963	**0.925**
Probcat	**0.814**	**0.967**	0.908
Transformer	0.743	0.953	0.904

Table 3: F-scores of our best runs and the baseline system (i.e. HeLI) on the offical test set.

The scores of our final 4 runs of the transformer model are shown in Table 4.

Run	Track 1	Track 2	Track 3
Track 1, run 1	0.718	0.928	0.898
Track 1, run 2	0.737	**0.953**	**0.904**
Track 3, run 1	**0.743**	0.928	0.899
Track 3, run 2	0.615	0.830	0.784

Table 4: F-scores of our 4 final runs of the transformer model on the offical test set.

These results suggest our development sets were not very good estimators for model selection, as a model that we (slightly) tuned for track 1 was best on tracks 2 and 3, whereas a model we tuned for track 3 was best on track 1. If we check how many training steps each of the four models did before early stopping, we see that the model that stopped earliest produced the poorest results on the test set:

- Track 1, run 1: step 649375
- Track 1, run 2: step 651875
- Track 3, run 1: step 726875
- Track 3, run 2: step 590625

We also see that the model that stopped the latest produced the best results on track 3; since the batch size was 32, that model observed about 23 million samples from the training set (including duplicate samples from rare classes), which is less than the total number of available training samples. Given these observations, it seems likely that we could have obtained better results by fine-tuning longer. Other ways of improving the accuracy of this model include: trying multiple random initializations; exploring the hyperparameter space more extensively or efficiently; fine-tuning on the complete training set; or adapting the model to the unlabeled test examples (e.g. through self-supervised MLM or self-training on the language identification task).

We could not conduct extensive error analysis because we did not have access to the test labels at the time of writing, but we did inspect the predictions of our systems to try to gain insights on their behaviour or the properties of the data.

If we look at the cumulative predicted frequency of the 29 relevant languages, we find that Probcat predicted a relevant language for 21,051 or 1.4% of the 1,510,315 test cases. Since Probcat achieved 0.967 on track 2, this must be very close to the actual number of relevant examples in the test set. Thus, the distribution of relevant vs. non-relevant examples is very different than the one we assumed when we constructed our dev set. Furthermore, the worst of our four transformer runs seems to have over-detected relevant examples, as it predicted a relevant language for 27,901 test cases.

If we look at the top off-diagonal values in the confusion matrix between Probcat and our best transformer run (i.e. track 1, run 2, which performed best overall) for all 178 languages, assuming Probcat's predictions as ground truth (as it performed better), we find that the 10 most frequently confused pairs (Probcat prediction, transformer prediction) are:

1. Indonesian, Sundanese (10110)
2. Tatar, Bashkir (9897)
3. Indonesian, Wu Chinese (6184)
4. Indonesian, Standard Malay (5957)
5. Javanese, Sundanese (5550)
6. Croatian, Bosnian (5312)
7. Mandarin Chinese, Wu Chinese (4453)
8. Japanese, Wu Chinese (4136)
9. Iranian Persian, Pushto (3806)
10. Italian, Lombard (2574)

These contain pairs that are notoriously hard to distinguish, e.g. Croatian and Bosnian.

If we restrict this analysis to pairs involving a relevant language, we find that the top 10 most confused pairs are:

1. Standard Estonian, Võro (467)
2. Võro, Standard Estonian (388)
3. Standard Estonian, Veps (86)
4. Finnish, Tornedalen Finnish (51)
5. Ludian, Veps (44)
6. Ludian, Livvi (43)
7. Tornedalen Finnish, Finnish (35)
8. Russian, Eastern and Meadow Mari (32)
9. Haitian, Veps (31)
10. Finnish, Võro (15)

Note that several of these involve a non-relevant Uralic language, i.e. Standard Estonian or Finnish, which raises the question as to whether the Standard Estonian and Finnish training corpora contain noisy examples actually belonging to a relevant, low-resource language variety.

We manually inspected some of the test cases for which Probcat predicted a language that we understand, i.e. English, and looked for potential sources of errors. Without access to the gold labels, we could not glean much, but we did observe examples where English is used within sentences that are mainly in another language:

- Kanta horien artean ezagunenak "Cocaine", "After Midnight", "Call Me the Breeze", "Travelling Light" eta "Sensitive Kind" dira.
- 外国人以为皮蛋要腌交关年，所以叫渠Century egg（世纪蛋）。

And examples that are not in Standard English, but a closely related language or variety:

- The GT wis sauld alangside the GTi for a few months, but wis eventually phased oot.
- The population increased frae 76,254 inhabitants (1992 census) tae 77,566 (2001 census), an increase o 1.7 %.
- Ships o the Hudson's Bay Company wur regular visitors, as wur whalin fleets.

We plan on conducting a more extensive error analysis once the gold labels of the test set are made available.

6 Related Work

Thorough surveys of research on language identification are provided by Jauhiainen et al. (2019) and Zampieri et al. (2020). Language identification is one of the few tasks in natural language processing where deep learning methods have yet to provide convincing gains in accuracy or robustness. Simpler classifiers based on character n-grams continue to provide state-of-the-art results on many benchmarks. The winning submission by the NRC team to the Cuneiform language identification task at VarDial 2019 was the first time a neural system was ranked first on a language identification shared task (Zampieri et al., 2019). That task involved 7 language varieties, and less complex class imbalances. The results of this Uralic language identification shared task cast doubt on whether a character-based deep neural network can advance the state of the art in settings more representative of real-world applications of language identification, such as crawling the web to automatically compile monolingual corpora for low-resource languages.

7 Conclusion

For the Uralic language identification shared task at the 2021 VarDial evaluation campaign, the NRC team evaluated two different approaches: a probabilistic classifier exploiting only character 5-grams as features, and a character-based neural network pre-trained through self-supervision, then fine-tuned on the language identification task. The former method ended up being ranked first on two of the three tracks, and outperformed our neural approach on all three tracks. We do not exclude the possibility that deep learning approaches could improve accuracy or robustness on this task, but the results we were able to obtain within the limited time constraints of this shared task suggest that the simpler, n-gram based approach is still a very strong baseline.

Acknowledgments

We thank the organizers for their work developing and running this shared task.

References

Gabriel Bernier-Colborne and Cyril Goutte. 2020. Challenges in neural language identification: NRC at VarDial 2020. In *Proceedings of the 7th Workshop on NLP for Similar Languages, Varieties and*

Dialects, pages 273–282, Barcelona, Spain (Online). International Committee on Computational Linguistics (ICCL).

Gabriel Bernier-Colborne, Cyril Goutte, and Serge Léger. 2019. Improving cuneiform language identification with BERT. In *Proceedings of the Sixth Workshop on NLP for Similar Languages, Varieties and Dialects*, pages 17–25, Ann Arbor, Michigan. Association for Computational Linguistics.

Bharathi Raja Chakravarthi, Mihaela Găman, Radu Tudor Ionescu, Heidi Jauhiainen, Tommi Jauhiainen, Krister Lindén, Nikola Ljubešić, Niko Partanen, Ruba Priyadharshini, Christoph Purschke, Eswari Rajagopal, Yves Scherrer, and Marcos Zampieri. 2021. Findings of the VarDial Evaluation Campaign 2021. In *Proceedings of the Eighth Workshop on NLP for Similar Languages, Varieties and Dialects (VarDial)*.

Jacob Devlin, Ming-Wei Chang, Kenton Lee, and Kristina Toutanova. 2019. BERT: Pre-training of deep bidirectional transformers for language understanding. In *Proceedings of NAACL*, pages 4171–4186.

Eric Gaussier, Cyril Goutte, Kris Popat, and Francine Chen. 2002. A hierarchical model for clustering and categorising documents. In *Proceedings of the 24th BCS-IRSG European Colloquium on IR Research: Advances in Information Retrieval*, pages 229–247. Springer-Verlag.

Cyril Goutte and Serge Léger. 2016. Advances in Ngram-based Discrimination of Similar Languages. In *Proceedings of the Third Workshop on NLP for Similar Languages, Varieties and Dialects (VarDial3)*, pages 178–184, Osaka, Japan.

Cyril Goutte, Serge Léger, and Marine Carpuat. 2014. The NRC system for discriminating similar languages. In *Proceedings of the First Workshop on Applying NLP Tools to Similar Languages, Varieties and Dialects (VarDial)*, pages 139–145, Dublin, Ireland.

Mihaela Găman, Dirk Hovy, Radu Tudor Ionescu, Heidi Jauhiainen, Tommi Jauhiainen, Krister Lindén, Nikola Ljubešić, Niko Partanen, Christoph Purschke, Yves Scherrer, and Marcos Zampieri. 2020. A Report on the VarDial Evaluation Campaign 2020. In *Proceedings of the Seventh Workshop on NLP for Similar Languages, Varieties and Dialects (VarDial)*.

Tommi Jauhiainen, Heidi Jauhiainen, Niko Partanen, and Krister Lindén. 2020. Uralic Language Identification (ULI) 2020 shared task dataset and the Wanca 2017 corpus. In *Proceedings of the Seventh Workshop on NLP for Similar Languages, Varieties and Dialects (VarDial)*, pages 688–698.

Tommi Jauhiainen, Krister Lindén, and Heidi Jauhiainen. 2017. Evaluating HeLI with non-linear mappings. In *Proceedings of the Fourth Workshop on NLP for Similar Languages, Varieties and Dialects (VarDial)*, pages 102–108, Valencia, Spain.

Tommi Jauhiainen, Marco Lui, Marcos Zampieri, Timothy Baldwin, and Krister Lindén. 2019. Automatic Language Identification in Texts: A Survey. *Journal of Artificial Intelligence Research*, 65:675–782.

Nils Reimers and Iryna Gurevych. 2019. Sentence-BERT: Sentence embeddings using Siamese BERT-networks. In *Proceedings of the 2019 Conference on Empirical Methods in Natural Language Processing and the 9th International Joint Conference on Natural Language Processing (EMNLP-IJCNLP)*, pages 3982–3992, Hong Kong, China. Association for Computational Linguistics.

Ashish Vaswani, Noam Shazeer, Niki Parmar, Jakob Uszkoreit, Llion Jones, Aidan N Gomez, Łukasz Kaiser, and Illia Polosukhin. 2017. Attention is all you need. In *Advances in Neural Information Processing Systems*, pages 5998–6008.

Thomas Wolf, Lysandre Debut, Victor Sanh, Julien Chaumond, Clement Delangue, Anthony Moi, Pierric Cistac, Tim Rault, Rémi Louf, Morgan Funtowicz, Joe Davison, Sam Shleifer, Patrick von Platen, Clara Ma, Yacine Jernite, Julien Plu, Canwen Xu, Teven Le Scao, Sylvain Gugger, Mariama Drame, Quentin Lhoest, and Alexander M. Rush. 2020. HuggingFace's Transformers: State-of-the-art natural language processing.

Marcos Zampieri, Shervin Malmasi, Yves Scherrer, Tanja Samardžić, Francis Tyers, Miikka Silfverberg, Natalia Klyueva, Tung-Le Pan, Chu-Ren Huang, Radu Tudor Ionescu, Andrei Butnaru, and Tommi Jauhiainen. 2019. A Report on the Third VarDial Evaluation Campaign. In *Proceedings of the Sixth Workshop on NLP for Similar Languages, Varieties and Dialects (VarDial)*. Association for Computational Linguistics.

Marcos Zampieri, Preslav Nakov, and Yves Scherrer. 2020. Natural language processing for similar languages, varieties, and dialects: A survey. *Natural Language Engineering*, 26(6):595–612.

Social Media Variety Geolocation with geoBERT

Yves Scherrer
Department of Digital Humanities
University of Helsinki
yves.scherrer@helsinki.fi

Nikola Ljubešić
Department of Knowledge Technologies
Jožef Stefan Institute
nikola.ljubesic@ijs.si

Abstract

This paper describes the Helsinki–Ljubljana contribution to the VarDial 2021 shared task on social media variety geolocation. Following our successful participation at VarDial 2020, we again propose constrained and unconstrained systems based on the BERT architecture. In this paper, we report experiments with different tokenization settings and different pre-trained models, and we contrast our parameter-free regression approach with various classification schemes proposed by other participants at VarDial 2020. Both the code and the best-performing pre-trained models are made freely available.

1 Introduction

The SMG (Social Media Geolocation) task was first introduced at VarDial 2020 (Gaman et al., 2020). In this task, the participants were asked to predict latitude-longitude coordinate pairs. This contrasts with most other VarDial tasks, in which the goal is to choose from a finite set of variety labels. The second edition of the SMG task is run at VarDial 2021 (Chakravarthi et al., 2021), with the same three language areas as in the previous year: the Bosnian-Croatian-Montenegrin-Serbian (BCMS) language area, the German language area comprised of Germany and Austria (DE-AT), and German-speaking Switzerland (CH). All three datasets are based on social media data, Twitter in the case of BCMS (Ljubešić et al., 2016) and Jodel in the case of DE-AT and CH (Hovy and Purschke, 2018).

This paper describes the HeLju (Helsinki–Ljubljana) submission to the SMG task. Following our successful participation in 2020 (Scherrer and Ljubešić, 2020), we again propose systems based on the BERT architecture in both constrained and unconstrained settings. We report experiments with different tokenization parameters and with newly available pre-trained models. Furthermore, we compare our parameter-free double regression approach with three classification schemes proposed by other participants at VarDial 2020. The models and code used in our final submissions are available at `https://github.com/clarinsi/geobert`.

2 Related work

One of the first works focusing on predicting geolocation from social media text is Han et al. (2012). The authors investigate feature (token) selection methods for location prediction, showing that traditional predictive algorithms yield significantly better results if feature selection is performed.

There has been already a shared task on geolocation prediction at WNUT 2016 (Han et al., 2016). The task focused not only on predicting geolocation from text, but also from various user metadata. The best performing systems combined the available information via feedforward networks or ensembles.

Thomas and Hennig (2018) report significant improvements over the winner of the WNUT-16 shared task by separately learning text and metadata embeddings via different neural network architectures (LSTM, feedforward), merging those embeddings and performing the final classification via a softmax layer.

During the last iteration of the VarDial social media geolocation shared task (Gaman et al., 2020), most teams submitted constrained systems, i.e., they did not make use of any form of transfer learning from other tasks or pre-training self-supervision. Two approaches emerged during the shared task – a direct one, modelling the problem as multi-target regression, and an indirect one, which converts the coordinates into a finite set of dialect areas and uses a classification model to predict one of the areas. Interestingly, both approaches obtained similar results in the constrained setting, while only multi-target regression was tested in

Proceedings of the 8th VarDial Workshop on NLP for Similar Languages, Varieties and Dialects, pages 135–140
April 20, 2021 ©2021 Association for Computational Linguistics

Instances	BCMS	CH	DE-AT
Training	353 953	25 261	318 487
Development	38 013	2 416	29 122
Test	4 189	2 438	31 515

Table 1: Data characteristics.

the unconstrained one. We will inspect last year's submissions in more detail in Section 4.2.

3 Data

The VarDial evaluation campaign provides training, development and test data for the three subtasks (Chakravarthi et al., 2021). Table 1 gives an overview of the data. It can be seen that the BCMS and DE-AT datasets are roughly equivalent in size, whereas the CH dataset is more than one order of magnitude smaller. The BCMS test set is much smaller than the development set, whereas the two are roughly equal in size in the Jodel-based subtasks. Note that the instances from the Twitter dataset (BCMS) correspond to single tweets, while the instances from the Jodel datasets correspond to entire conversations and are much longer on average.

The task organizers also provide a simple baseline for the geolocation task. They compute the centroid ("average location") of all instances in the training data and then predict the coordinates of this centroid for all development or test instances.

While the official metric of the shared task is median distance (in kilometers) between the gold and predicted geolocations, the organizers report back both the median and the mean distance metrics. In the previous iteration of the shared task, the two metrics showed to correlate in most, but not all cases.

4 Experiments

Due to lack of time (the two evaluation campaigns were held just a few months apart due to the *ACL conference bidding procedure), all our experiments are based on our successful 2020 submissions (Scherrer and Ljubešić, 2020): we use the BERT architecture (Devlin et al., 2019) with a fully connected layer on top of the `CLS` token. This fully connected layer implements double regression with a two-dimensional output vector and Mean Absolute Error loss.

We provide both constrained submissions, where

Task	Vocab. size	Median distance	Mean distance	Eps.
BCMS	3k	92.74	129.14	28
	30k	59.93	109.51	23
CH	3k	22.94	33.01	11
	30k	21.20	30.60	9
DE-AT	3k	182.76	205.90	4
	30k	160.67	186.35	2

Table 2: Effect of different vocabulary sizes on constrained model performance, evaluated on the development set. *Eps.* refers to the number of fine-tuning epochs to reach minimum median distance.

BERT models are pre-trained from scratch using the VarDial training data, and unconstrained submissions, where we use pre-trained off-the-shelf BERT models. For all our experiments, we rely on the *simpletransformers* library, which is built on top of the HuggingFace *Transformers* library (Wolf et al., 2019), and use the same hyperparameters as in our 2020 submissions (Scherrer and Ljubešić, 2020).[1]

In the following subsections, we discuss some additional experiments carried out for the 2021 edition.

4.1 Tokenization

The BERT architecture requires a fixed vocabulary that is defined during the pre-training phase. Automatic word segmentation techniques are used to represent all tokens present in the data with a fixed-size vocabulary. Most off-the-shelf pre-trained models are based on a vocabulary size of 30 000 units. However, we hypothesize that when dealing with language variation, a more aggressive split that approaches a character-by-character split might be beneficial.

On the basis of the constrained setup, we trained BERT models from scratch with vocabulary sizes of 3 000 and 30 000 units, with masked language modeling as pre-training task and geolocation pre-

[1]The maximum length of the instances was capped at 128 tokens for BCMS and CH and at 256 tokens for DE-AT. Intermediate models were saved every 2000 training steps and the savepoint with the lowest median distance value measured on the development set was selected for testing. For the regression models, we converted the coordinates using joint scaling and used the MAE loss. For the classification models, we used the default cross-entropy loss.

Pre-training from scratch is done with the masked language modelling task and default parameters.

Task	Approach and parameters	Number of classes	Train. reconstr. error (median)	Dev. reconstr. error (median)	Median dist.	Mean dist.	Eps.
BCMS	Regression	—	0	0	62.21	110.56	28
	K-means: $k = 35$	35	5.15	5.07	46.74	111.77	5
	K-means: $k = 75$	75	2.67	3.00	**41.84**	**107.38**	4
	Fixed cell numbers: 9×9	60	31.98	31.25	57.32	129.00	2
	Fixed cell size: $1^\circ \times 1^\circ$	38	39.92	36.68	46.92	119.79	3
CH	Regression	—	0	0	**21.20**	**30.60**	9
	K-means: $k = 35$	35	4.42	4.48	23.06	32.77	4
	K-means: $k = 75$	75	0.28	0.35	22.18	32.48	3
	Fixed cell numbers: 9×9	55	8.36	8.36	21.69	33.56	3
	Fixed cell size: $0.2^\circ \times 0.2^\circ$	61	7.52	7.52	22.95	34.12	3
DE-AT	Regression	—	0	0	**160.67**	**186.35**	2
	K-means: $k = 35$	35	30.20	31.07	177.03	215.71	3
	K-means: $k = 75$	75	17.41	17.92	183.17	210.04	2
	Fixed cell numbers: 9×9	69	36.82	36.92	182.63	210.67	3
	Fixed cell size: $1^\circ \times 1^\circ$	75	35.23	35.17	176.78	207.91	3

Table 3: Regression vs. classification approaches. *Median dist.* and *Mean dist.* are reported on the development set. *Eps.* refers to the number of fine-tuning epochs to reach minimum median distance.

diction as fine-tuning task. The corresponding results on the development sets are shown in Table 2. Our hypothesis was not verified, since for all three subtasks, the model with the large vocabulary yielded lower distances and converged faster than the model with the small vocabulary. We were not able to test other parameter settings due to time constraints.

4.2 Regression and classification approaches

The SMG task takes text as input and produces two outputs on a continuous scale, the predicted latitude and longitude. It is thus formulated most straightforwardly as a double regression task. However, three VarDial 2020 participants chose to convert the task into a classification task, grouping data points with similar coordinates into a discrete set of classes. We decided to replicate these three approaches on top of BERT and contrast them with our double regression approach.

K-means clustering Benites et al. (2020) apply k-means clustering to the VarDial training data, grouping instances with similar coordinates together. Each instance is then annotated with the centroid of its respective cluster. K-means clustering requires setting the parameter k, i.e. the number of clusters. Benites et al. (2020) choose a value of $k = 35$ for all subtasks on the basis of the CH development set. Besides $k = 35$, we also provide results for a second parameter choice, $k = 75$.

Grid with fixed number of cells Jauhiainen et al. (2020) lay a grid with 9×9 cells over the area of study. Each of the 100 corner coordinates of the 81 grid cells functions as an anchor point, and each instance is associated with its nearest anchor point. This approach yields thus a theoretical maximum of 100 labels, but not all of them are effectively assigned any instances.[2]

Grid with fixed cell size Hulden et al. (2015) also use a regular grid, but fix the size of its cells rather than the number of cells in the grid. Each instance is then associated with the center point of the grid cell it falls in. They experiment with roughly square grid cells of $0.5^\circ \times 0.5^\circ$ to $10^\circ \times 10^\circ$ on a different data set covering the USA. It is unknown which cell size was used in their VarDial 2020 submissions.[3] We decided to use a cell size of $0.2^\circ \times 0.2^\circ$ for the CH subtask and of $1^\circ \times 1^\circ$ for the BCMS and DE-AT subtasks.

[2]Note that Jauhiainen et al. (2020) introduce a second step in which they move the anchor points away from their initial (fixed) locations to the centroid of the data points assigned to them. With this second step, their approach can be conceived as a variant of k-means clustering with a specific initialization. For our experiments, we do not apply this second step.

[3]Note that Hulden et al. (2015) apply kernel density estimation after classification for smoothing. We did not implement this step to keep the approach comparable to the others.

The central part of Table 3 shows various statistics regarding the different approaches to space discretization. The number of effectively used classes is identical to the value of k for k-means clustering, but is typically a subset of the maximally available amount of grid cells, since the areas of study are not densely populated and do not fit into a square. The number of effectively used classes varied between 38 and 75.

We also computed the median reconstruction error, i.e., the median difference between the real coordinates and the coordinates of the assigned class labels. K-means turned out to provide lower errors than fixed-grid setups with comparable numbers of classes. This is again due to the uneven distribution of the SMG data points across space, most of which come from major cities and urban areas. For fixed-grid approaches, the reconstruction errors of the training and development set are expected to be similar, which is the case. For k-means, the development reconstruction error tends to be higher than the training one since the clusters were fitted to the training data alone. However, the k-means development reconstruction errors are still below the fixed-grid ones.

The right side of Table 3 contains the results of the experiments on the development data. In terms of distance, the (parameter-free) regression approach performs best on the CH and DE-AT subtasks, whereas the k-means approach with 75 clusters yields the best results for BCMS. The most likely reason for better performance of the classification approach on the BCMS data is high concentration of tweets in large cities, i.e., smaller dispersion of data than in the other two Jodel-based datasets. Classification approaches generally converged faster than regression. Among the different discretization approaches, no clear winner can be identified, despite the low reconstruction errors of k-means clustering.

4.3 Hyperparameter optimization

We performed hyperparameter optimization via the **wandb.ai** platform (Biewald, 2020), allowing for 30 iterations. We search for the optimal initial learning rate (we search between 9e-6 and 1e-4) and batch size (32, 64, 128, 256). Our experiments show that no significant improvements can be obtained by modifying the default hyperparameter values of the 5e-4 learning rate, setting with the batch size of 64 for all subtasks.

Pre-training	Median	Mean	Eps.
dbmdz + SwissCrawl	18.25	26.78	59
SwissCrawl (30k voc.)	22.10	31.16	10
SwissCrawl (3k voc.)	22.37	31.62	8

Table 4: Effect of different pre-training schemes for the CH unconstrained model, evaluated on the development set. *Eps.* refers to the number of fine-tuning epochs to reach minimum median distance.

4.4 Pre-trained models

Our unconstrained 2020 submissions showed that language-specific BERT models clearly outperformed multilingual BERT. For DE-AT, we continued using the DBMDZ model[4]. For the BCMS and CH subtasks, we carried out additional experiments.

BCMS While last year we achieved significant improvements by using the CroSloEngual BERT (Ulčar and Robnik-Šikonja, 2020)[5] in place of multilingual BERT, this year we had the opportunity to test a new model, BERTić (Ljubešić and Lauc, 2021).[6] Comparing the two models on the development data showed significant gains for the BERTić model, with a median distance of 30.11 in comparison to a median distance of 40.05 for the CroSloEngual BERT.

CH In the absence of a generally available pre-trained BERT model for Swiss German, our 2020 submission took the DBMDZ model as a starting point and continued pre-training for 10 epochs on the SwissCrawl corpus (Linder et al., 2020). We wanted to test whether pre-training (and defining the word segmentation model) on SwissCrawl alone would benefit classification performance. (SwissCrawl contains 562k sentences and 9.2M words, compared to 2350M words for DBMDZ.) Table 4 shows that this is not the case, neither with a 30k nor with a 3k vocabulary. Consequently, we stick to the 2020 setup for the final submission.

5 Final submissions

We present the final results of our constrained and unconstrained systems in Table 5. Unconstrained

[4]https://huggingface.co/dbmdz/bert-base-german-uncased

[5]https://huggingface.co/EMBEDDIA/crosloengual-bert

[6]https://huggingface.co/CLASSLA/bcms-bertic

Task	Setting	Development set		Test set	
		Median dist.	Mean dist.	Median dist.	Mean dist.
BCMS	Unconstrained	30.11	87.43	15.49	76.04
	Constrained	60.83	109.44	52.06	98.74
CH	Unconstrained	18.32	26.68	17.55	25.84
	Constrained	21.20	29.77	20.70	29.62
DE-AT	Unconstrained	147.88	172.04	149.33	172.52
	Constrained	160.03	184.53	161.13	184.97

Table 5: HeLju final submission scores.

systems, similar to last year, consistently outperform constrained systems. The results on the development and test set are consistent among all datasets, except for the BCMS task where our unconstrained system achieves a two times better score than on development data. The reason for this improvement is probably to be found in the way the 2021 data for the BCMS task was constructed. In this subtask, the test data consists of tweets that were published exclusively after March 2020, i.e., in times of COVID. It is quite likely that the limitation in overall mobility made the BCMS task significantly simpler.

6 Conclusion

In this paper, we presented our BERT-based approach to the problem of social media geolocation. This year we experimented primarily with tokenizer vocabulary size, space discretization and hyperparameter tuning. The hypothesis that a smaller tokenization vocabulary might improve generalizability and performance proved wrong. We showed that it actually performs worse and converges slower than if standard vocabulary size of 30k wordpieces is used. Converting the geolocation task to a classification task yielded worse results in all except the BCMS subtask. This is probably due to high concentration of BCMS Twitter data in the few large cities in the respective area. Hyperparameter tuning did not yield any consistent improvements and simply selecting the optimal epoch number on development data showed to be the best approach to this problem. Similarly to last year, unconstrained systems performed better than constrained systems. We share our code as well as the best-performing models via `https://github.com/clarinsi/geobert` and the HuggingFace models repository.

Acknowledgments

This work has been supported by the FoTran project, funded by the European Research Council (ERC) under the European Union's Horizon 2020 research and innovation programme (grant agreement No 771113). This work has also been supported by the Slovenian Research Agency and the Flemish Research Foundation through the bilateral research project ARRS N6-0099 and FWO G070619N "The linguistic landscape of hate speech on social media", the Slovenian Research Agency research core funding No. P6-0411 "Language resources and technologies for Slovene language", and the European Union's Rights, Equality and Citizenship Programme (2014-2020) project IMSyPP (grant no. 875263).

References

Fernando Benites, Manuela Hürlimann, Pius von Däniken, and Mark Cieliebak. 2020. ZHAW-InIT - social media geolocation at VarDial 2020. In *Proceedings of the 7th Workshop on NLP for Similar Languages, Varieties and Dialects*, pages 254–264, Barcelona, Spain (Online). International Committee on Computational Linguistics (ICCL).

Lukas Biewald. 2020. Experiment tracking with weights and biases. Software available from wandb.com.

Bharathi Raja Chakravarthi, Mihaela Găman, Radu Tudor Ionescu, Heidi Jauhiainen, Tommi Jauhiainen, Krister Lindén, Nikola Ljubešić, Niko Partanen, Ruba Priyadharshini, Christoph Purschke, Eswari Rajagopal, Yves Scherrer, and Marcos Zampieri. 2021. Findings of the VarDial Evaluation Campaign 2021. In *Proceedings of the Eighth Workshop on NLP for Similar Languages, Varieties and Dialects (VarDial)*.

Jacob Devlin, Ming-Wei Chang, Kenton Lee, and Kristina Toutanova. 2019. BERT: Pre-training of deep bidirectional transformers for language understanding. In *Proceedings of the 2019 Conference of the North American Chapter of the Association for Computational Linguistics: Human Language Technologies, Volume 1 (Long and Short Papers)*, pages 4171–4186, Minneapolis, Minnesota. Association for Computational Linguistics.

Mihaela Gaman, Dirk Hovy, Radu Tudor Ionescu, Heidi Jauhiainen, Tommi Jauhiainen, Krister Lindén, Nikola Ljubešić, Niko Partanen, Christoph Purschke, Yves Scherrer, and Marcos Zampieri. 2020. A report on the VarDial evaluation campaign 2020. In *Proceedings of the 7th Workshop on NLP for Similar Languages, Varieties and Dialects*, pages 1–14, Barcelona, Spain (Online). International Committee on Computational Linguistics (ICCL).

Bo Han, Paul Cook, and Timothy Baldwin. 2012. Geolocation prediction in social media data by finding location indicative words. In *Proceedings of COLING 2012*, pages 1045–1062, Mumbai, India. The COLING 2012 Organizing Committee.

Bo Han, Afshin Rahimi, Leon Derczynski, and Timothy Baldwin. 2016. Twitter geolocation prediction shared task of the 2016 workshop on noisy user-generated text. In *Proceedings of the 2nd Workshop on Noisy User-generated Text (WNUT)*, pages 213–217, Osaka, Japan. The COLING 2016 Organizing Committee.

Dirk Hovy and Christoph Purschke. 2018. Capturing regional variation with distributed place representations and geographic retrofitting. In *Proceedings of the 2018 Conference on Empirical Methods in Natural Language Processing*, pages 4383–4394, Brussels, Belgium. Association for Computational Linguistics.

Mans Hulden, Miikka Silfverberg, and Jerid Francom. 2015. Kernel density estimation for text-based geolocation. In *Proceedings of AAAI*.

Tommi Jauhiainen, Heidi Jauhiainen, and Krister Lindén. 2020. Experiments in language variety geolocation and dialect identification. In *Proceedings of the 7th Workshop on NLP for Similar Languages, Varieties and Dialects*, pages 220–231, Barcelona, Spain (Online). International Committee on Computational Linguistics (ICCL).

Lucy Linder, Michael Jungo, Jean Hennebert, Claudiu Cristian Musat, and Andreas Fischer. 2020. Automatic creation of text corpora for low-resource languages from the internet: The case of Swiss German. In *Proceedings of The 12th Language Resources and Evaluation Conference*, pages 2706–2711, Marseille, France. European Language Resources Association.

Nikola Ljubešić and Davor Lauc. 2021. BERTić - the transformer language model for Bosnian, Croatian, Montenegrin and Serbian. In *Proceedings of the 8th Workshop on Balto-Slavic Natural Language Processing*, Kiev, Ukraine. Association for Computational Linguistics.

Nikola Ljubešić, Tanja Samardžić, and Curdin Derungs. 2016. TweetGeo - a tool for collecting, processing and analysing geo-encoded linguistic data. In *Proceedings of COLING 2016, the 26th International Conference on Computational Linguistics: Technical Papers*, pages 3412–3421, Osaka, Japan. The COLING 2016 Organizing Committee.

Yves Scherrer and Nikola Ljubešić. 2020. HeLju@VarDial 2020: Social media variety geolocation with BERT models. In *Proceedings of the 7th Workshop on NLP for Similar Languages, Varieties and Dialects*, pages 202–211, Barcelona, Spain (Online). International Committee on Computational Linguistics (ICCL).

Philippe Thomas and Leonhard Hennig. 2018. Twitter geolocation prediction using neural networks. In *Language Technologies for the Challenges of the Digital Age*, pages 248–255, Cham. Springer International Publishing.

Matej Ulčar and Marko Robnik-Šikonja. 2020. FinEst BERT and CroSloEngual BERT: less is more in multilingual models.

Thomas Wolf, Lysandre Debut, Victor Sanh, Julien Chaumond, Clement Delangue, Anthony Moi, Pierric Cistac, Tim Rault, Rémi Louf, Morgan Funtowicz, and Jamie Brew. 2019. HuggingFace's Transformers: State-of-the-art natural language processing. *ArXiv*, abs/1910.03771.

Association for Computational Linguistics
209 N. Eighth Street
Stroudsburg, Pennsylvania 18360

CURRAN ASSOCIATES INC.
proceedings.com

ISBN 978-1-7138-2971-3

9 781713 829713